CONTENTS

THE TOP FIVE
REGRETS

of the DYING

A Life Transformed by the Dearly Departing

BRONNIE WARE

HAY HOUSE, INC.
Carlsbad, California • New York City
London • Sydney • Johannesburg
Vancouver • Hong Kong • New Delhi

Published and distributed in the United States by: Hay House, Inc.:
www.hayhouse.com® • *Published and distributed in Australia by:*
Hay House Australia Pty. Ltd.: www.hayhouse.com.au • *Published
and distributed in the United Kingdom by:* Hay House UK, Ltd.:
www.hayhouse.co.uk • *Published and distributed in the Republic
of South Africa by:* Hay House SA (Pty), Ltd.: www.hayhouse.co.za
• *Distributed in Canada by:* Raincoast: www.raincoast.com • *Published in India by:* Hay House Publishers India: www.hayhouse.co.in

Previously published by Balboa Press (ISBN 978-1-45250-234-2)

Library of Congress Control Number: 2012933481

Tradepaper ISBN: 978-1-4019-4065-2
Digital ISBN: 978-1-4019-4066-9

16 15 14 13   6 5 4 3
1st edition, March 2012
3rd edition, February 2013

Printed in the United States of America

INTRODUCTION

On a balmy summer's evening in a little country town, a conversation was underway that was like many cheerful conversations taking place simultaneously all over the world. It was two people simply catching up with each other and having a yarn. The difference with this conversation, though, was that it could be later identified as one of the most significant turning points of a person's life. And that person was me.

Cec is the editor of a great folk music magazine in Australia, called *Trad and Now*. He is equally known and loved for his support of folk music in Australia, as he is for his big cheerful smile. We were chatting about our love of music (which was very appropriate, since we were at a folk music festival). The conversation also touched on the challenges I was currently facing, to find funding for a guitar and songwriting program that I wanted to start in a women's jail. "If you get it up and running, let me know and we'll print a story," Cec said with encouragement.

I did in fact get it up and running and some time afterwards, I wrote a story for the magazine about my experiences. When I finished writing, I questioned myself as to why I wasn't writing more stories in my life. After all, I had always written. As a freckle-faced little girl, I wrote to pen friends all over the world. This was in the days when people still wrote letters by hand that went into envelopes and mailboxes.

Writing didn't stop at adulthood either. Handwritten letters to friends continued, as did years of journals. And I was now a songwriter. So I was still writing, as such (just with a guitar, as well as a pen in my hands). But the enjoyment I experienced in writing the story about the jail, which I did at the kitchen table with an old-fashioned pen and paper, reignited my love of writing. So I sent thanks to Cec and soon after, I decided to start writing a blog.

The events that followed changed my life's direction in the very best of ways.

'Inspiration and Chai' began in a snug little cottage in the Blue Mountains of Australia, naturally enough, over a cup of chai tea. One of the first articles I wrote was about the regrets of dying people whom I had cared for. The role of a carer had been my most recent occupation before the jail job, so it was still fresh in my life. Over the following months, the article gained momentum in ways that only the Internet can explain. I began receiving emails from people I didn't know, connecting with me on the article and then on other articles I'd written since.

Almost a year later, I was living in a different little cottage, this one in a farming district. One Monday morning as I sat at the table on the verandah to write, I decided to check the stats on my website, as one does from time to time. A puzzled but amused look crossed my face. The next day I returned for another look, and the next. Sure enough, something big was happening. The article, also called 'The Top Five Regrets of the Dying' had found its wings.

Emails began pouring in from all over the world, including requests from other writers to quote the article on their blogs and for it to be translated into numerous languages. People read it on trains in Sweden, at bus stations in America, in offices in India, over breakfast in Ireland, and on and on it went. Not everyone actually agreed with the article, but it prompted enough discussion to continue its ride around the world. As I said to the few who didn't agree, if I did reply, 'Don't shoot the messenger'. I was simply sharing what dying people had shared with me. At least ninety five per cent of the feedback that came in from the article, though, was beautiful. It also reinforced just how much we all have in common, despite cultural differences.

All the while this was happening, I was living in the cottage, enjoying the bliss of the birds and other wildlife that the creek out the front drew in. I sat at the table on my verandah each day and kept working, saying "Yes" to opportunities that began presenting themselves. In the months that followed, over one million people read 'The Top Five Regrets of the Dying'. Within a year, that number had more than trebled.

It was due to the enormous amount of people who connected to this theme, and at the requests of many people who contacted me afterwards, that I decided to elaborate on the subject. It had always been my intention to write a full-length book one day, as many other people also wish to do. As it turned out, though, it was only through telling my own story here that I could fully articulate the lessons that were given to me while caring for dying people. The book I had wanted to write was ready to be written. It is now this book.

As you will read from my story, I've never been one to follow any traditional ways in life, if such a thing truly exists. I live as I am guided and write this book simply as a woman who has a story to share. Also, I am Australian, and as much as I have written as universally as possible, Australian spelling and language is used.

Almost all of the names in the book have been altered to protect the privacy of the families and friends. My first yoga teacher, my boss at the pre-natal centre, the caravan park owner, my mentor with the jail system, and any songwriters mentioned, are all original names, however. The chronological order has been shifted slightly, too, in order to share common themes between clients.

My thanks go to all who have assisted my journey in so many different ways. For support and/or positive influence professionally, special thanks go to: Marie Burrows, Elizabeth Cham, Valda Low, Rob Conway, Reesa Ryan, Barbara Gilder, Dad, Pablo Acosta, Bruce Reid, Joan Dennis, Siegfried Kunze, Jill Marr, Guy Kachel, Michael Bloeme, Ana Goncalvez, Kate and Col Baker, Ingrid Cliff, Mark Patterson, Jane Dargaville, Jo Wallace, Bernadette, and all who support my writing and music by connecting with it in a positive way.

Thank you also to the many people who helped to keep a roof over my head at various times, including: Mark Avellino, Auntie Jo, Sue Greig, Helen Atkins, Uncle Fred, Di and Greg Burns, Dusty Cuttell, Mardi McElvenny, and all of my wonderful house-sitting clients whose homes I have loved as my own. Thank you also to every kind person who has ever fed me.

For personal support along the winding road, I thank all friends past and present, near and far. Thank you for enriching my life in so many ways. Special thanks to: Mark Neven, Sharon Rochford, Julie Skerrett, Mel Giallongo, Angeline Rattansey, Kateea McFarlane, Brad Antoniou, Angie Bidwell, Theresa Clancy, Barbra Squire, all who serve at the meditation centre in the mountains that led me to a road of peace, and my partner. You have all been my stretcher when I've most needed to rest.

Thanks of course to my mother, Joy, the most appropriately named person to ever walk the Earth. What a sacred lesson in love you have given to me, by natural example. Endless thanks, beautiful woman.

To all of the wonderful people who have now passed on – whose stories not only make up this book, but have also influenced my life significantly – this book is a tribute to you. I also thank the families left behind, for the loving, memorable times we experienced together. Thank you all.

Lastly, thank you to the magpie singing in the tree by the creek as I write this. You and all of your fellow birds have kept me delightful company whilst writing these pages. Thank you, God, for sustaining me, and for sending so much beauty my way.

Sometimes we don't know until much later that a particular moment in time has changed our life's direction. So many of the moments shared in this book changed my life. Thank you, Cec, for reigniting the writer within me. And thank you, the reader, for the goodness of who you are and for our connection.

With loving kindness,
Bronnie.

The Verandah at Sunset
Tuesday Afternoon.

FROM THE TROPICS
TO THE SNOW

෬ඟ෬

"I can't find my teeth. I can't find my teeth." The familiar call flowed into the room as I attempted to have my scheduled afternoon off. Placing the book I was reading on the bed, I wandered out into the living area.

As expected, Agnes was standing there looking both confused and innocent, smiling her gummy grin. We both burst out laughing. The joke should have worn thin by now as the misplacement of her teeth happened at least every few days. But it never did.

"I am sure you do this just to get me back out here with you," I laughed as I began today's search in now familiar places. Outside snow continued to fall, enhancing the cosiness and warmth of the cottage. Shaking her head, Agnes was adamant. "Not at all, Darling! I took them out before my nap, but when I awoke, I couldn't find them anywhere." Other than her memory loss, she was as bright as a button.

Agnes and I came to be living together four months earlier when I had responded to an advertisement for a live-in companion. As an Australian in England, I had been doing a live-in job in a pub to keep a roof over my head. It had been fun and some lovely friendships were made with other staff and the locals. Bar skills were definitely handy and had enabled me to start work immediately on my arrival in the country. So for that, I was grateful. But it came time for a change.

The two years prior to going overseas were spent living on a tropical island, as picturesque as any postcard could ever portray. After more than a decade of working in the banking industry,

I had needed to try an existence that released me from the Monday to Friday, nine to five grind.

One of my sisters and I ventured to an island in North Queensland for a holiday, to gain our scuba diving certificates. While she cracked onto our diving instructor, which was of course very beneficial for us in passing our tests, I climbed a mountain on the island. While sitting on an enormous boulder in the sky, smiling, I had an epiphany. I wanted to live on an island.

Four weeks later, the bank job was no more, and my belongings were either sold or sent to a shed on my parents' farm. Two islands were chosen from a map simply for their geographic suitability. I knew nothing else about these islands, other than I liked their location and there was a resort on each of them. This was before the Internet, where you could find out anything about everything in a flash. With application letters in the mail, I headed north, destination unknown. It was 1991, also before mobile phones arrived en masse in Australia a few years later.

Along the way, my carefree spirit was given a timely and cautious warning, as a hitch hiking experience saw me retiring from that occupation very quickly. Finding myself on a dirt road in the middle of nowhere, way off track from the requested town, rang enough warning bells for me to never put my thumb out again. He said he wanted to show me where he lived, as houses faded away and bushland thickened, the dirt road showing few signs of regular visitors. Thankfully I stayed strong and determined, managing to talk myself out of the situation. Only a few slobbery kisses were attempted from him as I finally exited the car, *rather* quickly, in the right town. So that was the end of my hitch hiking.

I stuck to public transport then. Other than that dodgy experience, it was a great adventure, particularly not knowing where I would end up living next. Travelling on various buses and trains ensured my path also crossed with some great people while I was being transported to warmer climates. A few weeks into the trip, I called my mum who had received a letter telling me there was a job waiting on one of the chosen islands. Being so desperate to escape the banking grind, I had made the ridiculous mistake of saying I was willing to take any job, and a few days later was living on a beautiful island, up to my elbows in filthy pots and pans.

Island life was a fantastic experience, though, not only releasing me from the Monday to Friday grind, but also effectively releasing me from even knowing what day of the week it was. I loved it. After a year of being what was not so affectionately known as a dish-pig, I worked my way into the bar. The time in the kitchen had actually been a lot of fun and taught me a wealth of things about creative cookery. But it was hot, hard, and sweaty work in a non-air conditioned kitchen in the tropics. Days off at least were spent wandering magnificent rainforests, hiring boats and cruising to nearby islands, scuba diving, or just kicking back in paradise.

Volunteering in the bar eventually opened the door for me into this coveted role. Overlooking a million dollar view of perfect calm blue waters, white sands, palm trees swaying, the whole thing, it was not a hard job. Dealing with happy customers who were having the holidays of their lives, and becoming adept at mixing cocktails worthy of travel brochure photos, was a world away from the previous life I'd known in banking.

It was over the bar I met a man from Europe who offered me a job at his printing company. Travel yearnings had always been a part of me, and after more than two years of island life by then, I was starting to crave some change and to enjoy being somewhat anonymous again. When you live and work within the same community day in day out, privacy in your every-day living can start to become sacred.

Culture shock was to be expected for anyone returning to mainland life after a couple of years on an island. But to throw myself from that into a foreign country where I couldn't even speak the language was challenging to say the least. Some nice people crossed my path during these months, and I am glad to have experienced the time. But I needed some like-minded friends again, so eventually headed off to England. Arriving there with only enough money for a travel card to get to the one person I knew in the country, and with one pound sixty six left over, a new chapter began.

Nev had a lovely big smile and head of thinning white curls.

He was also a wine-loving expert, appropriately working in the wine department at Harrods. It was the first day of the store's summer sale and coming straight off the overnight ferry across the channel, I certainly looked like the waif I was wandering into this classy, busy joint. "Hi Nev. I'm Bronnie. We met once. I'm a friend of Fiona's. You crashed out on my beanbag a few years ago," I announced to him over the counter with a cheerful grin.

"Of course, Bronnie," I was relieved to hear. "What's happening?"

"I need a place to stay for a few nights, please," I said rather hopefully.

Reaching into his pocket for his key, Nev replied "Sure. Here you go". And with that I had a roof over my head, sleeping on his sofa, and directions to his place.

"May I also borrow ten quid, please?" I asked optimistically. Without hesitation, ten quid came out of his back pocket. Offering words of thanks and a cheerful smile in reply, I was sorted. I had a bed and food.

The travel magazine I had intended to find a job from came out that morning, so I picked up a copy, went home to Nev's and made three phone calls. By the next morning I was being interviewed for a live-in pub job in Surrey. By that afternoon I was living there. Perfect.

Life rolled on for a couple of years with friendships and romance. They were fun times. Village life suited me, reminding me of the island community at times, and I was surrounded by people I had come to love. We were also not terribly far out of London, so regular trips happened easily, most of which I thoroughly enjoyed.

But further travel was calling. I wanted to check out a bit of the Middle East. The long English winters were good experiences, and I was glad to have done a couple of them. It was a complete contrast to the long, hot summers of Australia. But I had a choice to stay or go, and decided to stay for one more winter, with determination to save some money for the trip. To do this I needed to remove myself from the pub scene and the temptation to be out socialising every night. I was never much of a drinker anyway and have since become a non-drinker, but being out and about every night still cost money that could take me travelling instead.

Almost as soon as I'd made that decision, the job advertisement for the role with Agnes caught my eye, as it was only in the next county to Surrey. The position was offered to me at my first interview, when the farmer Bill realised I was a farm girl myself. His mother, Agnes, was in her late eighties, had shoulder length grey hair, a cheerful voice, and a huge round stomach, covered almost every day by the same red and grey cardigan. Their farm was only about half an hour's drive away, so seeing everyone on days off was easy enough. But it felt like a different world while I was there. It was very isolating, as I was with Agnes around the clock from Sunday evening until Friday evening. Two hours off every afternoon didn't allow much time for socialising, though I did use that time occasionally to see my English man.

Dean was a darling person. It was humour that linked us from the very start, within the first minute of meeting. Our love of music also bonded us. We had met the day after I arrived in the country, just after the interview for the pub job, and it soon became obvious that both of our lives were richer and funnier by knowing each other. Unfortunately, though, it wasn't Dean's company I was most keeping by then. I was usually snowed in with Agnes – and more often than not, busy looking for her teeth. It was amazing how one could find so many different locations within such a small home to lose your teeth in.

Her dog, Princess, was a ten-year-old German Shepherd who moulted hair everywhere. She was a sweet natured dog but was losing strength in her hind legs from arthritis. It was a common condition in this breed of dog apparently. Learning from past experience, I lifted up her rump and looked underneath for her lady's teeth. No luck today. On another occasion, though, she had sat on them. So it was always worth the look. Princess wagged her big tail then returned to her dreams by the fire, forgetting the brief disturbance in a second. Time and again, Agnes and I crossed each other's path as we continued the search. "They're not here," she would call from the bedroom.

"They're not here either," I'd reply from the kitchen. Eventually though, I would find myself searching the bedroom, and Agnes the kitchen. There are only so many rooms to search in a little home, so we covered them all to be doubly sure. On this particular day they had slipped into her knitting bag, beside the lounge chair.

"Oh, you are a treasure, Darling," she said, putting them back in her mouth. "Come and watch television with me now that you're out here." This was a strategy that was often used, and I smiled as I went along with her request. She was an old lady who had lived alone a long time and was enjoying the company. My book could wait. It was hardly like the job was strenuous at the best of times. It was simply companionship, and if she needed that outside of my scheduled work-hours, no worries.

The teeth had previously been found under her cushion, back in the bathroom vanity, in a teacup in the kitchen cupboard, in her handbag, and numerous other half-believable places. But they had also turned up behind the television, in the fireplace, in the rubbish bin, on top of the fridge, and in her shoe. And of course, under Princess, the mighty German Shepherd's backside.

Routine works for a lot of people. Personally, I thrive on change. But routine has its place and it certainly works best for many people, particularly as they are getting older. There were weekly routines and daily routines with Agnes. Every Monday we went to the doctors, as Agnes had to have regular blood tests. The appointment was at the exact same time every week. One thing per day was enough, though, or it would ruin her afternoon routine of rest and knitting.

Princess came everywhere with us, rain, hail or shine. The tailgate of the pick-up would be lowered first. The old dog would wait patiently, always wagging her tail. She was a gorgeous creature. I would then lift her front paws onto the tailgate and quickly grab her rear and lift her up fully, before the rear legs gave way and we had to start over again. I would then be covered in sandy coloured dog hair for the remainder of the outing.

Hopping down was easier, though she still required assistance. Princess would drop down herself so that her front legs were on the ground, but would wait for me to lift her hind legs down. If Agnes needed me to help her in any way in between, Princess would wait in that position with her backside in the air until I was ready. Once down, she walked happily and painlessly, always wagging that big, old tail.

Tuesdays were spent grocery shopping in the nearby village. A lot of elderly people I have worked with since have been very frugal. But Agnes was the opposite. She was always trying to buy me things, particularly things I didn't need or want. Every aisle would see the same two women, one elderly and one younger, arguing with each other. Both would be smiling and sometimes laughing, yet both were determined. As a result, I would end up with half of what Agnes wanted to buy me. This could be various vegetarian delicacies, imported mangoes, a new hairbrush, a singlet, or some terrible tasting toothpaste.

Wednesdays were bingo, again in the local village. Her sight was deteriorating so I was Agnes's eyes, for confirmation at bingo. She could read the numbers OK and hear relatively well, but checked with me to be sure before she crossed off each number. I loved all of the old people there. I was in my late-twenties and the only young one, which left Agnes feeling very special. She would describe me as 'my friend'.

"Well, my friend and I went shopping yesterday and I bought her some new underpants," she would announce seriously and proudly to all of her elderly bingo friends.

Everyone would nod and smile at me as I sat there thinking, 'Oh, brother'.

On she would go. "Her mother wrote to her this week from Australia. It is very hot there at the moment, you know. And she has a new nephew." Again the heads would nod and smile.

It didn't take me long to learn about editing how much information I gave her. I hate to think what they would have known of my life otherwise, particularly when Mum posted me some lovely lingerie and other gifts, to pamper me from afar. But it was all innocent and loving with Agnes. So I managed to endure the blushing and cringing she sometimes caused me.

Thursdays were the only day we stayed out over lunch. It was a big day out for the three of us, Princess included, of course. We would drive to a town in Kent and have lunch with her daughter.

Thirty miles was a long way away by English standards, but just down the road for an Australian. Our perspective of distance is definitely a cultural difference.

In England, you can drive two miles and be in a whole new village. The accent will be totally different from the previous village and you may not know anyone, even if you've lived in the other village all of your life. In Australia you can drive fifty miles for a loaf of bread. Your neighbours can be so far away they ring you up or speak to you on the two-way radio to say hello, but they still think of you as their neighbour. I once worked in an area in the Northern Territory that was so remote they flew planes to get to the nearest pub. The little airstrip would be full of single and two seater planes early in the evening and totally empty by the next morning, when they had all flown home to their cattle stations, half full of grog.

So the big day out on Thursdays was indeed a big day out for Agnes, but a lovely leisurely drive for me. Her daughter was a gentle woman and the occasions pleasant. The two of them always had a ploughman's lunch, with beef, cheese, and pickles. I often marvelled at English people's love of pickles. It was a good country for vegetarians, too, though. So my choices were never terribly limited. Being so cold, I usually enjoyed a warming soup or a hearty pasta dish.

Fridays were spent very local. We lived on a cattle farm with its own butcher shop. The farm was run by two of Agnes's sons. Our outing on Friday mornings was to the butcher shop. Although Agnes insisted on taking her time and looking at everything in great detail, she bought the exact same things every week, exactly. The butcher even offered to deliver her order, but no. "Thank you very much, but I must come and make my choice here," she would reply politely.

In those days I was a vegetarian. I am a vegan now. Yet here I was living on a cattle farm, not unlike how I had grown up. Even though I didn't advocate eating meat, I did understand the business and the lifestyle. It was familiar territory after all.

We would wander back from the butcher shop and walk through the barn talking to the farmhands and to the cows. Agnes would plod along slowly with her walking stick, me close by her side, and

Princess behind us. It didn't matter how cold the weather, we would just wear more layers. Fridays were always spent this way, visiting the shop then the cows in their barn.

I marvelled at how differently English cows were treated to Australian cows, with their warm barns and individual attention. But Australian cows did not have to endure English winters. It still made me terribly sad getting to know these cows on an individual basis, though, knowing we would probably be buying their flesh from the butcher shop at a later date. It was a hard thing to come to terms with, and I never truly succeeded in doing so.

The vegetarian thing came up a lot at home despite my attempted silence and my respect for the family's chosen lifestyle. I was never the kind of vegetarian or vegan who would be overly verbal about it. Yet having seen what I have in my upbringing, and then being taken on a life-scarring school excursion to the abattoirs, I do understand why some Vegos get so vocal and passionate about it. It is heartbreaking when you find the bravery to look honestly at these industries and at what goes on behind the walls.

But I preferred to just live quietly and simply by example, respecting everyone's right to live the way that made sense to him or her. I only spoke of my beliefs if I was asked and was then happy to, since there was a genuine interest. It *is* interesting though, how almost-strangers from meat-eating paths have attacked me without provocation over the years, simply because of my choice *not* to eat animals. Perhaps this is partly why I chose to live a quiet vegetarian life. I just wanted peace.

So when Agnes started questioning me about why I was a vegetarian, I hesitated. Her very survival was based on the income from their cattle farm. In effect, I guess mine was, too, although I hadn't related to that immediately. I took the job simply with the intention of saving money and brightening up an old lady's life.

But she persisted with her questions. So I told her about my feelings of watching cattle and sheep killed when I was a child and how affected by it I was, how much I loved animals, and how I had noticed that cows mooed differently when they knew they were about to die. Their sounds of terror and panic still haunt me.

That was it. Agnes declared her vegetarianism on the spot. "Oh boy," I thought. "How am I going to explain this one to her family?" Speaking about it with her son soon after, he then spoke to Agnes of his desire for her to continue eating meat. But there was little budging at first. Agnes finally accepted eating red meat one day a week, fish one day per week, and chicken another day. The family fed her on my days off, so she would be eating meat then, too.

Over time my views have strengthened and now I would not even consider accepting a job that involved cooking flesh. But I did back then, and I hated that part of my role. I could never cook meat without being saddened that this was once a beautiful living thing, which had had feelings and a right to live. So I liked this arrangement instantly, even though fish and chicken were certainly still animals, by my way of thinking.

It turned out, though, that Agnes had only agreed with her son Bill in order to keep the peace. She had no intention of eating any meat at all during the week. So I spent the remaining winter and spring months cooking us up delicious vegetarian feasts of nut-loaf bakes, divine soups, colourful stir-fries, and gourmet pizzas. I think Agnes would have happily lived on boiled eggs otherwise and, of course, baked beans. She was English after all, and the English do love their beans.

The snow melted as the daffodils bloomed into spring. Days grew longer and blue skies returned. As the farm came to life again, newborn calves ran around on their wobbly, skinny legs. Birds returned and greeted us in song every day. Princess moulted even more. Agnes and I removed our winter coats and hats, and carried on with our same routine for another couple of months, enjoying the spring sunshine. We were two ladies of very different generations, walking arm in arm day after day, as we shared continuous laughter and stories.

Travel was calling, though. We had both known from the start that I would be going. I was missing Dean, too. The weekends were not enough time together anymore and we were keen to head off travelling together. My job was advertised before long, and our days started winding up. Those months with Agnes were a wonderful and special experience. Although I had accepted it mostly as a job for the benefit of my travel yearnings, companionship was beautiful work.

It was much more enjoyable for me than pulling beers. I would rather help someone walk steady because she is old and frail than someone who is young and drunk, or even old and drunk. Plenty of both had been done during my employment on the island and in the English pub. I much preferred looking for an old lady's teeth to removing dirty ashtrays and empty pint glasses.

Dean and I travelled to the Middle East, where we marvelled at vastly different but fascinating cultures (and ate heaps of delicious food). After a wonderful year or so away, I went back to visit Agnes. Another Australian girl had replaced me and we had an enjoyable long yarn, after Agnes had drifted off to sleep in her armchair. Sharing lots of stories, she admitted to being somewhat puzzled by the first question Bill had asked when he interviewed her. I asked what that was and cracked up laughing when she told me.

The very first question Bill had asked was, "You're not a vegetarian, *are you?*"

AN UNEXPECTED CAREER PATH

‿⊙⌒⊙‿

After those years in England and the Middle East, I finally came home to my beloved Australia. I was a changed person, as one is after travel. Returning to work in the banking industry, it soon became obvious that this work would never satisfy me again. Customer service was the only highlight of the role now, and while it was easy to pick up work in any town, I was restless and desperately unhappy in my working life.

Creative expression was also starting to flow from me. Now living in Western Australia, I sat by the Swan River in Perth one day and made two lists. One list was what I was good at. The other one was what I loved to do. From this I had to acknowledge there was an artist of sorts within me, as the only things that landed in both columns were creative talents.

"Dare I think I could be an artist?" I thought to myself. Despite growing up around musicians, the reliability of a 'good job' has also been instilled in me, hence why no one could understand my restlessness with a steady nine to five existence in the banking game. They were 'good jobs'; good jobs that were slowly but surely killing me.

Intensive soul searching unfolded, as I tried to work out what I could do well, but also enjoy. They were hard times as everything was changing within me. I finally came to the conclusion that I would have to eventually be working from the heart, as working only from the intellect had already left me too empty and dissatisfied. So I began developing my creative skills through writing and photography, which led to songwriting and performing eventually, in a long and roundabout way. All the while I was still working in banking jobs, though mostly as temporary staff now. The trappings of a full-time job were just not possible to endure anymore.

Perth was a long way from anywhere, though, and as much as I loved living there, the desire to be more accessible to those I cherished saw the eastern states calling me back. So across the mighty Nullarbor Plains it was, through the Flinders Ranges, along the Great Ocean Road, up through the New England Highway, until Queensland declared itself home for the next while. Some of this time found me working in a call centre for people subscribing to an adult movie channel. It was far more interesting than the banking industry at times.

"Um."

Silence.

"I'm just ringing up for my husband."

"So you would like to subscribe to 'Night Moves' then?" I would reply in a friendly, accepting tone, always putting the women at ease.

Or the guys would ask, "What's it like? I mean, do you see *everything?*"

"I am sorry, sir. I've not viewed it myself. But I can offer you a one night trial for $6.95 and if you like it enough, you can call back and subscribe to it on a monthly basis."

And of course, there were the expected calls of, "What colour knickers have you got on?" Bronnie hangs up. But when the giggles had subsided, it was simply another office job. Friendships were formed with other staff, which made it more enjoyable. But my restlessness continued to fester.

We moved back to my home state of New South Wales. Dean, the man I had been with in England and the Middle East, had moved back to Australia with me. Soon after we relocated back to New South Wales, our relationship came to an end. We had loved each other dearly for years now and had been best friends for most of that time. It was devastating to watch our friendship fall apart. But our numerous lifestyle differences could no longer be swept under the carpet or laughed off, as had once been done.

I was a vegetarian. He was meat eater. Working indoors all week, I longed for outdoor life all weekend. He worked outdoors all week and wanted to be indoors all weekend. The list went on and on, and seemed to grow larger by the week. The things each of us delighted in, no longer delighted the other. A mutual love of music still bonded us and kept us hanging in there for a while. But in the end, the communication channel between us lost its strength and we each battled with our own loss, watching our shared dreams disintegrate before our eyes.

It was a heartbreaking time as the relationship finished and the grief of such loss arrived. As I curled up in a ball sobbing, wishing we could have made it work, I knew in my heart we couldn't. Life was calling us in different directions, and the relationship was now hindering our paths rather than helping them.

The search for more meaning in my life intensified and as a result, the work issue increased in prominence. Waking up to the fact that being an artist is a very hard way to survive until your work has gained momentum and a healthy reputation, I had to find a new direction in the meantime. Surviving as an artist was going to be possible eventually. If I could dream it, I could do it, after all.

But I needed to get back to earning and I needed to do it in a field that allowed me to work from the heart and to be my natural self. The pressure of selling products within the banking industry had increased and I had changed too much. I no longer fitted into that world, if I ever truly had. Determined to continue on my creative journey, the choice was made to work as a live-in companion again. At least then I wouldn't be stuck in a rent or a mortgage grind, which would also free me up from the rigidity of routine.

Despite the years of soul searching that had led up to this point, the final decision was almost a casual, flippant one. Simply, I'd take a job as a companion for the benefit of my creative path and to also work from the heart, all the while enabling me to live rent-free. I had no idea then that my yearnings for a heart-felt job had been so clearly heard, and the years to follow were in themselves going to be such a significant part of my life and my life's work.

Within two weeks, I had moved into a harbour-side home in one of the Sydney's most exclusive suburbs. Her elderly brother had found my client Ruth unconscious on her kitchen floor. After more than a month in hospital she was allowed home, providing she had twenty-four hour care.

My experience in the care industry had only been companionship with Agnes those years prior. I had not looked after sick people and was honest about this to the agency employing me, but they didn't mind. Carers who were willing to live-in were a commodity and they were not going to let me slip through their net. "Just pretend you know what you're doing, and call us if you need any help." Holy dooly, welcome to the care-game, Bronnie.

My natural empathy enabled me to do the job reasonably well for a new person. I simply treated Ruth as I would my own grandmother, who had been precious to me. Catering to her needs as they surfaced, I worked it out as I went along. The community nurse would come in every few days and ask me questions about things I had no idea about. Because I was honest with her, she ended up helping me enormously as I learned about medications, personal care, and industry jargon.

My employers would drop in now and then, too. Happy that the client was happy was enough for them, and off they'd go. They had no idea I was becoming emotionally and physically exhausted in a rapid time. I am not sure I had yet realised it myself.

Ruth's family was pleased because I was spoiling Ruth rotten. There were foot massages, manicures, facials, and lots of lovely bedside conversations over cups of tea. Like I say, I treated her as I would my own dear grandmother. I didn't know any other way.

Ruth would ring her bell throughout the night, too, and I'd be down the stairs in a flash, helping her onto the bedside commode to go to the toilet. "Oh, you are glamorous," she would to say to me as I wandered in. Her impression of my glamour was that I sometimes wore my hair in a bun to bed, simply because I was too exhausted to get the knots out at the time. And my so-called 'glamorous' nightdress was due to my mother's insistence I take it.

"You can't go to this lady's place and sleep naked or in any old thing," Mum had pleaded. "Please take this and promise me you will wear it." So in respect of my darling mother's wishes, I found myself wearing a satin nightdress to bed. Glamorous I was, half sleepwalking into her bedroom four or five times a night, eyes struggling to open, longing for reprieve from my exhausted state. Ruth would need me all of the following day too, so little chance was ever presented to catch up on a few hours of sleep. I was also doing housework, which I tackled during Ruth's afternoon naps.

Sitting on the commode, she would also want to talk then. Ruth loved all of the attention after years of living on her own. I was enjoying our friendship, too – except for hearing about what cups and saucers they had used at whatever dinner party thirty years ago, while she urinated on the commode at three in the morning, my body just longing to return to bed.

Over the weeks, Ruth spoke of the years around the bay and of the children playing down by the harbour. Horse and dray, plodding along through all of the quiet streets, had done the milk and bread deliveries. Sundays would see the neighbourhood all dressed in their best clothes for church. Ruth spoke about her children when they were young and of her husband long since passed. Her daughter, Heather, whom I found to be delightful, would drop in every day or two and was a breath of fresh air. Ruth's son and his family lived out in the country and had Heather not also mentioned her brother, it would have been easy to forget his existence. He did not play an active role in his mother's life.

Heather was the rock that supported Ruth throughout her decades as a widow. Ruth's elderly brother, James, also helped. He would wander down from his home about a mile away, every afternoon. You could set the clock by his visit. There he was in the same sweater, day-in, day-out. He was already eighty-eight years old and had never married. With a mind as clear as they come, he was a wonderful character, and it was my pleasure to know him and to enjoy the simplicity of his life.

Ruth was not recovering from her illness, however, and was still in bed after a month. More tests were done, and it was then I was informed that she was dying.

Walking down to the harbour with tears in my eyes, everything felt surreal. Children were playing in the shallow water. The footbridge hanging over the bay swung lightly as happy people walked over it. Ferries cruised by on their way to Circular Quay in the city centre. I walked as in a dream, as laughter rang out from a group of people having a picnic.

Sitting against a sandstone cliff, the water almost at my feet, I looked up at the beautiful sky. It was one of those perfect winter days, when the warmth of the sun is like a balm. Sydney is never totally freezing in winter, not like European winters. It was a glorious day, where a light coat was sufficient. Having already grown close to Ruth, the thought of her passing left me tearful for my own inevitable pain. The shock that I would be losing her was my first reaction. My tears flowed as a yacht sailed by, full of happy, healthy people. It then also hit me that I would be her carer, the one nursing her until the end.

Growing up on the cattle farm, then a sheep farm, I had seen a lot of animals dying or dead. It was not new to me, although I was still always terribly sensitive to it. But the society I was living in, the modern society of Western culture, was not one that exposed its people to dying bodies on a regular basis. It wasn't like some cultures where human death is out in the open and a very visible part of everyday life.

Our society has shut death out, almost as a denial of its existence. This denial leaves both the dying person and the family or friends totally unprepared for something that is inevitable. We are all going to die. But rather than acknowledge the existence of death, we try to hide it. It is as if we are trying to convince ourselves that 'out of sight, out of mind' really works. But it doesn't, because we carry on trying to validate ourselves through our material life and associated fearful behaviour instead.

If we are able to face our own inevitable death with honest acceptance, before we have reached that time, then we shift our priorities well before it is too late. This gives us the opportunity to then put our energies into directions of true value. Once we acknowledge that limited time is remaining – although we don't know if that is years, weeks, or hours – we are less driven by ego or by what other people think of us. Instead, we are more driven by what our hearts truly want. This acknowledgment of our inevitable, approaching death, offers us the opportunity to find greater purpose and satisfaction in the time we have remaining.

I came to realise how detrimental this denial is in our society. But at the time, on that sunny winter's day, it simply left me completely ignorant of what lay ahead with Ruth and of my role in caring for her. Resting my head back against the sandstone wall, I prayed for strength. Having already faced plenty of challenges in my upbringing and adult life, I believed I wouldn't have been brought to this place had I not been capable of doing the job. This didn't particularly ease my personal sadness and pain.

But sitting in the warmth of the sun that day, quiet tears falling, I knew I had a job to do and would give Ruth all of the happiness and comfort I possibly could for her dying weeks. I sat for a long time, contemplating life and how I hadn't seen this coming. Yet I was also accepting that I had gifts to share and this is what I was being asked to do. Walking back to the house a strong resolve developed within me. I would give this situation the absolute best I had, and would catch up on sleep later.

My employer dropped in later that day. Explaining that I had never even seen a dead person, let alone cared for someone towards their passing, I heard my words fall on deaf ears. "The family loves you. You'll be right."

'You'll be right' (as in, 'You'll be alright'), is such a common expression in Australian language that I accepted I would be. Ruth's deterioration was quite fast from that point. Other carers came in to relieve me on days off and as her needs increased, I was relieved of night duty. I was still called on by the other carers, as I oversaw the running of things. But, at least sleep was now possible.

The days were still special and more often than not, it was mostly just Ruth and me. It was a quiet neighbourhood, with occasional laughter ringing up through the trees from the harbour-side park below. Heather would drop in on us, as would James and a string of specialists doing their jobs. The learning on offer was immense and I was growing enormously in my role, without then realising the full extent of it. I simply did whatever needed doing and asked a lot of questions from everyone I could.

One morning as I was about to leave for two days off, excited to be heading out of the city to visit my cousin and to enjoy some lightness after the weight of it all, I noticed the smell from the bedroom. The night carer had either not noticed it, or had not wanted to, hoping it could be left for the day carer who was about to come on. I saw a lot of this in coming years.

There was no way I could leave my beautiful friend lying in it for another minute. Her bowels had opened and evacuated completely. Lying limp, Ruth was only able to reply to me with quiet grunts. Her major organs were collapsing. The night carer reluctantly tore herself away from the gossip magazine she was reading and helped me, as we cleaned this gentle woman and changed her sheets from underneath her. It was a relief when the day carer arrived, dropped everything and pitched in immediately with pleasant cheer. We had Ruth clean and resting, and in no time she was in a deep sleep, exhausted.

Sitting out in the bush with my cousin later that day, my heart was still back at the house. Welcoming the lightness and humour his company always provides, I was glad to be hanging out with him. But it was not going to be possible for me to stay away for two nights. Ruth was in my thoughts too much, and I was sure she didn't have that long left. I had only been at my cousin's for a few hours when my employer called and said that Ruth was in her last stages and could I come?

Arriving back around dark, the somber mood of the house was palpable before even walking inside. Heather was there with her husband, as well as the new night carer who had just arrived. She was a lovely Irish girl.

Heather asked would I mind if she went home? I replied gently that she had to do whatever felt right for her. So home it was. After she had left, though, it was initially a little difficult for me to remove judgment from the situation. I could only imagine my own mother dying and how I would move heaven and Earth to be with her at her passing.

They say that everything comes down to love or fear: every emotion, every action, and every thought. I concluded that fear was driving Heather's decision and for that I felt a rush of compassion and love for her. From the start of our association, I had found her to be a very practical person and somewhat detached. But this situation was foreign to me. I didn't want my own beliefs and conditioning to hinder my regard for someone I had come to care for, simply because she handled things differently to how I would have.

Sitting in the darkened room with Erin, the other carer, I came to accept and respect Heather's actions. She did what she'd had to do, because she had done all she could. For decades, she had kept her mother's life in order as well as that of her own family. She was completely and totally exhausted by now, both physically and emotionally. She had given all she possibly could and wanted to remember her mum sleeping peacefully, as she was when Heather left. I smiled with respect and my assumed understanding.

In conversation with Heather in the days afterwards however, I found out that Ruth had implied to Heather that she wanted her to go. Heather knew her mother well enough to read her wishes. So it had been in love she left, not fear at all. Similar situations also became somewhat familiar in the years to come. Not every dying person wanted his or her family there. They said their goodbyes while conscious and occasionally preferred to be seen out by carers, allowing their families to keep other memories instead.

Erin and I chatted quietly in Ruth's room, the presence of death lingering. Erin explained how in her family, the room would be filled with everyone by now. Aunts, uncles, cousins, neighbours, and children – everyone would come along to say their farewell, to send the person out.

We fell into spells of silence, both of us looking at Ruth, watching and waiting. The night was incredibly still as I quietly sent Ruth love from my heart. Erin and I would chat a little again, then go back into silence. She was a beautiful person to share the experience with, as she cared. It was in her naturally to do so.

"She's opened her eyes," Erin suddenly said to me, startled. Ruth had been in a semi coma for the entire shift so far. "She's looking at you."

I moved closer to the bed and held Ruth's hand. "I'm here, Sweetheart. It's OK."

She looked directly into my eyes and a moment later her spirit began to leave the body. It shook for a short time. Then all was still.

Instantly, tears rolled down my cheeks. Speaking silently to her from my heart, I thanked Ruth for what we had shared, told her I loved her and wished her well on her journey. It was a very reverent moment, full of stillness and love. Standing in the darkened room, all of my senses alive, I silently thought what blessings I had been given by having this time with her.

Then Ruth's body surprisingly took another huge breath. I jumped back, swearing, my heart beating out of my chest. "Holy shit!" I said to Erin.

She laughed at me. "That's quite normal you know, Bronnie. It happens a lot."

"Yes, well, thanks for telling me," I replied in shock, smiling at her. My heart was pounding hard and all of the reverence of the moment was gone. I stepped back beside the bed with great hesitance. "Is it going to happen again?" I whispered to Erin.

"It could."

We waited in silence for another minute or so, hardly breathing ourselves. "She's gone, Erin. I can feel she's gone," I finally said.

"God bless her," we both uttered quietly, at the same time. Moving our chairs closer, we sat with Ruth for a while in sacred silence and loving respect. I also needed to settle a bit, after the fright of the moment before.

Heather and my employer had asked me to call them when it had happened, which I did. It was about two thirty in the morning. There was no more either of them could do now. I'd also been directed earlier that day with how to proceed from here. So I called the doctor to come and issue a death certificate. When that was done, the funeral home was called.

Erin and I sat in the kitchen until Ruth's body was taken away about the time the sun was coming up. During those hours of waiting, we both went back to look in on Ruth at times. It was a compulsion to still care for her body, even though she had departed from it. I didn't like her being in the room alone. The strange, dark time afterwards was very special in a way. But there was also a tangible emptiness in the home that night, after she had passed over.

Ruth's home was offered to me the next day as a house-sitting situation. Heather said it would take months for the estate to settle and rather than leave the house empty, the family would feel more secure to have someone living in it. So I went on to live in Ruth's home for some time afterwards, which was a blessing for my physical situation. It was also good to be somewhere that had now become familiar to me.

I had realised the around-the-clock live-in work was going to be too exhausting. Never being able to do anything by halves, I now understood I would need to remove myself from future patients between shifts, by going home each night. Care work asked much more of me than straightforward companionship.

Over the following months, I watched and assisted as Heather moved Ruth's belongings onto new places. Her physical world was dismantled one piece at a time, as happens to everyone. I had been nomadic for so long that I still had an aversion to owning too much. As a result, I declined many things Heather kindly offered to me. They were just things, after all, and while they had belonged to my friend Ruth, I knew her memory would stay on in my heart, as it has.

I did fall in love with a couple of old lamps, though, and they are with me to this day. Ruth's home was later demolished by the new owners and replaced with a modern concrete creation. The old frangipani tree that had thrown summer scents throughout the home for decades was crushed in the blink of an eye and replaced with a lap pool. An invitation arrived for me to the housewarming party of the new place.

The people who had bought Ruth's home had been uncomfortable with the spiders and their webs across the trees in the garden. Yet Ruth and I had previously sat in the sun room watching the Golden Orb spider weave a web so strong you could lift it up to walk under. It was a marvel we had both loved and shared. Standing near the lap pool, looking at all of the new, fashionable plants that had replaced an established garden of love and longevity, I was delighted to see a Golden Orb spider weaving her web high across one of the new plants.

I sent love to Ruth with a smile and knew that in her own way, she was visiting me there that day. Her home may have been gone, but her spirit was with me. I thanked the new owner for the invitation, had a chat, and walked down to the harbour. Sitting where I had the day I first heard about Ruth being terminally ill, I felt grateful for all we had shared and for all I had learned through our association.

On that summer's day, I smiled realising just how much more I had been given back then, a lot more than just living rent-free. As the happy day unfolded before me, I continued to smile in gratitude. And by having directed my vision to that Golden Orb spider, Ruth had already smiled back.

HONESTY AND SURRENDER

ᴄᴓᴓᴓ

A few random shifts came my way after Ruth's departure. At shift handover I met other carers. This was the only brief time of socialising with other staff. Throughout the long twelve-hour shifts, there was no team banter or laughter, as handover was the only time we ever saw each other. The client, family, and medical professionals who dropped in became the only contact.

This made the relationships even more personal. It also gave me time to occasionally read, write, continue my meditation practice, or do some yoga. Many of the carers went crazy with too much time to themselves, and it was not unusual to arrive at a house and find the television on before breakfast. Grateful that I loved my own company, the long hours of silence suited me quite well. Even if there were people around, with a dying person in the home they were usually peaceful environments.

Walking into Stella's home in the tree-lined suburb, this was definitely the case. It wasn't just the fact that she was dying. These were peaceful, gentle people. Stella had long, straight, white hair. Graceful was the first word that came to mind when we met, despite the fact she was lying ill in bed. Her husband, George, was a beautiful man and welcomed me naturally.

Having to accept a family member is dying is an enormous life changing time in itself. When that person reaches the stage of needing twenty-four hour care, however, everything about the life these people knew has disappeared. Their privacy and the special moments of just the two of them in the home are gone forever.

Carers came and went, changing shifts morning and night. Some were regular but some only came once, in between their own regular clients. So there were new faces to deal with, new personalities and varying work ethics. Before long, though, I became the regular day carer for Stella. A community nurse would also visit, as would the palliative doctor. He was a man I saw briefly with many clients over the following years and what a special, delightful, kindhearted person he was.

After the experiences with Ruth, my employer said I'd handled it beautifully and offered me more training in palliative care, if I would like to go down that road. I accepted this offer, as I felt that life was calling me in this direction for now. The time and learning with Ruth had had a profound effect on me, leaving a desire to grow and experience more in this field.

My training involved two workshops. One of these was to show myself and other carers how to wash our hands properly. The other was a very brief display in lifting procedures. That was pretty much it, my full extent of formal training. Then sending me off to work with Stella, my employer told me not to tell them I'd only ever had one palliative client. She believed I could do the job, as did I.

Honesty had always been a significant part of my personality. But when questions came up from the family about my experience, I found myself lying, all because I needed the work. New laws were also coming in about staff qualifications, of which I had none. Even though I couldn't prove my skills by speaking of previous experience, however, I did also want Stella's family to feel at ease with me. I knew in my heart I could do the job well, as it was about gentleness and intuition more than anything. So I went along with the lies, saying I had nursed more people than I had when they asked. Lying felt so uncomfortable for me, though, I could never do it with another client.

Stella was very much into hygiene and wanted clean sheets on the bed every day. But she was also a lady of style and insisted on wearing a matching nightdress to go with the colour or pattern of the sheets. George laughed to me one day that he had found himself in trouble for choosing the wrong sheets for the nightdress she wanted to wear. I said to him laughing, as I ended up saying to the families of almost all of my future clients, "Whatever makes her happy."

And so it was that this tall, graceful woman lay dying in her choice of sheets and nightdress when she asked me about my life.

"Do you meditate?" she asked.

"Yes, I do," I happily replied. It was not a question I had expected.

Stella continued. "What path do you follow?" I told her, and she nodded in understanding.

"Do you do yoga?" she asked.

"Yes, I do," I again replied, "but not as much as I'd like to."

"Do you meditate daily?"

I said, "Yes. Twice a day."

I couldn't help but smile, when after a moment she replied with a gentle voice, "Oh, thank God. I have been waiting for you for ages. I can die now."

Stella had been a yoga instructor for forty years, long before yoga had become an everyday thing in Western culture. Back then it was something strange from the East. She had been to India several times and was very devoted to her path.

Originally, because it was too out-there for the world they lived in, Stella had said she was an exercise instructor when asked, rather than a yoga teacher. As society thankfully evolved over time and yoga became more mainstream, she came out of her shell and taught many students the arts and wisdom of this path.

Her husband was a retired professional who still did a little work from home. He pottered about peacefully and I enjoyed his presence. The home library was full of spiritual classics. Many I had read, but many I had wanted to and as yet hadn't. It was a reader's dream come true, particularly for one so interested in philosophy, psychology, and spirituality. I devoured them as much as possible. Stella would stir from her sleep, ask what book I was reading, where I was up to in the book, and pass comment on it. She knew them all. When she was alert enough for long conversations, which wasn't often enough, it was always about philosophy. We shared many theories and found our thinking not terribly different from each other.

My yoga practice also improved greatly. I didn't feel I had to hide what I was doing, or go off into another room. The door to Stella's bedroom was never closed, so fresh air blew through unhindered at all times. It was a lovely space to work in. Stella's peaceful white cat called Yogi would lie on the end of her bed and watch me. As the afternoons in the neighbourhood were particularly peaceful, I used that time the most to stretch and breathe. Thinking Stella was asleep, I would be delighted when she would pass a comment on something I was doing and how to improve that posture or to try another similar one, perhaps more dynamic and challenging, before she dozed off again.

At the time, I had been doing yoga for about five years. It had begun in Fremantle, a suburb of Perth, whilst living over in Western Australia. Twice a week I would jump on my pushbike and ride down to Fremantle from a couple of suburbs away. Kale was the teacher. He truly was a wonderful introduction for me to yoga. He hadn't found his own way to it until late in life. Back injury drew him to it. Obviously life had big plans for him and he did find his calling, much to the benefit of his many devoted students.

When we had left Perth, life became unsettled for some time. But yoga continued to call. Wherever I was living, I would search for a new class and sometimes join one briefly. But finding a class I could connect with as much as I had Kale's was in vain. It was not to be found.

During my time in Stella's bedroom, I came to see how I hadn't truly connected with my practice, as I was still looking to the teacher for the connection, instead of myself. This was changed permanently thanks to her guidance. I have enjoyed other classes since, as they push me a bit further than may happen in my home practice. They are also a great way to meet up with like-minded people. But my home practice doesn't waver now, as the practice itself is the teacher. Stella had made her mark on her final student.

Her biggest frustration was that she was ready to die and it wasn't happening. I would arrive in the morning and ask how she was feeling. "Well, how do you think I am feeling?" she would reply. "I am still here and I don't want to be."

She was also unable to meditate anymore. After all of Stella's years of mental discipline and the connection she had experienced with herself through meditation, she thought it would be a natural thing now as she approached her return home. In fact, she thought her practice would intensify. But it was my practice that did. Every afternoon when she drifted off again, I would do my afternoon sit. "You're so lucky," she would say to me later. "This is so frustrating. I can't meditate and I can't die."

"Perhaps you are still here for me. Perhaps there are still things that I need to learn through you and that is why your time has not yet come," I suggested.

She nodded. "I can accept that."

As is always the case when any two people interact, we were there to learn through each other. When I broached the subject of surrender, Stella began to find more peace within. As I sat beside her bed and spoke of days gone by, of learning to let go, she listened with interest.

Over the years, I had lived from one leap of faith to the next. I told her how I had hit the road south years earlier with nothing but a full tank of fuel, fifty dollars, and an intention to move somewhere cooler for a while. With a town on the far south coast of New South Wales in mind, I headed off in that general direction. Visiting friends along the way, I found a couple of days' work, which allowed me to continue the trip. Having already been so nomadic, I had friends dotted all over the place, and it was wonderful to see them again, some I'd not seen for almost a decade. I eventually arrived in the town intended but with little money.

A caravan park on the headland had the best view in town, overlooking the mighty Pacific Ocean. So I stopped there for a night. The back seat of my old jeep had been removed and replaced with a mattress. Curtains went up before I'd hit the road and there it was, I was mobile. Checking out the work opportunities in the town, things looked a bit challenging initially. But it was autumn, my favourite time of year. So I just savoured the perfect weather for a couple of days and did a lot of walking.

Paying for my site at the caravan park, though, was not going to be possible on an ongoing basis. My money was running out, and I was really only there for a shower and as a base while I made some contacts. So I bought some food and headed into the bush, following signs to an inland river not far away. Having lived by leaps of faith before, I knew I would have to face my fears head-on yet again. If I was going to will something to me through faith alone, I had to get my head out of the way, and that is always the hardest thing.

Unhealthy patterns surfaced in my mind, results from my past conditioning and society telling me I couldn't live this way. Fear started rearing its ugly head as I wondered how on Earth it was all going to come together, yet again. Bringing myself back to the present moment was the only thing that had saved me before and was the only thing that would save me now. And there is no better place to face your fears than in nature, where you can get back into the true rhythm of life.

When fears were sleeping, I enjoyed wonderful days in a healthy, uncomplicated routine of eating simple, wholesome food, swimming in the cleansing, crystal clear river, watching the curious faces of wildlife come and go, listening to birds with a variety of songs, and reading. It was a reverent time, spacious and beautiful.

Almost two weeks went by before I saw another person. The day I did see people was pleasant. It was a family of three generations, out at the river for a picnic lunch. This told me it was probably the weekend. I left my jeep open and went for a big bushwalk, giving them the place to enjoy. In the late afternoon I lay in the back of the jeep, still with the back and windows wide open, and read for a while. The beautiful light of dusk filtered magically through the trees.

As the family was leaving, the woman – who was my age and the mother of the two children – broke away from the group. Her husband, parents and children continued to their car. She walked over to me quietly and lent inside my jeep. I looked up from my book a little startled and smiled, as she simply whispered to me "I envy your freedom." With that we both laughed, and she left, without another word or time for me to reply.

Lying in the jeep that night, the curtains open, frogs singing by the river, and a blanket of a million stars keeping me company,

I smiled thinking of her. She was right. I was as free as they come. I didn't have enough money or food beyond the next few days, but right at that moment, I was as free as a person could be.

People have often asked me since about the various trips I did to the bush and other places in the country, and if I was ever scared for my safety. The answer was no, rarely did I have reason to be. There were a couple of potentially dodgy situations, like the hitch hiking thing. But I came out OK and put those rare occasions down to good learning. As every move was done intuitively, I tried as best to always move forward with trust, knowing I would be looked after.

We are mostly social creatures, though, so I headed into town again. I phoned my mother, with whom I have a healthy and loving relationship. Being a mother, she was always a little concerned for my welfare. But another part of her understood that nomadic life was a part of me. She didn't judge my choices, but was always relieved to hear from me. The day before she had spent two dollars on a lottery ticket, with the intention of winning me some money. She is such a naturally generous person that life blessed her.

"You give to me in so many other ways," she said. "I insist you take this money. It was with the intention of helping you that it came to me anyway." So I gratefully found myself with money to get through another couple of weeks.

Waking up in my jeep at the caravan park the next morning, I headed down to the rocks to watch the sunrise over the ocean. I love that first glimpse of light, where there are still stars out but a whole new day is coming. As the sky turned pink then orange, I sat on the rocks watching a pod of playful dolphins swimming by, flipping themselves out of the water for pure delight. I knew then that everything was going to turn out just fine.

After a long and enjoyable chat about life and travel later in the day, the owner of the park returned to my jeep dangling a key. "I don't need van number eight for another ten days. It is yours and I will not allow you to pay one cent for it. If my daughter was sleeping in the back of her car, I would hope someone would do the same for her," Ted declared.

"Bless you, Ted, thank you," I said, fighting back tears of gratitude.

So I had a roof over my head for the next ten nights and somewhere to cook. During this time, though, fears were starting to rage fiercely in me again about my situation. I had to earn some money. My food supply was again diminishing. Each day I visited all of the businesses in town, and while I met plenty of fine people, no work was forthcoming. Walking back up the hill to the headland and caravan, I took a deep breath, trying to stay present, but trying to find a solution, too.

I hated this part of my life, this compulsion to always throw caution to the wind and create such challenging situations for myself, time and again. Yet it was also addictive. Each time I did this, I challenged my fears head-on, and somehow I always, always landed on my feet again. In some ways each leap of faith became harder, as it brought me closer to the core of my deepest fears within. Yet each leap also became easier. I had tested my faith to the limit on many occasions previously and had gained wisdom and stronger faith in myself through the process. Life also made more sense to me this way, regardless of how hard it was at times. I just didn't fit in with the way conventional society works.

It was at that point, as I watched the high tide wash back out, that I remembered the importance of surrender, of letting go and allowing nature to weave its magic. The same force that balances the flow of the tides, the force that sees seasons come and go perfectly and creates life, was surely capable of bringing the opportunity to me I needed. But I had to let go first. Trying to control the timing and outcome was a terrible waste of energy. My intentions were already out there, and I had taken what action I could. My only job now was to get out of the way.

I laughed gently at myself, remembering I had forgotten this. It was a lesson from previous times. When I was out on the very end of a thin, flimsy, bending limb, the only thing to do was surrender and see where I landed. It was time to let go again.

Surrender is not giving up, far from it. Surrender takes an enormous amount of courage. Often we are only capable of doing so when the pain of trying to control the outcome becomes too much to bear. Reaching that point is actually liberating, even if it is not fun. Being able to accept that there is absolutely nothing more you can do, other than hand it over to the greater force, is the catalyst that finally opens the flow.

The next morning I headed down the rocks to the water, where dolphins at play greeted me again at sunrise. I was feeling completely empty and drained after the onslaught of fear, pain, and resistance, finally leading to the surrender. Emotional exhaustion had worn me out. But watching the dolphins, I absorbed the new dawn and slowly, gently, allowed myself to be refuelled by hope.

In casual conversation with some people on holidays in the caravan park a few days later, a job was offered to me in Melbourne, another seven or so hours south. "Why not?" I thought. I was free to go anywhere and had wanted to live in a cooler climate anyway. Melbourne soon became my favourite Australian city and remains so. But I hadn't considered moving there at the time and had no idea how much I would benefit from living in such a creative city. It was only through surrendering and staying present that I could allow the job opportunity to flow my way.

As I finished telling my story to Stella, we both smiled. She ate her half a strawberry, agreeing without ego. She had been trying to control the moment of her passing. It was time to surrender that control and as much as she didn't particularly like the idea, she accepted it might still be some time before her day came. It takes the body nine months to form. Sometimes it takes a little while for it to close down, too.

By now, though, she was very weak and almost off her food entirely. There was no energy to eat, but she accepted small pieces of fruit simply to taste things. The day before, it had been two grapes. Today it was half a strawberry.

Her illness should have seen her in a lot of pain, especially for how far along it already was, before she was diagnosed. But there was very little pain, which amazed her doctor. It was mostly exhaustion she experienced as it spread. All of the work she had done on her spiritual journey gave her a very strong connection with her body, now blessing her with being almost pain free. It was also what allowed her a smooth departure when the time came.

Two or three days previously, I had noticed her fingers had swollen to the point that her wedding ring was now causing deep indentations in her finger. It looked like it was affecting the circulation there. Phoning my employer, I was advised by the nurse that the ring had to come off. With George lying on the bed beside her, I worked on the finger with water and soap, gently removing it. It took so long to do, and by then both Stella and George were crying. I felt like the devil's advocate, except that by the time I had succeeded in removing this symbol of their love that had been there for more than half a century, I was crying, too.

Always such a dear man, George called her by a special, affectionate name that had been a part of their married life for so long. I left the room while they shared a rare moment of private closeness, lying in each other's arms for perhaps the last time ever. As I stood in the bathroom crying, I felt blessed to witness the depth of love that was between them. It was unlike any I had seen previously. They were true friends and both gentle, considerate people with everyone, and especially with each other. But it was still painful for me, watching them cry as the wedding ring was removed from Stella's finger forever.

Their son and daughters visited regularly and were there a great deal more now, as time was drawing in. I liked them all. They were very different to each other. But each of them was a decent and lovely person. One of the daughters in particular, though, I had grown especially close to.

A cool change came along unexpectedly one day, and I found myself at work without enough layers. George had insisted I put on one of Stella's cardigans. Both he and Stella then agreed how much it suited me. It was one of those things you wouldn't normally notice in the shop, as it wasn't your style. But when you put it on, you fell in love with it instantly. On this day the family, including Stella, gave me the cardigan to keep. Years later I still wear it. She had style, our Stella.

That night, she fell into a coma when I was at home sleeping.

I returned the next morning to find a solemn house. George and their son David were there. As the soft breeze blew in through the bedroom door George laid on the bed beside his beautiful wife. His hand held hers, which was now getting cold. Stella was still alive; but in these cases, as death gets closer, the circulation is affected in the extremities. Her feet had also lost their warmth. David sat on a chair holding her other hand. I sat on a chair farther down the bed, my hand on her foot. I guess I just needed to touch her, too.

After more than twelve hours of being in a deep coma, Stella opened her eyes and smiled at something towards the ceiling. George sat up. "She's smiling," he declared, startled. "She's smiling at something."

Stella had no awareness of us anymore. But the smile she gave to whomever or whatever she was looking at cemented something in me that has never waivered. Having had meditations previously that took me to blissful places well beyond the usual human plane, I had never doubted an afterlife. But looking at Stella's amazing happiness as she smiled to the ceiling with her eyes open, I knew now with total conviction that nothing would ever sway me from this belief. There is something more to go to, or return to.

After she smiled, Stella let out a small sigh, her eyes rolled back, and all was quiet. George and David looked to me for confirmation. Having only experienced Ruth's passing before now, I waited for the big breath, which was not forthcoming. "Is she dead? Is she dead?" they asked in despair and heart-broken sorrow.

I tried to find the pulse in her neck, but my own heart was beating so hard, I could only feel that rhythm. I was under immense pressure and had no idea what I was doing. They looked at me desperately. I didn't want to declare she had died and then find her living for another day or two, or even just taking one more big breath. So I prayed for guidance.

A calm came over me as I looked at her then, and I knew she had left. It had been such a smooth, graceful, and gentle departure I hadn't been able to tell. But this wave of love now sweeping through me confirmed she had gone. I nodded, and then George and David left the room immediately. The most heartbreaking sob echoed through the house as George acknowledged his beloved wife was gone. I sat in silence with Stella, as my own tears then also fell.

A couple of hours later, with the rest of the family there and practical details attended to, we said our goodbyes to each other. The morning had now warmed into a very hot day, and I was contemplating what to do with myself, really just wanting a superficial distraction. Still driving the same jeep from all of those miles travelled previously, I had to slam the driver's door to get it closed properly. It had been this way for some time. As I did so this day, the whole driver's seat window shattered and fell inside the door panels. I sat there staring at it, already numb from the morning's events and now even more shifted, due to the huge bang that came with the shattering. I looked out of the window, glass free except for a few fragments, and accepted that perhaps the best thing for me was just to go home.

It took three days for the replacement window to arrive. So I spent those days at home and down by the harbour. I thanked Stella constantly during this time for sending me home. It was the best thing, allowing me to simply be. A couple of months later I received a letter from Therese, the daughter of Stella's I had grown close to. The day after Stella had passed, Therese was walking down the street, naturally thinking of her mum. A huge white cockatoo flew right down in front of her, so close she could feel the wind from its wings. Stella was that sort of woman, capable of sending us signs, and I delighted in reading Therese's letter.

A year or so went by, and I visited the family for dinner. I was looking very forward to the night, especially to see darling George again and to see how he was getting on. Therese and her husband came along, too. The evening started out well and it was lovely to hear how George was becoming quite social, playing bridge and other things. Then somehow the dinner conversation ended up back in the "lie" department. Therese was asking questions as to how different her mum's passing had been to all of my previous clients, or something along those lines. That was my big chance to come clean and tell them how I had been so inexperienced when caring for Stella.

I really don't think they would have minded by then, as they were more than happy in the service they had received. But I couldn't come clean, as George was just so delighted to have me there and kept making a point of how beautiful it was for us all to be together again. It took him back to Stella, I am sure. I wanted to get Therese alone that night and tell her the full story, but no chance came up.

We lost touch soon after that night as life moved on. Some years later, though, we all reconnected and I was given the chance to tell the family of my inexperience, and of my regret in not being straight with them from the start. They were beautifully accepting and forgiving about it, saying I more than made up for it with empathy and compassion. They had felt from the start I was the right person to care for their mother, as had I. It was lovely to re-connect and remember what we had all shared together. Every winter, I still wear my cardigan and I think of Stella at times. Last winter I was wearing it as I re-read a book she had given me, pausing and smiling at my own memories. This work sure introduced me to some beautiful people.

But either way, the lying thing was a great lesson. After my time with Stella, I decided I would never again lie to clients. The main thing was that I had learned from it. I was an honest person and regardless of how difficult honesty may be to deliver, it was the only path I would ever walk comfortably.

Learning from what happened then allowed me to forgive myself, and this, is the greatest forgiveness of all.

REGRET 1:
I WISH I'D HAD THE COURAGE TO LIVE A LIFE TRUE TO MYSELF, NOT THE LIFE OTHERS EXPECTED OF ME

ᴄᏯᎧᏗᎧ

It took no time at all for Grace to become one of my favourite palliative clients. She was a tiny woman with a huge heart. This flowed on to her children; all of whom were parents themselves by now, and equally beautiful people.

Grace lived in a totally different part of the city, which was unusual for our clients. It was a suburban street like many others, with no mansions looming on either side. My first impression was it would be a good street for a television series, as it oozed with family energy. The thing I most liked about Grace herself, and her family, is they were very down to earth and genuinely welcoming.

My early days with her began as usually happened with clients, sharing stories to get to know each other. Familiar comments were heard in the bathroom about the loss of dignity Grace was experiencing, with someone else having to wipe her bum, and how a nice young thing like me shouldn't have to do such an awful job. I became used to that part of my work, though, and tried to lighten up the situation for Grace and for all of my clients by making no fuss of it. Being sick is certainly a way to dissolve the ego. Dignity disappears into the past forever when you are terminally ill. Acceptance of the situation and of someone else wiping your backside becomes inevitable, as clients become too sick to worry about such things after a while.

Married for more than fifty years, Grace had led the life expected of her. She had raised lovely children and now rejoiced in the lives of her grandchildren as they lived through their teenage years. Her husband had apparently been a bit of a tyrant, though, making married life for Grace very unpleasant for decades. It was a relief for everyone, especially Grace, when he had been admitted into a nursing home permanently only a few months before.

Grace had spent her married life dreaming of living independently from her husband, of travelling, of not living under his dictatorship, and mostly just of living a simple, happy life. Although she was in her eighties, she had still been fit for her age and healthy. Good health gives freedom of mobility, and this had been present for her when he was admitted into the nursing home.

Within a short time of her newly found and long awaited freedom, however, Grace began to feel very ill. A few days after this turning point, she was diagnosed with terminal illness, already quite advanced. What made this even more heartbreaking was that her illness was due to her husband's long-term smoking habit within the home. The illness was aggressive, and by the time a month had passed, Grace had lost all of her strength and was bedridden, other than hobbling slowly to the bathroom with a walking frame while assisted. Dreams she had waited all of her life to live were now never going to happen. It was too late. The anguish she suffered over this was ongoing and tormented her enormously.

"Why didn't I just do what I wanted? Why did I let him rule me? Why wasn't I strong enough?" were questions I heard regularly. She was so angry with herself for not having found the courage. Her children confirmed the hard life she had experienced and their hearts felt for her, as did mine.

"Don't you ever let anyone stop you doing what you want, Bronnie," she said. "Promise that to this dying woman, please." I promised and went on to explain how I was fortunate to have an amazing mother who had taught me independence by example.

"Look at me now," Grace continued. "Dying. Dying! How

can it be possible I have waited all of these years to be free and independent and now it is too late?" There was no denying this was a tragic situation and one that was going to be a constant reminder to live my own way.

In her bedroom, dotted with sentimental artifacts and photos of her family, we shared hours of conversations over those first weeks. Her decline was happening quite fast, though. Grace explained that she wasn't against marriage, not at all. She thought it could be a beautiful thing and a great opportunity to grow, through shared learning. What she was against was the doctrine of her generation, stating that you had to stay in a marriage regardless of anything. And so she had, all the while forfeiting her own happiness. She had dedicated her life to her husband, who had taken her love completely for granted.

Now that she was dying, she didn't care what people thought of her and anguished over why she hadn't worked this out sooner. Grace had kept up appearances and lived the way others expected her to, only now realising the choice to do so had always been her own and was based on fear. Although I offered support, including the need to forgive herself, the fact that it was all now too late continued to overwhelm her.

Most of my assignments were of this one-on-one kind, longer-term clients whom I would care for until they passed. There came to be many others dotted in between these over the years, though, clients whom I would see just a few times in between their own regular carers. These words from Grace – filled with anguish, despair, and frustration – became familiar words from many others I also came to meet. Of all of the regrets and lessons shared with me as I sat beside their beds, *the regret of not having lived a life true to themselves* was the most common one of all. It was also the one that caused the most frustration, as the client's realisation came too late.

"It's not like I wanted to live a grand life," Grace explained in one of many conversations from her bed. "I am a good person and I didn't wish to harm anyone." Grace was one of the sweetest people I have ever met and wouldn't have been capable of harming anyone anyway. It just wasn't in her. "But I wanted to do things for me, too, and I just didn't have the courage."

Grace now understood it would have been better for everyone had she been brave enough to honour this desire. "Well, everyone except for my husband," she said with disgust towards herself. "I would have been happier and would not have let this misery permeate our family for decades. Why did I put up with him? Why, Bronnie, why?" Her heartbreaking sobs burst out and continued to flow as I held the dear lady close.

When her tears subsided, she looked at me with fierce determination. "I mean it. Promise this dying woman that you will always be true to yourself, that you will be brave enough to live the way you want to, regardless of what other people say." The lace curtains blew softly, allowing the day outside to enter the bedroom, as we looked at each other with love, clarity, and determination.

"I promise, Grace. I am already trying to. But I promise you now that I will always continue to do so," I replied with heartfelt truth. Holding my hand, she smiled, knowing that at least her learning wasn't going to be totally wasted. Explaining to Grace that for over a decade of my adult life I had worked in those unsatisfying banking, administration, and management roles, she started to understand me more and listened with great interest. Further years in banking had been added to this tally later, when I had returned from overseas. But I called those my weaning years, weaning myself out of the industry.

The first couple of years out of school were fun. There were many trainees and work was a social thing above all else. All of the trainees were seventeen or eighteen years old. So work was really just about catching up with friends and earning money to fund our weekends. The work itself was very easy for me at first and may have stayed that way, if my heart had been in the job. It never was, though. After those first years, I quickly became restless and began questioning life. Yet I carried on with the life expected of me for a decade more, the whole time knowing there was something else waiting but not having the courage to seek it.

What kept me there most was the fear of ridicule I would face from some family members, if I broke out of the mould they expected me to fit. I was living someone else's life through my shoes and it was never going to work. Yet I carried on, changing bank jobs, uniforms, and locations regularly. As a result, I found myself on an accelerated career path, due to having worked for most of the banks and in more roles than a normal person my age would have. I was a success by default.

Desperately unhappy, I continued to give my working week to an industry that did nothing for my soul. There are plenty of people who love their jobs in banking, and I am happy for them. Banking needs such people. These days, too, there are opportunities to work in areas where you are giving back to the community and other noble avenues. But like Grace, I had been living the life others expected of me, not the life I wanted to.

As I could do no right with some of my family and was struggling to be who they wanted me to be, staying in a 'good job' would at least keep them off my back in that area of my life. I was trapped by fear and the potential pain that would be created by setting myself up for even more judgment than I had already endured.

Being the black sheep in any family is never an easy task. Black sheep have a different role to play in family dynamics. But it is not always easy. When some of the main players in the unit gain their power by reducing the strength of others, it is a hard road upwards. But working amongst so many families in this line of work, I came to observe that very few families are free of conflict on some level. Every family has its learning, every one of them. Mine was no different, though this realisation didn't necessarily ease my own pain at the time.

Making jokes of me had been a family sport for as long as I could remember. I was a swimmer amongst a family of horse riders, a vegetarian from a sheep farming family, a nomad in a family of settlers, and on it went. Often things said were in jest, and the person saying so may not have realised the pain they were causing at the time. But jokes tend to wear thin after a few decades of hearing them. At other times, though, too often things said were intentional and just outright cruel. Even if you had the strength of a thousand people, it does wear you down after years. Particularly when you have trouble even recalling a period of your life when being ridiculed, yelled at, or told you were hopeless, were not a part of it.

Consequently, up until this time I had never particularly enjoyed family dynamics. So the easiest way to handle this back then was just to keep living the life expected of me. Eventually, though, I did begin to withdraw and close down around them. It was my own coping mechanism.

Artists the world over are also a misunderstood lot, and I was an artist. I just hadn't realised it yet. All I knew was that selling insurance products to people just wanting to bank their pay cheques was really not up my alley. The branch sales at the end of the month held absolutely no relevance to me. I didn't care about anything except giving the customers friendly, warm service, which I did very well. But that was not enough in the changing face of the banking industry. It was all sell, sell, sell.

They say that we do more to avoid pain than we do to gain pleasure. So it is when the pain becomes too much that we finally find the courage to make changes. Until then, the pain within me was just continuing to fester until it did reach the breaking point.

When I left yet another 'good job' to go and live on the island, confusion reigned. 'Why would she do that? Where is she going to this time?' And through all of this I was just thinking with excitement, 'I'm going to live on an island!' The farther away, the happier I was. My life was my own there, and it was a good life. Any contact I did have with the mainland was to my dear mother, who was my rock and treasured friend.

It was during these years on the island that I first dabbled in meditation. Later I found my way to the path that would offer me the opportunity to connect with my own goodness in ways no other had. Through this path, I began to understand and experience compassion. It is such a beautiful and powerful force.

The pain I had accepted from others had been their own suffering projected onto me. Happy people do not treat other people that way. They don't judge others for living a life true to his or her self. If anything, they respect it. Recognising the pain carried into my generation from previous ones, I had the choice to break free of it in my own life. I was never going to be able to control another and had no desire to. People change because they want to and when they are ready.

Learning to view life compassionately, and accept that I may never have the understanding or loving relationships I had once yearned for, was liberating. It transformed my life on so many levels. Knowing the ongoing pain of my own healing, I accepted that not everyone has the courage to face his or her past, at least not until it becomes unbearable.

To a degree, the same dynamics persisted for some years after, but began to affect me less and less. It took strength and time, but I now saw that it was not about me. It was about whichever person was trying to give me their criticism or judgment.

A Buddhist story is that a man came shouting angrily at Buddha, who remained unaffected by him. When questioned by others as to how he remained calm and unaffected, Buddha answered with a question. "If someone gives you a gift and you choose not to receive it, to whom then does the gift belong?" Of course it stays with the giver. So it was with words that were still unjustly dumped onto me sometimes. I stopped taking them on, and instead I felt compassion. After all, those words were not coming from a place of happiness.

The most important thing I have ever learnt in life though – the most, most important thing – is that *compassion starts with yourself.* Developing compassion for others allowed the healing to begin and continue. It removed me from the equation somewhat when the old behavioural patterns still tried to reign. I could recognise the suffering and see it wasn't about me at all. It was someone else's own pain coming up and out. This didn't just apply to family relationships, of course. It was relevant to all relationships, personal, public, and professional. We all suffer at some time. We all have pain, every one of us.

But learning how to develop compassion for myself was much harder, and though I didn't know at the time, it was going to take years. We are all so hard on ourselves, unfairly so. Learning to give myself loving kindness and acknowledge that I too had suffered enormously was such a difficult change to make. It was *almost* easier to listen to unfair opinions from others and take them on, as it was so familiar. It may not have brought happiness, but learning to be kind to myself and give myself compassion above everything else was certainly a process I had to grow into. But the healing had at least now begun.

With this new intention of self-love, self-respect and self-compassion, the old family dynamics started losing power. I found the strength to speak back, allowing myself to finally be heard, rather than continuing to withdraw. Of course, this was my own pain now being expressed and not really about the people I addressed at all. We all interpret things that happen to us in our own way. So it was about me expressing and releasing my own suffering. Breaking the patterns of decades took a lot of guts. But my pain gave me that, and I had nothing to lose anymore. As it was, I just couldn't carry the pain of silence any longer.

In the end, though, it was really only the desire to be loved, accepted, and understood by each other that was truly fuelling the pain in us all. So compassion was the only way forward: compassion and patience. In spite of everything, love, in its own fragile disguise, still existed between us.

It was as if I had been swimming down the same river over and over, and each time I would come across a large rock blocking my natural flow. It was always there. One day, though, I realised that it may *always* be there. So rather than have to face that same rock, that same blockage, repeatedly, I was choosing somewhere different to swim, somewhere that would allow me to move forward freely and naturally. I didn't have to set myself up for that hurdle over and over, one that hindered my natural progress, causing blockages and pain every time without fail.

It was time to do things differently. It was time to choose a different way, to speak up and say 'enough'. I wasn't willing to tolerate the same patterns anymore. Even if it turned out lonelier, at least it may lead to peace. The other path certainly wasn't peaceful.

After speaking up, things started to change within myself. I grew stronger in self-respect and clearer in self-expression. Some new and healthier seeds had finally been sown. I didn't yet know how to nurture them, but they were planted at least. It was time to start living as who I wanted to be, one small step at a time.

After sharing all of this with Grace, we grew closer without effort. She agreed that all families have their learning. She couldn't think of one family that hadn't had its challenges, and believed that families bring the greatest gifts of learning for most people. We discussed how the only way to experience love is to accept people totally as who they are and have no expectations of them. While it may be much easier said than done, it was the most loving approach possible.

Grace shared many stories with me – reflecting on her life, of the children growing up, the neighbourhood changing, then often back to her dying regret. She wished she'd had the courage to live a life true to her own heart, not the life others expected of her. When there is limited time left, there is little to lose by being totally honest. What we shared with each other now was straight to the core of important things. There was no idle chatter anymore as all of the subjects covered were deeply personal. Opening up to Grace was unexpectedly very healing for me, and my listening ear became healing for her.

Eventually we also came onto the subject of where my life was now, my musical directions and how I had started to write songs and perform. Over a cup of tea, Grace insisted I bring my guitar to work the next day and play her something, which was an absolute pleasure for me. With a heart of happiness, I sang to Grace as she smiled and hummed, sitting up in her bed. She embraced every song I shared, receiving them as if each one was the best song in the world. Her family came to hear some of them, too, and was equally beautiful and supportive. One song in particular Grace absolutely loved, as she had always wanted to travel. It was called 'Beneath Australian Skies'.

After that day, she would ask me to sing to her regularly. There was no need for a guitar, Grace had said. So I'd sit there in her bedroom, singing to this delightful little lady, as she closed her eyes smiling, absorbing everything I sang. Songs were requested over and over, and I never tired of singing them to her.

Each day Grace's health deteriorated. Her tiny size reduced even more. Old friends came to say their goodbyes. Relatives sat by her bed, chatting and fighting back their tears. Her family was a hands-on one, very involved, and their visits regular. I liked that. There was also gentleness in them that I was drawn to. When they were all gone, though, it was just Grace and me again, and the request for more singing resurfaced. They were special times.

She was not able to walk well now, and though Grace had accepted the use of the commode by the bed, she refused when it came to her bowel movements. She wanted to use a proper toilet so I didn't have to clean the commode. There was no budging her on this, even when I tried to assure Grace it was no big deal for me to do. So ages passed as we made our way to the bathroom, which thankfully was next to her bedroom. She was very weak. When the business was done and she was clean, I assisted her with standing up then pulled her underpants back up. Balancing her while doing the undies thing had to be quite a swift move.

As we then started our hike back to the bedroom, Grace leaning on her walking frame and me following, holding her hips, I noticed that in the rush I had tucked a little of her nightdress into the back of her underpants. Smiling at this dear little woman in her last days, tottering back to bed, I was then overwhelmed with joy as she started to sing 'Beneath Australian Skies' as she walked. A few of the words were in the wrong places, but that just made the moment even more endearing.

I knew then that I had just experienced the high point of my musical career. Nothing that could ever happen again would ever top the joy I experienced at that moment. If I never wrote another song it would not have bothered me. To have brought this dear person so much pleasure through my music, and to then receive that pleasure back by hearing her singing my song in her final days, opened my heart more than anything I had ever hoped for musically.

Arriving at work a couple of days later, it was obvious that today was to be the last for Grace. Explaining that I was going to call her family, she initially shook her head no. Weak and exhausted, she reached up and hugged me. To save her little arms the effort, I lay on the bed and held her in my own. She liked that and we lay talking softly for a while, as her fingers stroked my arm. Asking why she didn't want the family there, she said she didn't want to cause them any more pain. She loved them too much.

But they needed to say goodbye, I said, and not giving them that choice may end up causing them both pain and guilt that they would have to live with. She understood and agreed, accepting that she didn't want them to feel guilty for not being there. So phone calls were made, and the family soon arrived. But just before they did, she said to me through her exhaustion, "You remember our promise, Bronnie, don't you?"

Nodding through my tears, I said, "Yes."

"Live true to your own heart. Don't ever worry what others think. Promise me, Bronnie," her voice now a barely audible whisper.

"I promise you, Grace," I said gently. Squeezing my hand, she drifted off to sleep, waking again only for brief moments to acknowledge her lovely family who then sat by her bedside until the end. Within a few hours, Grace drifted off. Her time had come. Sitting quietly in the kitchen afterwards, my promise to her was still fresh in my ears. But it was not just Grace I had made the promise to. It was also to myself.

Standing onstage launching my album a few months later, I dedicated that song to her. Grace's family was in the audience. The spotlight blacked out most of the faces but I didn't need to see them. I could feel the love they were sharing as I remembered that dear little woman who hadn't lived as she wanted, but who had inspired me to instead.

PRODUCTS OF OUR ENVIRONMENT

Anthony was only in his late thirties when we first met one Saturday afternoon. He had dark-blonde curly hair, and despite being ill, had a natural look of mischief about him. It was a big change for me to be caring for someone younger. Striking up a friendship was a breeze, and despite the circumstances, we enjoyed an element of humour from the start.

With a younger brother, four younger sisters, and a high profile family in the business world, he had been very indulged throughout his life. Whatever Anthony wanted was his and he used it to his advantage as a younger man. But he also had big shoes to fill due to the financial success of his family. This pressure worked in reverse, and despite intelligence and opportunities, he had very low self-esteem. He masked this quite well beneath his humour and mischief. Anthony could not be what his family wanted him to be; as the oldest son in the family, this created a lot of pressure within him.

His years as a young adult were spent driving fast cars, being chased by police, hiring the most expensive working girls, and causing havoc to anyone who crossed his path. This was territorial land between the young men of the wealthy suburbs. Some of the actions Anthony had employed in his past were hardly endearing. But due to being a man of little self-worth, he also lived quite recklessly, challenging life to some dangerous levels. One such act left him in hospital with damaged organs and limbs, with the potential of losing his health forever, and the freedom that comes from such health.

The doctors were doing what they could to return his freedom to him, but things were not looking hopeful. Anthony was pretty resigned to it, though. Already realising he had probably done some permanent damage, he asked the doctors for the next operation to go ahead as soon as possible, so he could know either way. A couple of surgical procedures were done. Then painkillers kept him sleeping for the first week or so, as I sat beside his bed in the hospital room. After that it was a case of wait and see, hopefully allowing for a gradual recovery.

We fell into the habit of me reading to him. It started one evening when he asked me what I was reading. After spending that time living in the Middle East previously, I wanted to spend more time there. The book I was reading was an intelligent, unbiased look at the way of life in that region and the history. While I was not in denial about the subjugation of women in some of these countries, or the extent that some of the extremists from these nations go to in the name of religion (just as extremists from any religion lose sight of the teachings of kindness that are common in all religions), I had also seen a side of this culture that is unfortunately never portrayed in the media.

These warm-hearted people were wonderfully family orientated, and some of the most hospitable hosts that I had come across. Beautiful hearts were opened, and they welcomed me without hesitation. This has also been the same with people from that region I have since come to know in Australia. We have lost so much of the family connection in the West, particularly where the older generation is concerned. I was seeing this first hand by the amount of lonely people in nursing homes, during the random shifts I sometimes had to do in them.

Other cultures and how differently we all choose to live fascinate me. So do the culinary delights to be discovered through other cultures. Yet we are all very much alike in other ways, too. Racism is something I will never understand. The majority of us are the same, in that we just want to be happy. And on some level, we all have hearts that suffer.

Anthony was keen to hear more of what I was learning. So after making us a pot of herbal tea, its aroma wafting gently through the room, I brought him up to date on the book so far. The reading then continued, but now out loud. We would share an hour or two like this every day, and it became a time we both enjoyed. Because we had quite a few weeks of this, I was able to introduce Anthony to books he would have never come across otherwise. Offering him a choice of topics, he always insisted he would be happy with whatever I read.

So I introduced some spiritual classics to him. Books came to be shared about life, philosophy, and thinking outside of the square. Discussion would flow on naturally afterwards as I tended to his needs: lifting up an arm that was not working, another in a plaster cast, dressing the wound on a leg that was not working; then feeding him, combing his hair, and attending to other personal grooming needs.

In the end, though, the physical damage resulting from his actions meant the operations were not wholly successful. Some things were fixed. But some parts of him were damaged for life. So he was unable to go home, due to life ahead now requiring assistance with permanent personal care. It was then decided he would go into a nursing home, one of the best in the city, at least according to the brochure and the price.

Anthony was a young man now surrounded by drab coloured walls, and dying, elderly people. It was an awful environment, and I longed to take to the walls with brighter coloured paint. Initially, he was happy enough, though. It brought him peace that the pressure had been lifted from his family, as they knew he was being cared for. He was also able to bring good cheer to the older residents, and they loved him. Yet over time, his light grew dull, and the shortage of outside stimulus numbed his intelligence from lack of use. He started to become a product of his environment.

We are all fairly malleable, bendable creatures really. While we have the choice to think for ourselves and have free will to live the way our hearts guide us, our environment has a huge effect on us all, particularly until we start choosing life from a more conscious perspective.

Another example of being influenced by the surrounding environment is watching down-to-earth and already happy people get caught up in the chase for more, more, more after a job promotion. The desire to keep up with new friends on the new level of income often sees people change within to suit their environment.

The area they were once happy living in is no longer good enough, so they move to somewhere more suitable, for example. Sometimes this will bring happiness, sure, but not always.

Many country people also adapt to city life and become affected by city fashions and busier lifestyles. Not that there isn't fashion in the country. There definitely is. But again, it is a case of being influenced by where you live. Some people raised in cities also adapt to country life and slow their lifestyles down, ditching their labels and finding happiness in jeans and gumboots, as they plod around on their acreage. Wherever we are, our environment influences us enormously if we hang around long enough.

During my mid twenties I was having a lot of fun. The start of that decade had been hard for me. By the time I was nineteen years old, I was engaged to be married and had a serious life complete with mortgage commitments. It was an unhealthy relationship for the most part. Somehow I survived that time, though. Looking back, I have no idea how. An excess of mental abuse, psychological games, and being exposed to various states of rage expressed by my partner continuously diminished my confidence.

It all became too much around the same time as I scored a new job, not surprisingly, in a bank. The team at work was fantastic, and I found myself starting to enjoy life again. Having steady work also allowed me to dream of a life beyond my current situation, and I moved out. Before too long, I transferred to the north coast with my job, for a fresh start.

In no time at all dancing and frivolity were given free license and became a happy, carefree part of my life. There were also a lot of drugs around me. By now I knew drinking wasn't for me – although I hadn't yet reached the point where I would give up alcohol forever, drinking was not a big part of my life. There was plenty of other stuff on offer, though, and within a year I experimented with most of it. These were the days before synthetic drugs like ice and others I don't even know the street names of. Homegrown pot was common in my circle of friends, and when another friend gave me the opportunity to try opium, I did.

I was in a space where I felt I could try new things but was clear enough in myself to let most of it go after one experience, though I never tempted that theory with heroin, thank goodness. I never went near it. Thankfully only one experiment was the case with opium, magic mushrooms, LSD, and cocaine, all of which I tried within that twelve month period but never again. There was a need in me for some recklessness I think, after the confines of my upbringing and the previous relationship. But underneath all of this, on an unconscious level, was a total lack of self-worth that had become a part of me and was still being nurtured.

The life of excessive drug indulgence wasn't for me, though, and I knew that immediately. While I was happy to try some things, I told myself it was more out of a desire to experience life than the need to be 'off my face'. Consciously, it didn't take me long to work out that I preferred a healthier life. Unconsciously, though, there was still so much to be undone after decades of allowing the opinions of others to dominate my belief system. Happiness was still very dependent on external forces.

A few years afterwards, and following the island stint, I was living in England pulling beers in the village pub. Speed was around a lot. After doing a couple of lines, the local lads would come into the pub with huge dilated pupils, whilst grinding their teeth all night. Their regular routines were the same year in, year out. So when someone scored speed, it altered their realities enough to give them a different view of the same scene. It was merely boredom they were trying to escape from – and watching them on the days after, with the melancholy and exhaustion that followed, I had to wonder if the price was worth it.

There were a few occasions where my partner and I decided to join in. But it didn't take us long to realise it wasn't our thing. The comedown from speed was awful and I hated myself for doing this to my body. Yet about a month or so later, I found myself experiencing a life changing time, again being influenced by my environment and the lack of will and conscious choice to live a better life.

Dean was working all weekend, so I joined the ranks of the other village lads and jumped on a train up to London for the night. Despite being in my late-twenties, I had never been to a rave, simply because they didn't play my sort of music. But rather than see me at home on my own, the lads convinced me to join them, promising me the time of my life. They were all my mates, so off I went.

A previous experience on ecstasy, the only occasion I had tried it, had been OK. I'd had a silly night and survived the comedown, although definitely not enjoyably. My stomach felt awful, and my energy was incredibly low for days. It had felt like enough of an experience, though, and I had declined any offers of it since. I also lived with self-loathing afterwards, and I could do without any more of that. There were enough of those thoughts in me already. Yet here I was on the train to London with eight guys convincing me to have an ecstasy pill.

Those in the city scene were dropping several pills every week, so what was the big deal about me having one little one? I don't blame the guys at all, though, not in the slightest. They enjoyed that stuff and were only trying to get me to join them. The final choice was ultimately mine as the pill slid down my throat, just as the train pulled into Victoria Station. It was the middle of winter and absolutely freezing outside, as London is at that time of year.

From the moment we walked into the club, I hated the music and wanted the night to be over. Acoustic music was always going to be my thing, much more than anything digital (though each to their own, of course). Techno music blared out through the speakers. Making a conscious choice to stop judging the situation and accept I was there until sunrise, I loosened up and joined the lads on the dance floor. While they were having a blast immediately, I was merely enduring it.

Then the pill kicked in with full intensity, and I knew I had to get out of the crowd. Sweat poured off me. Every bump of anyone's body on the dance floor made me claustrophobic. I stumbled around trying to find some space. The bass thumped through the floorboards and through my body. Smiling faces from the lads who were dancing nearby blurred into somewhere else. I was losing control fast, and I had to get to a safe place.

Noise, laughing faces, and lighting were increasingly distorted as I made my way in a desperate haze to the women's toilets. I couldn't keep a cubicle all to myself for the whole night, as much as I wanted to. After contemplating this for some time while in the cubicle, I reluctantly surrendered the private space when girls started knocking on the door to see if anyone was in there.

It was too cold to go outside of the club and the first train home wasn't until six am. The noise of the ladies' toilets and the laughter of people coming and going left me in a swirling daze. Then I spotted the window ledge. My haven, I decided. Climbing onto the sink I managed my way onto the ledge, which was plenty wide enough for me to sit on without any risk of slipping off. Sliding across, I found a nice little corner out of the way, overlooking the sinks in the ladies room. Busyness and chaos were below. But I could now rest my back and head against the window and try to find some peace.

Sweat continued to pour from me. The icy window I was leaning against brought much-needed reprieve. I was in my own world now and could possibly handle things better. My poor heart was beating faster than could ever be natural for a human heart, and I prayed it would survive the night. It didn't slow down. Yet it didn't cross my mind to ask for medical help either. Maybe it was a subconscious fear of the law and illegal drugs. I don't know. But sitting with my head resting back against that icy cold window was what I felt I most needed.

"Are you alright, Love?" an English girl asked me, tugging at the hem of my jeans, which were at eye level to her.

I vaguely heard her but sat open mouthed, head resting back, staring at the ceiling. It was just too hard to answer. My heartbeat was out of control and I couldn't move.

"Are you alright, Love?" she persisted. With every ounce of effort I could muster, I looked down at her and nodded.

"Do you have any water?" she asked. I shrugged my shoulders to which she disappeared, only to return with a bottle of water for me. "Drink this," she insisted. Obliging, I then watched her re-fill the bottle from the bathroom tap.

"Thanks," I managed to say with a slight smile. The conversation was good for me, as difficult as it was. I had to concentrate rather than be lost in the trip my mind and body were taking. We managed to chat for a while. She was an angel.

Throughout the whole night I remained on that window ledge, unable to move, my heart still pounding out of my chest, the freezing night air on the window behind me balancing the excess heat within my body. That beautiful woman continued to come in regularly and check on me, topping up my water bottle and chatting with me each time. I don't know who she was to this day, but I hate to think what would have happened to me without her.

About half an hour before the club shut, she helped me down. I was still terribly off my head and not enjoying it one bit, but I could speak more clearly now. We managed to smile and chat a little. But even though we made slight jest of it, we both knew the seriousness of what I had been through, and I hugged her in thanks. She then led me back out into the club to find the lads. They had been looking for me for half the night and were frightfully relieved to see me. "Keep an eye on her," the woman told them, handing one of them my hand and saying goodbye to me with a kiss and a smile.

On the train home, the lads couldn't stop laughing with each other and talking about what a fantastic night it had been, wishing they were still there and sorry the drugs had worn off. I lent my head against the window and feigned sleep, knowing it would be some time before that was truly possible. My heart was still beating out through my chest, and my only thought was that I wished it would all just wear off.

The days of messing my precious body up with toxic chemicals were behind me from that day onward. Sleeping for two solid days afterwards, I awoke as a new woman grateful for the huge lesson I had been given. Lying there looking at the ceiling, exhausted from the ride my poor body had been through, my biggest relief was that I had survived it. It was time to treat myself with more respect and look after the gift of health I had been given.

Several years later I was offered an ecstasy pill at a gig, which I declined politely without hesitation. It felt so foreign to my world by then. I realised I had again grown into a product of my environment, thankfully, my new environment. My lifestyle had become one of health. Social times with friends were spent over healthy food, drinking tea around fires, long walks, and swimming in rivers. It was an environment that suited me much better. I didn't mind at all being a product of this environment.

Anthony, though, had become a product of his environment in the worst possible way. During my visits over his first year in the home, he would love to discuss current affairs from the radio or television. He was astute and always ready to offer an intelligent opinion or a bit of cheek. He also encouraged me to share stories with him, as to what was happening in my own life and was genuinely interested.

Yet over time, his light faded to the point that he would even decline my offer to take him outside. Previously we'd had delightful times, soaking up the sunshine and talking to passers-by. Sometimes we would just sit in the garden of the home, watching the birds and catching up with each other that way. Either way, they were always fun times with lots of laughter and conversation.

If any one of his friends or family suggested he try to learn new skills and create a better life than his current one, he would shut off from listening. "I don't see the point," he said to me time and again. "Things are fine here, I accept this lot in life." Anthony felt he deserved what had happened to him due to the harm he had done to others in the past.

"You've paid your dues, Anthony," I would say. "You've learnt from it, and that's what matters." But he wouldn't forgive himself. Also, he couldn't be bothered to create a better life. Anthony had slowed down to the pace and routine of the nursing home and had no aspirations to return to regular life in society again. His disabilities somehow gave him a sense of relief in a way, as if he didn't have to try anymore. This was despite plenty of people with various disabilities living full and inspiring lives elsewhere. But most of all, with these excuses he couldn't set himself up to fail. When questioned, he admitted to me he didn't have the courage to try anymore. If he didn't try, he couldn't fail. Not one ounce of motivation remained in him, and as the sun rose and set each day, Anthony chose to sleep his life away instead.

I continued to visit him occasionally for another year or so, as oppressive as his environment was. But one-sided friendships are exhausting for anyone, and this is what it was becoming. Anthony had lost the motivation to phone anyone, including me, as he always used to in between visits. When I did see him, our conversations now revolved around how well his bowels were working and how rude the employees were. His lack of interest in his appearance, too, was impossible to ignore.

Anthony had grown old before his time, and while he was still at least thirty years younger than most of the other residents, he now fit right in. He was a product of his environment. Watching this lovely man's light fade offered another reminder about how important having courage is in order to live the life your heart desires. Sadly, his life was an example of what I didn't want.

A phone call from his younger brother a few years later told me Anthony had passed away. Until then, his life had not changed at all and he had continued to refuse any outings from the home, including family gatherings. Anthony said he just couldn't be bothered, his brother told me. I couldn't help but wonder what his final thoughts were when he was lying there looking back over his life.

The impact of Anthony's sense of failure drove me forward. With a total lack of effort, Anthony had given himself absolutely no opportunity to improve or change. Failure was not about whether he would have been successful or not in whatever he tried. Just having a go would have been a success in itself. Anthony's biggest failure lay in becoming a complete product of his environment, lacking any desire to challenge himself and hence, improve his life. It was such a waste of a good and intelligent person, and of the natural gifts he had been born with.

So if we were all to become a product of our environment, myself included, the best thing I could do was to choose the right environments from here on, ones that would suit the direction I wanted my life to move toward. It was still going to take courage to live the way I wanted. But this new awareness, of the potential effects the surrounding environment could have on me, would make the journey easier.

And so it was with this consciousness and renewed bravery that I became more mindful about the life I was creating, and the power that lies in the freedom of choice.

TRAPPINGS

ఌఐఞౚ

Not all of the relationships formed with clients started out positive. While the bulk of my work was with dying people, sometimes clients needed care due to mental illness. Because I'd had a positive, calming effect on some other short-term clients, some more difficult cases started coming my way. No experience in life is wasted. My past had exposed me to plenty of irrational behaviour that now seemed to help me with difficult people.

A lot of the time I was not terribly fazed by challenging clients. I say a lot of the time, though, not all of the time. Sometimes, my calm persona couldn't appease the client at all, no matter what I tried. Arriving at a magnificent mansion, surely one of the best in the city, the warnings I had been given about the lady came back to mind. Florence was terribly defensive about needing care, insisting she didn't need it at all. This was not new. Plenty of elderly people were reluctant to accept that they were not as independent as they once were. It was not always easy for them to acknowledge that such a time had come.

But I wasn't prepared for the mad woman who came chasing me down the driveway brandishing a broom and yelling at the top of her voice. Her hair had not been attended to in goodness knows how long. Fingernails were full of dirt or possibly worse. Wearing only one slipper, she hardly represented the Cinderella fairytale. And it looked like she had not changed her dress for a year.

"Get out! Get off my property!" she screamed. "I'll kill you first. Get off my property. You're just like the rest of them. Get out or I'll kill you!"

The broom swished through the air, missing me only slightly.

Now, I can handle a lot in life, but I am not stupid. Nor am I a martyr. I did try for one sentence to placate Florence. But with my words falling on deaf ears and her threats of breaking my windscreen with the broom still lingering, I needed no more convincing. "OK, OK," I said, "I'm going, Florence. It's OK." She looked wild and untamed as she stood at the end of the driveway defending her territory, a firm hold still on the broom.

Driving off, that image stayed in my rear view mirror until I was completely out of sight. She didn't budge. As much as it may have appeared to an outsider as a pretty funny scenario, my heart couldn't help but feel sorry for her, too. I wondered who she once was, what her life had been, and what had driven her to become who she now was.

A month later those answers were offered when I was returned to the same address. Since then, Florence had apparently been taken by force and sedated. This image is one I hated to imagine. How scared she must have felt. But the last month had seen her in a temporary home for those with mental illness, and now she was doing well. Doctors were happy with her response to the medications and were sending her home with advice to have around-the-clock care.

The community nurse was waiting when I arrived. "She's asleep now, but is due to wake soon. So I will wait with you until after that," she explained. Opening the double doors into the mansion, I was greeted by an enormous marble staircase, chandeliers, and a house full of beautiful, antique furniture. I was also greeted by a stench that was absolutely rotten.

"We've finished the entrance. I'll show you through the rest of the house," the nurse said, referring to the team of cleaners we came across in the next room. Florence had been living in a filthy rubbish dump for over ten years with no one realising until recently, when a neighbour commented to the community nurse about some unusual and erratic behaviour. When the nurse came to see Florence, the extent of her squalor was revealed. Not directly by Florence, of course – no one could approach her – but by looking in the window and seeing the state of her home.

She was surviving on tinned food and had about a year's supply in her pantry. I saw no evidence of anything else, certainly nothing fresh or anything able to be cooked. It was almost impossible to see the floor of the kitchen for the rubbish. The little bit of floor that was revealed was inches thick in black grime. Florence's bathroom was no better. It was an unhealthy pit of dirty towels, dried up cakes of soap and obvious signs that no one had used the shower or bath for a very long time.

The nurse led me downstairs where another six or so bedrooms and a couple of bathrooms lay in similar neglect. The cleaners were contracted to do the whole house and it was expected to take them a few weeks. Downstairs the doors opened to a filthy swimming pool; uninhabitable even for frogs, I am sure. Standing by the pool and looking back up to the main level of the home and all of its grandeur, I wondered what the walls of this place would say if they could talk.

Florence had been through a positive transformation with hygiene while in hospital and was resting in a lovely, clean nightdress. Her hair was untangled and had been washed and cut, and her fingernails were clean. It was almost like looking at a different woman.

A hospital bed had now replaced her original bed. I was given very firm instructions that she was to stay in the bed, with the sides up at all times, whenever I was in the home alone with her. Another carer would come in for two hours morning and afternoon to assist me. The mornings were for showering, toileting, and breakfast. The afternoons were focused on getting Florence out into the garden or onto the balcony to enjoy some fresh air. Heavy sedation was to be a big part of Florence's management. The rest of the time she would just be mildly doped. As a result of this patient management plan, she became much more obliging.

A month passed by and we were now hanging out in a sparkling mansion. The cleaners were finally finished, but were contracted to attend to the home on a weekly basis. Some lovely moments of clarity began flowing from Florence, and she was able to start sharing stories with me. Her life had been grand and exciting. She had sailed the world on the most luxurious ships and visited many fabulous places. When she pointed to drawers nearby, I would hand photos to her as she told me about each one. It was hard to believe this was the same person, except at times I did recognise her as the young, beautiful woman laughing in the photos.

I wouldn't say we grew close, but we grew fond enough of each other to accept the situation that had brought us together. There were still moments I glimpsed that mad, wild woman in her, though. Having another carer was definitely required for her outings from the bed. She was obliging in taking her medications – yet even so, still put up an enormous fight every day with the shower routine, and I came to dread hair wash day immensely. But once out of the shower, she was a delight and would pamper herself by the mirror, laughing like the grand woman she was in those days gone by.

Her fortune had been in the family forever. Old, old money, she called it. Her husband had also come from money, but nothing like the league from which she had originated. After some dodgy business dealings, he was jailed for several years. The one relative Florence allowed into her life told me it was at this time that Florence started to become suspicious and paranoid of everyone.

Her husband then died within a year of getting out of jail. So no opportunity to heal or reduce her paranoia ever presented itself again and her mental stability worsened. She had trusted him completely and believed everyone else was out to get her money and it was other people who were the cause of his incarceration. It made little difference to my association with her whether he was guilty or not, so I didn't ponder it for a moment.

Florence accepted life in the hospital bed most of the time. She was just happy to be in her own home and on occasions admitted to loving the company we carers brought to her. However, a few hours before the other carer returned each afternoon, Florence visited the other side and became a totally different woman again. I could have almost set a clock to it.

"Let me out. Let me out of this damn bed. Help! Help! Help! HELP!" she would scream, her voice echoing throughout the mansion and off the marble floors. Walking into her room, I would sometimes manage to settle her for a few seconds, but only a few. I mean, three seconds maximum. Then off it would start again. "Help! Help! Help! HHHEEEEELLLLLLPPPPP!"

If we weren't in such a luxurious mansion with thick walls and distance between neighbours, I am sure there would have been people ringing the police daily to report someone screaming. In the end, it made no difference if I was in the room or not. She would scream for help and to be let out of the bed constantly until the other carer had arrived and we let her out.

There was no reasoning with her during these times, and while I felt for her and was tempted to let her out, I knew her other side. It was not worth risking my own safety for. That image of her chasing me with the broom and her wild determination had never left me. It was glimpses of this belligerent personality that I would see in her afternoon shouting match, convincing me to listen to the professionals who had set the management routine the way they had. I did feel for her, though. How awful it must have been to be trapped inside your own home.

Side rails on her bed, legalities, and professional decisions were the combining factors currently trapping Florence. Prior to this, paranoia had trapped her. Florence's illness had robbed her of the freedom to leave her own home, with an obsessive mistrust of people and what they might steal from her if she did. While most people may not live trapped in a bed, it is possible to create lives where the traps that hold us back are self-created and desperately need releasing.

One of my earliest memories is of being trapped inside a box. But I didn't actually feel trapped. It was a large wooden box off the side of the house in the garden. One of my older siblings convinced me to climb in and then locked the door on me. I can still remember sitting in the darkness and feeling safe and happy, though. Even when I was only two or three years old I knew I liked my own company, and the peace was beautiful. My mother's panicked voice came calling some time later, so I called back and all was well. I was let out and returned to the chaos of busy family life.

Other trappings were present in my adult life now, however. While I was finding the courage to honour my own directions, one step at a time, old thought patterns were not helping me at all. Overcoming my dread of performing was a particularly hard process, as I tried to release myself from these self-made traps.

If someone had told me that photography and writing would eventually have led me to performing on a stage, I may have once laughed at the absurdity of such a thought. It started by me selling my photographic work at markets, then galleries. Not enough of them sold to create a livable income, but there were sufficient moments of encouragement to keep me on the slow and steady path.

From these small signs of support, I decided to work within the photography industry and landed a job in a professional lab in Melbourne. Unfortunately, it was an office job; and after a year of boredom, fluorescent lights, and no windows, I acknowledged it was no more satisfying for me than any of my previous banking jobs. No opportunity had arisen either for me to get into the creative side of the business, and I came to hold no interest in the job at all, eventually starting to make mindless mistakes. I remember sighing a lot in that job; leaning on my elbows, chin in the palm of my hand, trying to find the solution for satisfaction in my working life – then sighing again.

From this role, though, I did come to see how I didn't need to work in the photography industry to take nice photos. With the help of a couple of new and digital savvy friends, I then created a small photography and inspiration book. Again, much support about the quality of my work was forthcoming, but not enough to get the book published. The cost of colour printing was a significant factor in the advice I received back from publishers, though some commented it was a beautiful book.

For a few years I gave it everything I had, every ounce of focus and energy. But the rejection letters continued to pile up, despite some continuing to come with sincere encouragement. It was during the tears and frustrations of these efforts that I picked up my guitar. I could hardly play it, but proceeded to half write my very first song. Little did I know the significance of that moment.

Having learned about the power of surrender, I came to accept that whether the photography book was ever published or not, it didn't really matter in the end. I was already a success in my own eyes, for having had the courage to try. Success doesn't depend on someone saying yes, we will publish your book or no, we won't. It is about having the courage to be you regardless. Feeling the lessons I had learned through that whole book process had already brought gifts in themselves, I was finally able to let it go. Perhaps it was simply for my own learning that this book had flowed through me anyway. Or maybe it would find its feet at another time, when I was more ready.

Either way, it didn't matter. I had to let go. My efforts had left me drained, and I had placed too much emphasis on the book being published. It was time to live again and to stop trying to control the outcome. The song I had half written also remained semi-forgotten while I searched for answers, devoting more and more time to my meditation path and healing. After one of many stints away in silence and meditation, though, I felt a strong urge to finish that half written song. From that day onwards I knew that songwriting was a part of my life's work, as not only did I finish the song, but I also wrote another one the same day. I just couldn't get enough of it once started. They poured out of me.

As children, we had put on concerts for relatives and friends. Music was in my genes. Despite their other so-called 'sensible' careers, my father was a guitarist and songwriter when he met my mother, who was a singer at the time. Yet I had never experienced a conscious yearning to be on the stage. I certainly wasn't experiencing it now either. In fact, the thought terrified me. It wasn't just the idea of being on a stage. It was that my work was calling me into the public arena. I was happy to be anonymous. Plenty of songwriters don't perform, and I wanted to be one of those. But to get my work heard initially, performing my own songs was going to be the way.

This terrified me and created enormous turbulence within for a long stretch. Trying to find work I loved had already been such a painful challenge for me, one I never seemed to be able to move past completely. Now I couldn't accept that the work I was very clearly being guided to do would actually put me in the public eye, when I had always loved and guarded my privacy so much. I definitely didn't want to live the life I saw ahead.

We are given lessons to heal, though, not necessarily to enjoy. It was a terribly confronting time. It didn't help that I was also receiving a lot of negativity from particular people in regards to my new directions. Either way, I just longed for life to swallow me up and let me go on unnoticed.

Spending a lot of solitary time at one of my favourite rivers, I swam for weeks trying to accept that this was where life was going for me. The fresh water cleansed me with every stroke I took. When I swam underneath, the other world slipped away. There were never any sounds out by the river, except for birds singing and the breeze blowing softly through the trees on the banks. The peace was healing, so I drank it in often. One day I even saw a platypus, known to be a very shy creature that rarely comes out around people. Such a blessing restored me.

As I sat on the bank, allowing nature to weave its magic on my very weary soul, the breeze so soft on my face, I had to be honest with myself. When all of my life experiences to this point were considered, I saw that deep down, a part of me had always known I would be in the public eye to some degree. The choice to keep some of my life for me was still going to be my own, and I could manage that. It was my life after all, and it was my choice how I handled what unfolded.

So in the end I accepted that if this work was a part of my life's path and I could help others by doing so, then hopefully I would somehow grow into my role. Trusting that the learning would also help my own growth, irrespective of who else would ever hear my music, also assisted my acceptance. The support of a couple of friends who were musicians was also life-saving at the time.

Thinking back to when I first started performing, I feel for the audience as much as myself. Even if the music was tolerable, it was obvious for a long time that I found performing painful. My hands would shake, the guitar would bounce, I'd miss strings, and my voice would choke up completely. I hated it immensely and was often sick with nerves. Meditation helped me a lot in this regard. So did practice. Like anything you persevere with, you do eventually get better with practice. Yet through all of these nerves and dread, something drove me on. It was the acceptance that this was a part of my life's work and a yearning to contribute. It was also the desire to be heard. An avenue had been presented to share thoughts that had been suppressed for too long.

I was well into my thirties when I finished that first song and another year or two passed before I started performing. Not drinking alcohol at all by now meant I had to face my fears head-on, without artificial assistance. Performing helped me to open up and brought so many of its own gifts. At the time that I was caring for Florence, I was also doing the songwriting circuit in the city pubs. Most of this I hated. I was very lonely during this time, as my emotional wounds had seen me withdraw a long way into myself. Getting up on a stage and singing my songs was something I managed, but didn't enjoy for a long time.

It all helped me to grow, though. When you are sharing your personal thoughts with a room full of strangers, it certainly opens you back up again. The consistently positive response to my songs and what I had to say also encouraged me as a songwriter.

Later I came to appreciate that I was playing in the wrong sort of venues for my style and personality. After one too many noisy gigs over the following years, I said goodbye to pub gigs forever. I had done my apprenticeship by now. It may have meant there wouldn't be much opportunity to gig, but as performing live in pubs and gaining recognition that way wasn't what drove me, this didn't bother me at all. By then I was also getting into some folk festivals and had experienced the bliss a performer gets when you have a respectful audience who not only listens to your songs, but also understands them totally. That connection with like-minded people is a fantastic feeling. So from then on, it was beautiful venues or suitable festivals only.

Thinking back to who I was when I first started performing, I hardly recognise that fragile creature. Now when I play live I am confident, because I am playing in the right venues, to the right audience. My songs are meaningful and mostly gentle. They can be. They're allowed to be. I am not competing with the meat raffle being called out over the microphone in the pubs anymore, or losing the connection with the audience because the boxing comes onto the television screens on the walls. If I make a mistake, I laugh gently with myself and carry on. After all, performers are human, too.

It is also refreshing that Mr. Invincible is no longer ogling me. You know, the guy who has had the most to drink in the pub and suddenly decides he is Johnny Depp's twin brother. He stands there right in front of the stage, leering at you as he rocks back and forth, somehow managing not to spill a drop of his eighteenth beer. He knows without a doubt that he is God's gift to women as he graces you with a nod and a wink, while gyrating his hips just for you. *And* if you are good enough, he will wait for you side-stage to answer all of your prayers in the department of men and great lovers. Yes, I have known them all. Bless them.

So as well as having to face my initial terror in performing, every day I continued to walk the creative path was one of courage. I had also recently finished a year of music study. Deciding I'd like to learn more about the industry, I taught myself some very basic music theory, at least enough to pass my audition to the program. The audition also included a very shaky version of one of my own songs. But I was in. I was a student in my thirties and I loved every minute of it.

I had to employ different tools when conquering my nerves while performing, though. Practice was one for sure. Consistently putting myself out there improved my playing, singing, and confidence more and more. But the two things that helped me most of all were the tools I used to set myself free of my mind. These tools apply to anything, not just performing, and have helped in other ways since.

When my nerves would kick in or when negative thoughts surfaced, like *"What on earth did I think I was doing up there?"* I would return to my meditation practice mid-song. I didn't actually stop the song or sit on the stage in the lotus position. It wasn't quite that way. The singing would continue, as would my guitar playing. But I would change my focus to the breath, observing it going in and out. All the while I would put total trust in my muscle memory, that it would remember where to put my fingers on the guitar and the words would continue to flow. It was the breath I had to focus on at that moment. This worked incredibly well, as it calmed me down enough to then return to the song with better expression and more presence.

The other thing that changed my thinking and truly said goodbye to the nerves was when I removed myself from the equation and saw it as a time of giving to those in the audience. A simple prayer was silently said beforehand, thanking the music for flowing through me and bringing these people pleasure. Then I would just get out of the way and enjoy the music as much as the audience.

Performing has taught me many great things. I am very grateful life kept me going with it when I didn't particularly want to. How can we ever know what gifts are awaiting us through the lessons on hand if we don't go through them? We can't know until we proceed through. Whether I continue to perform or not in future is really of no relevance to me anymore. I will if I do, and I'll enjoy it immensely. Or I won't if I don't, and I'll enjoy whatever I do instead immensely. It doesn't matter either way. I'll just go where my path leads.

But through mastering my nerves in performing, I had started to master my mind in other ways, too. I was setting myself free of the trappings I had created through a lifetime of unhealthy thinking patterns. We all have trappings we need to free ourselves from. Most of those are not physical ones; if they are, it is likely they originated from non-physical trappings, such as unhealthy thinking and negative belief systems.

Unfortunately for dear Florence, though, she was still trapped in her bed at least until the other carer arrived. Because my presence did not lessen the volume of her yelling, it was naturally kinder on myself to not be in the room. Occasionally I would poke my head in. She would pause for about two seconds, look at me, then look away and start screaming "Help!" again. This lady should have been a singer. She sure had the lungs for it.

Yachts sailed by on Sydney Harbour. Remembering back to a time when I had been friends with some great guys who sailed, I smiled wondering where they had all ended up. The sound of the doorbell interrupted my reminiscing.

As we lowered the sides on her bed, the yelling ceased in a

microsecond. Just like that. Florence smiled at us. "Well hello to you both. How has your day been so far?" she asked. We both looked at each other smiling, as we helped her out of bed. Although the other carer did not have to endure a few hours of Florence's screaming every day, she was still welcomed by it each afternoon.

"Great, thanks, Florence, and yours?" I asked.

"Oh, not too bad, Darling. I've just been watching the boats on the harbour. They race on Wednesdays, you know."

Agreeing with her I said, "They sure do, Florence."

Wandering around the garden together, we all marvelled at the colours. It too had been neglected over the years. But the relative who had recently gained power of attorney over Florence's money had insisted the place look beautiful in case Florence had any moments of clarity to enjoy it. So gardeners had been in to weave their magic and the pool was clear and clean again.

"Look at my beautiful garden," she told us. "How spectacular it looks at this time of year." We both agreed sincerely. Underneath all of the neglect, a lovely garden had remained and was coming back into its full glory.

"I was only out here the other day planting these flowers, you know. You have to stay on top of gardening, especially with all of these creepers." We smiled and again agreed. Considering this place was an overgrown, grungy-looking jungle only a month or two earlier, it was fun to listen to how Florence saw it.

Pulling some vines away from the flowers, she continued. "You can't get lazy with gardens. They need a lot of love and time." We asked her about some of the flowers and she replied with amazing clarity and knowledge. "This vine will trap the flowers and strangle them," Florence told us, as she pulled some more of the vine away. I nodded as she continued, "I would never let anything trap me, you know, and I won't let anything trap my flowers."

And as Florence continued to break the constraints around her beautiful garden, I silently said a prayer of thanks for having found the courage to start breaking free of my own constraints. Like a flower, I too was now free to grow and to bloom.

REGRET 2:
I WISH I HADN'T WORKED SO HARD

∽ↂ∾

Drying the dishes, I could hear my client John in his office giggling like a schoolboy. "Yes, she's just the right age, too," he chuckled, continuing to describe me to his friend on the phone. John was almost ninety. I was still in my thirties. Recalling a line a seventy-year old man had once told me, 'all men are boys,' I smiled to myself, shaking my head.

Coming out of his office later, John was the diplomatic gentleman I knew, with no sign at all of his mischief. He wanted to take me out to lunch, though, and did I have a pink dress to wear? If not, could he buy me one? I laughed and politely declined his offer of buying me a dress, because I did in fact own a pink one. While it was not a part of my uniform for care work, I informed him I was happy to oblige an old dying man. His delight was wonderful.

A table for two was booked at a very expensive restaurant. It was the prime table, front and centre, overlooking a park across to the harbour. John looked dapper in his navy jacket with gold trimmings, a fresh dose of aftershave lingering in the air. With his hand on the small of my back, he guided me to our table. After looking out at the view, I glanced back to catch him winking to the four men sitting at a table nearby. They were all giggling while checking me out, but instantly dropped to straight faces when they realised they were busted.

"Friends of yours then, John?" I asked smiling. He stammered and admitted that he wanted his friends to see how lucky he was to have a carer of such great physical quality. I cracked up laughing. "Any woman my age is of great physical quality to a room full of eighty-nine year olds." I must admit, though, his manners were impeccable and I did wish more men from my generation still carried the charm and dinner etiquette he bestowed upon me. We had a lovely lunch. John had phoned ahead and explained he was bringing a vegan to the restaurant. They had obliged with a beautiful vegetable loaf, especially baked.

It turns out that his friends were all banned from interrupting our lunch or even coming to the table. He would introduce me afterwards. So while their lunch had long finished, they all sat patiently until John and I had finished our lunch and conversation. Then, again with his hand on the small of my back, he guided me to their table where I played the perfect girlfriend by charming them all, but ensuring John received the most attention. He reminded me of a rooster with all of his feathers up in pride and mating. It was a fun time.

Underneath all of this, though, there was a man dying. What harm did it do to oblige such a harmless game in what would be one of his last outings? Once home and out of my pink dress into more practical work clothes (much to John's disappointment), I assisted him to bed. The outing may have delighted him, but he was exhausted, too.

The energy of dying people is so weakened that a small outing becomes like working an eighty-hour week lifting bricks. It completely drains them. Family and friends also don't often realise how their well-intended visits can exhaust sick people. When they are in their last week or so, visits of more than five or ten minutes can become hard work for the patient, yet this is when they are usually bombarded with visitors.

It was just John and me this afternoon, though, and he slept deeply. Folding my pink dress away in my bag, it was lovely to have brought him the pleasure he gained from the lunch. It had brought me pleasure, too.

John had also benefitted from my youth in other ways. Understanding computers better than he did, I returned to the job in his office that had begun the previous month. For a man of his age, his approach to computers was admirable as he embarked on grasping the age of technology. His files were a mess, though, as he hadn't known about folders and ordered filing. While he slept, I carried on creating categories and finding homes for hundreds of documents, all the while creating an index so things could be found. But like I say, for a man his age, he was already doing remarkably well on the computer.

When I saw the deterioration in John the following week, I felt very grateful we had already been out to lunch. He would not be leaving the house again. There may still be a few weeks to go, or maybe not, but his strength was disappearing very quickly. Sitting out on his balcony late that afternoon, we watched the sun set over the Harbour Bridge and the Opera House. John was in his dressing gown and slippers, trying to eat a little, but struggling. "Don't worry about it, John, only eat what you can or want to," I said, as we both knew the unspoken words behind that sentence. John was dying, and it wouldn't be too far away. Nodding, he put the fork on the plate, handing them to me. I sat the tray aside, and we continued to watch the sunset.

Out of the afternoon peace John stated, "I wish I hadn't worked so hard, Bronnie. What a stupid fool I was." Sitting in the other lounge chair on the balcony, I looked across at him. He needed no encouragement to continue. "I worked too damn hard and now I am a lonely, dying man. The worst part is that I have been lonely for the whole of my retirement and I need not have been." I listened as he told me the whole story.

John and Margaret had raised five children, four of whom now had children of their own. The other one had died in his early thirties. When all of the children were adults and gone from the home, Margaret asked John to retire. They were both fit and healthy and had enough money behind them to retire well. But he always said they might need more. Margaret replied each time that they could sell their huge, now almost empty, house and buy something more suitable if required, freeing up more money. For fifteen years this battle went on between them, while he kept working.

Margaret was lonely and longed to discover their partnership again without children or work. For years she devoured travel brochures, suggesting different countries and regions to visit. John also had a desire to travel more and agreed with wherever Margaret suggested. Unfortunately, he also enjoyed the status his work gave him. He told me he didn't particularly like the work itself, just the role it gave him in society and amongst his friends. The chase of closing a deal had also become a bit of an addiction for him.

One evening with Margaret in tears, begging him to finally retire, he looked at this beautiful woman and realised that not only was she desperately lonely for his company, but they were both old people now. This wonderful woman had waited so patiently for him to retire. Looking at her, she was still as beautiful as the day he had met her. But it was the first time in his life John considered they were not going to live forever.

Although petrified for reasons he could now not justify, he agreed to retire. Margaret had jumped up and hugged him, her tears switching from sadness to joy. But the smile didn't last long, disappearing the minute he added "in one more year." There was a new deal being negotiated at the moment in the company and he wanted to see it through. She had waited fifteen years for him to retire. Surely she could wait for one more. It was a compromise, but one she reluctantly agreed to. As the sun dropped out of view, John told me he felt selfish for his choice even then, but he couldn't retire without doing just one more deal.

Dreaming of this time for years, things started to become real for his beloved wife. She made some actual plans, on the phone to the travel agent regularly. Each night as he wandered in, she would be waiting for him with dinner prepared. As they ate at the table that had once accommodated their whole family, she shared her thoughts and ideas with great excitement. John was starting to warm to the idea of retirement now, too, although still insisted on seeing the twelve months out if Margaret ever suggested otherwise. With four months since his acceptance to retire and eight still to go, Margaret began feeling queasy. At first it was a bit of nausea, but after almost a week it had not passed. "I've made an appointment with the doctor tomorrow," she told him as he came in from work. The night was already dark. Traffic continued in the distance, as other workers headed home. "I'm sure it's nothing, though," she said with attempted cheerfulness.

While John was concerned she was not feeling well, it didn't cross his mind it may be more until the following night, when Margaret said the doctor had suggested some tests. Even if the results had not said so within the following week, however, the increase in her discomfort and then pain would have told them something was wrong. They just hadn't expected how wrong. Margaret was dying.

We spend so much time making plans for the future, often depending on things coming at a later date to assure our happiness or assuming we have all of the time in the world, when all we ever have is our life today. It was not difficult to understand the deep regrets John was now living with. I understand how people can love their work, and there is no need for guilt in doing so. I too now loved my work, despite the sadness that often accompanied it.

But when asked if he would have enjoyed his work so much if he hadn't had such a supportive family life, John shook his head. "I liked the work enough, sure. And I definitely loved the status, though what's the point of that now? I gave less time to what truly kept me going through life: Margaret and my family, my dear Margaret. Her love and support were always there. But I wasn't there for her. She was a lot of fun, too. We would have had such a good time away together."

Margaret had died three months before John was due to retire, though he *had* retired by then due to her health. John shared how his retirement had been plagued with guilt ever since. Even when he was able to come to a certain place of acceptance about his 'mistake', as he called it, he longed to be travelling and laughing with Margaret now.

"I think I was scared. Yes, I was. I was petrified. My role had come to define me in a way. Of course now as I sit here dying, I see that just being a good person is more than enough in life. Why do we depend so much on the material world to validate us?" John thought out loud, random sentences filled with sadness for both past and future generations who wanted everything, basing their importance on what they owned and what they did, rather than on who they were in their heart.

"There's nothing wrong in wanting a better life. Don't get me wrong," he said. "It's just that the chase for more, and the need to be recognised through our achievements and belongings, can hinder us from the real things, like time with those we love, time doing things we love ourselves, and balance. It's probably all about balance really, isn't it?"

Agreeing, I quietly nodded. A few stars were out above us now, and the colourful city lights were reflected on the water. Balance had always been a bit of a challenge for me, too. It seemed to be all or nothing, even in this role. Twelve-hour shifts were my normal working day, and as the clients neared the end, they and their families wanted as much consistency with the carers as possible. So it wasn't unusual to work six days per week during their last month, sometimes even taking on a sleepover shift in between, meaning I was there for thirty-six hours straight. An eighty-four hour week is not healthy for anyone, even if you love the work you do.

Sometimes the clients would sleep, but I still had to be there. Plenty of other duties called. It felt like my own life was on hold, though in hindsight it wasn't, of course, as this too was a part of it. When the client's life had passed, I was exhausted. It usually turned out that another regular client would not arise for some time after a run like that. So I welcomed the time off, caught up with friends again, returned to my music and writing, and then did it all over again. The time off was wonderful, particularly in large blocks with only a random shift or two somewhere in between. But the inconsistency put a lot of pressure on my income. If the work stopped, the money stopped.

Around this time, I was offered one day a week as an office manager in a pre-natal centre. It was steady work and I loved it. The centre ran birthing courses for pregnant women and mothers' groups. There were weeks when I would go from nursing people who were ready to die that week or very soon after, to having toddlers climbing over me while I worked, placing sloppy kisses on my cheeks.

It was a healthy reminder about the joys of life and the full circle. As a client passed on, a new babe would arrive at the centre. The little ones were so incredibly fragile and beautiful. My boss, Marie, was one of the most wonderful people I have ever known, with a heart as big as they come. I loved her and still do. Part of my role would be to update the course material for the pre-natal classes. As a result, much of my day would be spent reading about how women of different cultures around the world approached pregnancy and the whole birth process. It reinforced how fear is conditioned into us as Westerners, when I saw how naturally many cultures approached things and how reduced the pain of birth was for some. It was treated as a joyous, beautiful celebration from start to finish.

Being around birth and life was very healthy for me. Hanging out with the dying and having such a strong empathy for the clients and families did wear me down sometimes. There are people all over the world who devote their whole lives to working with dying people. Perhaps they have mastered detachment more than I had. Or balance. I don't know. My full respect goes out to them regardless. What I do know is that having one day a week revolving around the beginning of the life cycle rather than the end brought lightness to my life I hadn't known was missing during these years. The energy was fresh and alive, like someone had opened the windows for me and let clean air blow through.

Having the contrasts on a weekly basis also helped me to see my dying clients as babies once. And as new mums proudly showed me their dear newborns, I too considered the babies would hopefully grow older and live a full life. Then one day they would reach the end of their lives, just as my clients were doing. It was a pretty interesting time, to be so exposed to both ends of the spectrum. It was a blessing.

From that time, I was able to grow in compassion more for others in my life, as I recognised that they too were once just fragile little babies and they too will one day die, as will I. I started to see my parents, siblings, friends, and strangers as babies and young children, once trusting in life with the innocence and hope that young children do. I thought about who they were before the wounds of others – whether that be family, peers, or society – were dumped on them, affecting the natural trust and openness they were born with. The goodness of people's hearts became clear to me, and I began to love them all with the protectiveness of a caring mother.

No longer did I see the hurtful things said over the years as truly coming from them. The words were coming from their wounds, not the beautiful, pure beings they were born as. Each of those precious babies born decades ago were still a part of them. A dear, little, innocent child also still lived within each of them. And one day they would also receive the wisdom of hindsight that comes to so many people with the dying process.

There may be times I thought I didn't love particular people in my life. But I saw it was only their behaviour and words I did not love. Now I loved their innocent hearts, hearts that once trusted the world would bring them happiness and look after them. When it didn't, suffering kicked in, and their pain and disillusionment saw them reacting in ways that were not wholesome. I was no different. I too had caused others pain, through my own suffering, and my own disappointment that life hadn't turn out as I'd hoped. That little girl whose trust had been broken by being exposed to others' pain had then reacted with pain of her own.

The hearts of my dear family, and of everyone, still contained that original purity. It was just clouded over with pain and life. Whether I would ever find the happiness and friendship I had once hoped for with some people was still to be determined. Either way, it didn't really matter anymore. I now saw that they were all once beautiful little babies, with all of the trust and innocence bablies have. Anything said that was not kind to others was simply the suffering, manifesting from a little child who had lost their way, as I had. And for that alone I could continue to love them.

Sitting beside John on the balcony, I saw the fragile child in him, too; a precious little boy who somehow decided through whatever he was exposed to that proving himself through his work was going to make him happier than to go travelling with his wife. He was an old man now, yet that little innocent child within him was still obvious. Slow tears fell down his cheeks occasionally as he sighed deeply. Leaving him to his thoughts and privacy, I took the dishes inside and cleaned up. On returning I placed a rug over his legs and kissed him on the cheek before sitting down again.

"If I can tell you one thing about life, Bronnie, it's this. Don't create a life where you are going to regret working too hard. I can say now that I didn't know I was going to regret it until I was at this time facing the very end. But deep in my heart, I knew I was working too hard. Not just for Margaret, but for me, too. I would love to have not cared what others thought of me, as I do now. I wonder why we have to wait until we are dying to work things like this out." Shaking his head, he kept talking. "There is nothing wrong with loving your work and wanting to apply yourself to it. But there is so much more to life. Balance is what is important, maintaining balance."

"I agree, John. It has been a lesson for me already, but I'm working on it, don't worry," I admitted honestly. He knew what I meant. We had shared enough stories by now for him to understand me. John then started laughing to himself. So I questioned him, encouraging him to share the joke.

"Well, I said if there was one thing I could tell you, it is to not regret working too hard. But I just thought of another, almost as important."

"Go on then," I smiled.

He looked at me with mischief in his eyes and said, "Don't you ever throw out that pink dress!"

Laughing, John pointed to my chair then tapped the side of his, indicating for me to bring my chair over, which I did as I laughed, too. Another couple of hours passed as we sat side-by-side overlooking the harbour, a rug each over us. Now and then the conversation would drift into a comfortable silence, before more conversation resumed. Other moments of silence, though, were simply broken by a deep sigh from John. I took his hand, and he squeezed mine in response.

Looking across at me with a sad smile, he told me, "If I can leave any good in this world besides my family, I leave these words. Don't work too hard. Try to maintain balance. Don't make work your whole life." Smiling back gently, I lifted his hand up and kissed the back of it.

John passed away not long after that night. Although I didn't know it then, his words were to be repeated to me time and again by others I came to care for. He had made his point, though, and it was one I would never forget.

PURPOSE AND INTENTION

꒰ઓ꒱

Word of mouth had begun working in my favour with my living situation. The time at Ruth's house had now well passed. But a network of wonderful people had started to see the mutual benefit of me looking after their homes when they were away. While there were occasions that it wore me down, moving house every few weeks or months, it also exposed me to many beautiful homes. One of them even backed onto the home of the wealthiest man in the country. So I was certainly living in some affluent surroundings.

With many of the house-sits came a cleaner and a gardener, sometimes a separate window washer, too. My only role was to live in the home as if it was my own and to enjoy it. Needless to say, this was not difficult. As well as this network being of very wealthy people, some were also incredibly creative. So the homes were often bright, colourful, and welcoming.

It was through one of my house-sitting clients I came to care for Pearl. Her home was cheerful, as was she, at least as much as is possible for a dying person. We liked each other instantly. She also had three dogs, one of which was usually very timid with strangers, but was sitting on my lap within minutes. (Animals know animal lovers.) The little black dog's response to me helped Pearl's and my rapport immediately.

Some months earlier, just prior to her sixty-third birthday, Pearl had been diagnosed with terminal illness. Because of her dogs and the love of her home, she was determined to die in her own bed. A friend had already offered to adopt all three dogs when the time came, so Pearl was peaceful they would be able to stay together. She was also quite accepting of her approaching passing.

Many of the clients I had cared for by now had been in denial initially about their situations. They would go through a range of emotions before finally accepting the inevitable outcome. Other clients were in shock as the news had been delivered to them in such a way that it was too much to bear. The conveyer of such news occasionally did so in a manner that was just too matter-of-fact, not understanding the full impact of their delivery. Sometimes this was family. Sometimes it was medical professionals. True gentleness is definitely needed on such occasions, though.

Pearl, however, was very much at a place of acceptance that her time had come. A part of what made this easier, she told me, was that she had lost her husband and their only child, a little girl, a year apart more than thirty years ago. She knew in her heart she would be seeing them again soon.

Her husband had been taken suddenly in a work accident, although she didn't like to use the word 'accident', as she believed there was no such thing. "It was meant to be," she told me. "It brought me enormous pain, but with more than thirty years of living since, I have come to see how that loss helped me to become the person I now am and to help others. I wouldn't be who I am without having experienced his passing."

She was philosophical about losing her little girl, too. Tonia had died of leukemia at eight years old. "Losing a child is as bad as everyone says it is. No parent should have to experience it. But they do, you know, all over the world, every single day. I am merely one of many." I listened and appreciated the peace that came from her, as she discussed her daughter. "I am glad for her that she didn't suffer for too long. I believe she came into my life to teach me the joy of unconditional love. Since then I have been able to give that to others, even without being related to them. Dear Tonia, my dear little angel."

The memories had faded from being clear pictures in her mind, but had not diminished at all in her heart. Pearl's love for her daughter was as strong as ever. Love doesn't die, she told me joyously. She went on to share how life had been difficult for some time after Tonia's passing, taking quite a few years for the wheels to start turning again properly. But she didn't ever see herself as a victim. Although she knew the pain of losing a child and wouldn't wish that on anyone, she'd also known the joy of having a child, which, as she pointed out, not everyone has such opportunity to.

We agreed there is always a gift in any challenge. "People play the victim forever," she continued. "But who are they kidding? They are only robbing themselves. Life doesn't owe you anything. Neither does anyone else. Only *you* owe yourself. So the best way to make the most out of life is to appreciate the gift of it, and choose not to be a victim."

I explained to Pearl how I had known quite a few victims in my time, but the biggest wake-up call was when I had recognised it in myself at one stage. It had taken me completely by surprise when I saw that I had become so caught up in my wounds, I was only able to focus on how hard my life had been.

She agreed without judgment. "We can all be guilty of it at some time. There is a fine line between compassion and a victim mentality. Compassion, though, is a healing force and comes from a place of kindness towards yourself. Playing the victim is a toxic waste of time that not only repels other people, but also robs the victim of ever knowing true happiness. No one owes us anything," she said again. "We only owe ourselves to get off our backsides, count our blessings, and face our challenges. When you live from that perspective, the gifts pour forth." I loved this woman.

She continued speaking about how hard many people's lives are, how some folks are given such enormous challenges, yet they still manage to soldier on and find happiness in little things along the way. Yet others complain non-stop about their life when they have no idea how good they really have it, compared to others. Agreeing with Pearl on this was easy, as despite the pain I still carried at times, I didn't lose sight of the blessings I received, too. There was always someone much worse off.

When Pearl did manage to get her life on track again after the loss of her husband and daughter, she threw herself into her work for several years. It was work that she liked enough. She loved her co-workers and the customers, and felt a part of her reason to be there was to keep them inspired and happy, which she did well. There was always emptiness in her, though. For almost two decades, she had put it down to the loss of her family.

A passing comment one day changed her life, and she found herself helping a customer outside of hours who was developing a new community program. Without being terribly conscious of it, Pearl became more and more involved, simply because she loved the project and what these people were about. "For the first time in more than twenty years, I knew passion again. And do you know why?" she asked, as I waited. "I had purpose, true purpose. That was what the emptiness had been with my work. It didn't have enough purpose for me."

It was not difficult for me to relate to this. I shared my previous work history with Pearl, including the struggles I went through until I found myself working in palliative care and in music, both of which were bringing increasing contentment. She agreed that my work truly had purpose, particularly compared to other roles I had done. But like me, she believed anyone could find true purpose in his or her work if they are in the right field for who they are. It was just a matter of perspective.

Pearl's home had a beautiful conservatory where the winter sun would shine in on us through the glass roof. It was bright and lovely. Each morning I would wheel her out there, usually with at least one dog on her lap, sometimes all three. We would drink gallons of fresh herbal teas while delighting in the gift of each new day. When I commented to her that being there didn't feel like work at all for me, she brightened up and said, "Of course, that is how it should be. When you are doing work you love, it doesn't feel like work. It is simply a natural extension of who you are."

The community project evolved into Pearl finding her life's work. Within a year she had resigned from her old job and was fully devoted to her new role. The pay was less initially, but she didn't care. Over time it did increase, though. "Sometimes you have to take some steps back to get a run-up before you jump," she laughed. "Money is so misunderstood. It keeps people in the wrong jobs forever because they think they won't be able to make money doing what they love. When it can really be the other way around. If you totally love what you do, you can become more open to the flow of money because you are more absorbed in your work and are happier as a person. Of course, it takes some time to change your thinking and to stop trying to work out how the money will come."

A friend of mine had once put it well, and I shared this with Pearl. We put too much emphasis on the money. What we need to do is work out what we want to do, what project, and work toward that with focus, determination, and faith. Don't make it about the money. Make it about the project instead. Then the money will attach itself to you naturally, often through unimagined sources.

My leaps of faith had also taught me this already. When the money stopped, it was usually because I was focusing on that fear of lack, so I received more lack. When I focused on the beauty of the day, counted my blessings, and worked towards whatever I was being guided to do, what I needed would flow my way.

One of the greatest rewards for having the courage to keep working towards what I wanted was when I recorded my first album. The timing was going to be perfect, as I would be living in one of my favourite and most regular house-sits, where we could record. It was a gorgeous dark pink house that overlooked a pocket of rainforest. The same block of time worked well for all involved. My producer particularly was a very busy man, but had managed to allocate the time. Other musicians were also happy with the schedule. There was only one thing missing. Money! I had some, but not enough.

Everything in me though said to prepare as if it was happening, so I did. Musicians were booked in. I dedicated time to rehearsing, fine-tuning songs. But as the days drew nearer, the faith that had propelled me to this point began to waver. I knew deep down I wouldn't have been guided to do this if it wasn't possible. So during stronger moments, total belief existed that it would all go ahead. After all, I had done other leaps of faith in the past. I believed in myself and in my ability to draw the things I needed to me. But fear was starting to bubble to the surface, to the point where my faith could no longer keep the lid on it.

We were due to begin recording on Monday. It was Friday

afternoon and still the money had not turned up. Fear began raging. The producer could not afford the time off unpaid. The other musicians had limited time available as well. Beginning to panic, I went straight to my meditation cushion and sat. Tears sprang forth. They had been building for a few months as I had tried to stay totally focused and strong. Now they were pouring out. Sobbing, I released all of my frustrations, admitting that I couldn't do it anymore. I had no strength left. I had done what I was guided to, but couldn't keep going. It was all too hard. I just could *not* do it anymore.

Then "Ahh!" That beautiful moment of surrender! There it was. There was nothing more I could do. I simply had to hand it over to the greater forces. Feeling frightened and drained, I decided to go out and see some music as a distraction. A friend phoned just then, not knowing my situation, and invited me to come out with her and another friend. They were going to a café/bookshop. It felt more appealing than heading out alone to see a band, so I accepted. Promising myself to enjoy the night and forget about my situation, I headed out happily. Tomorrow was a new day, and I would deal with things then. But tonight I just needed to forget about it.

As my friend Gabriela browsed through the books, I sat on the lounge in the café chatting with her friend. Leanne and I had met only once, very briefly in passing, a few years earlier and had not crossed paths since. She asked where I lived so I explained my house-sitting life. This intrigued and also assisted her, as she was about to go into the housing market and valued my opinions of the different suburbs I had lived in by now. On being questioned further, I told her how I had fallen into this lifestyle as a result of wanting to be rent-free and to work on my creative stuff, particularly music.

Leanne was going through a very messy divorce, and welcomed the distraction from her own life as much as I did from mine. So the conversation continued to flow naturally. She then asked about my album, and I was brought back to my current situation, regretful that I had allowed the conversation to get onto this topic. But I told her honestly where things were at, and how I was waiting on a miracle to save me.

She asked me more about the album, about the people working

on it with me, what instrumentation we had planned, where I'd come from with my music and what drove me to perform, which I told her. Then without another moment's hesitation, she declared that she had always wanted to support the arts, did not know who to support, was going through a crappy time in her own life, needed to do something positive, and would be at my place on Monday morning with the cash I needed.

Tears of relief and joy burst out of me. I couldn't believe it. Without a thought, I hugged her sincerely, fighting back the urge to sob completely. It was over. I had done it. The album was happening. The money had attached itself to me.

Leanne came along for some of the recording. It was lovely to have her there, lying on the long carpet listening through headphones as we sang and played, recording each new track. She was pretty detached from it all, though. Just happy to see it happening was enough for her. What a beautiful, generous woman she was. This incident gave me strength for every leap of faith afterwards, too. The help does come. We just have to get out of the way.

Pearl delighted in this story as it reinforced everything she believed in. "That's exactly right. Fear blocks us up entirely. Money is just another kind of energy, an energy that wants to bring good and happiness to us all. But we use it wrongly – giving it power, chasing it, fearing it, unbalancing our lives in its pursuit as we obsess over it," she stated. "It is as available as the air we breathe. We don't waste our time worrying if there will be enough air. We shouldn't waste our time worrying if there will be enough money. Those very thoughts are what block the natural flow of this loving, creative energy to us." I understood and agreed.

When Pearl had first joined the community project, funding had been a constant concern for the people already working there. All of their energy had been going into how the money would be found, not *why* it was needed. Thankfully, the team of workers was open to Pearl's philosophies. While they didn't initially have enough faith in themselves to believe they could attract the funds needed for each section of the project, they had faith in Pearl's faith. So they agreed to keep working towards the project's success, with the trust that the funds would come, but all the while taking whatever active steps were possible to assist this. They were also learning to let go when there was no more that could be done in that regard and to just keep working as if the funds were already on their way. Pearl's faith was unwavering, though, and as a result, she inspired the team enormously.

Money soon began to flow to the project from numerous unexpected sources, creating great joy amongst the workers. The program expanded into another suburb, helping more people. In a few years, Pearl and some others were all earning decent money, expanding the program yet again, helping more and more people in need and never for a moment feeling like it was work.

The sun had now moved over the house, and we returned to the living room, where I had lit the fire a little earlier. Pearl was exhausted but didn't believe in going to bed until it was evening, if she could help it. She took her rests during the day on the settee in by the fire. Making her comfortable, I adjusted the pillows and placed a lovely big rug over her. Like Pearl and all of her home, it was also colourful. The fire threw beautiful light across the room, offering a feeling of comfort. When she was settled, the dogs jumped up and snuggled in. It was a beautiful scene – Pearl, the dogs, the fire, the colours of her home – and is one that remains clear in my mind these years later.

"It is about intention mostly, though, this money thing," she declared. Carrying a chair over to be closer, I continued to listen, enjoying her thoughts. "Money flows best when the intention is honorable. We were able to find funds for the project because it was for the good of others. Of course we benefitted from this, too, by earning money doing what we loved, as well as enjoying a sense of purpose in our lives."

Pearl said this is why purpose was so important in our work. If we find purpose in it, we naturally approach it with the right intention. Any work with purpose will benefit someone else somehow. The money will come to support that intention; providing we take what action we can and don't block the flow with fear. People of middle age, in particular, find many questions arising and feel a longing to somehow connect with the world through their work. This is the natural yearning for purpose Pearl spoke of.

She was an intelligent and wise woman and shared her thoughts freely. I imagined it would have been the same easy flow between us even if she hadn't been dying. Pearl continued, stating that parents, for example, don't always believe their own worth and how their intention to raise happy children is one of the greatest contributions anyone can make to society. It breeds good adults. She hated to hear any mother say they were *just* a mum, when it was the most important thing and a job of true purpose. The same even went for people in their gardens, celebrating the beauty of the earth.

Thinking of a lovely lady I had known when I was living over in Perth, I shared how her garden had brought me happiness every morning as I walked to the train station. It brought so much pleasure with blooming flowers and colourful trees that I ended up putting a card in her mailbox to thank her for the delight she gave me. The garden truly did make every day better for me. Colourful flowers and exotic plants worked in beautiful symmetry with each other, each day revealing another change, another view. People don't always realise the joy they bring to others. One day I finally saw the gardener herself, an eighty-year old woman, and told her how much I loved her place. It took Yvonne no time to work out that it was me who had written the card, and a new friendship began.

"Yes, that was her purpose – the garden. Finding purpose in life is one of the most important things ever," Pearl went on. "In some ways, I wish I hadn't wasted all of those years in a job that was pleasant but of very little significance to my true life's work, the work I found through the project. It led me to where I was meant to be ,though, as it was a customer from there who helped me to find my way to that change. It can take years to work out what you want to do, and it did for me. But the satisfaction that awaits will make the search worth it for anyone."

Considering the struggle I too had gone through to find work that satisfied me, I agreed it was worth it. Sitting by the fire with this beautiful woman and three sweet natured dogs, I felt very grateful to be able to call this my work. I told Pearl this, and she smiled in agreement.

"If I had any regrets, Bronnie, it would be that I wish I'd not spent so many years in an average job. Life is over so quickly. I knew this from losing my family. But sometimes we can know things for a long time before we are ready to act on them, unfortunately. So I could regret it, but I am not going to. Instead I prefer to be gentle, forgiving myself for not being able to leave that job sooner, for not seeing the signposts clearly enough until later." Agreeing that self-forgiveness was a much healthier state than regret, I told Pearl how much I was learning through my clients.

She laughed, saying, "That's right. You have no excuse. You cannot go to your deathbed and say you wished you'd worked it out sooner. You are being blessed by all of your mistakes instead." Laughing, I shared her opinion. But I could see the talking was now also exhausting Pearl, and she agreed. So I made sure she was comfortable then closed the curtains, leaving her to rest in the light of the fire. Standing at the door watching her and the three dogs for a moment, a slow tear rolled down my cheek.

Although I was still learning to realise my true worth, I was overwhelmed with gratitude that I at least now had a job with heart. Smiling then, I headed into the kitchen. After making a cup of chai, I enjoyed another peaceful room of the house while Pearl slept. It was a quiet afternoon in the neighbourhood, though it would have made no difference here. It was always a peaceful home, both in volume and energy.

I shared another few weeks with Pearl, but she grew weaker every day until finally accepting that getting out of bed was just too hard. Acknowledging that she had appreciated her home to its fullest, she asked me to continue appreciating it for my remaining time there, on her behalf. I smiled and said no worries. But it was Pearl I appreciated much more than her lovely home.

Friends came to say their goodbyes, including those she had worked with on the community projects. They spoke of how she had changed their lives and how her work had left a permanent footprint, helping so many others. It doesn't need to be grand work

to have purpose, though. Some people are able to help thousands. Some may only help one or two. Either way, the work is just as important. We all have a purpose, and working towards finding that purpose contributes to the good of all. And, of course, it helps each of us, too. Work, then, is no longer work, but as Pearl said, a satisfying extension of ourselves.

When I closed the door behind me on the day of Pearl's passing, I walked out into a day of beautiful winter sunshine. Pausing and taking a deep breath, I welcomed the winter sun shining down on my face. Through all of that searching during my years in banking, it had only ever been my intention to find work I loved.

Now in the winter sunshine, I smiled thinking of Pearl and the wonderful person she was. I had indeed found work I loved, and for that I felt blessed. It took some time for me to move off from her front garden, lost in my thoughts and gratitude, and sending Pearl love. But either way, it didn't matter. I was smiling, and I had my work to thank for that.

SIMPLICITY

❧◌❧

Understandably, the families of those dying also suffered enormously during the clients' last weeks. The general age range for most of the families was early forties to late fifties, with the majority of them having children themselves.

The fear of losing their parent, and perhaps the fear of their own pain, triggered some intense behaviour. This was one of the areas where I was often reminded how detrimental it is to live in a society that tries to keep death hidden. People are not only unprepared to deal with the enormity of emotions that surface, but they become desperately scared and vulnerable, the families often more so. The clients found their peace before they departed. But the children often had emotions that were totally out of control, ruled by fear and panic.

Working within private homes exposed me to the lifestyles and dynamics of a huge amount of families. It taught me that almost all families have challenges on some levels, things to heal and to learn through each other. Some were not even completely aware of the triggers each person served to ignite. But they were definitely there. When I would hear siblings getting impatient or upset with their brother or sister, I would respectfully stay out of it, and try to view the situation as compassionately as possible.

Control issues were paramount at this time, too. Often there was one sibling who wanted to control everything: the running of the home, the grocery list, the carers, the approaching funeral, everything. When other siblings tried to contribute or have a say, arguments sometimes broke out. Everyone has a right to contribute, particularly as limited time left increases this desire for everyone.

But the controlling person in the family often intensified their need to rule even more. It was heartbreaking to watch this exhibition of power, or attempted power, as it was so fear driven.

The wellbeing of the client was my first priority, though, over absolutely everything else. So when I heard a screaming match begin and intensify over Charlie's bed, I was into the room in a flash. My lovely client lay beneath his adult children, Greg and Maryanne, as they screamed desperately at each other across the bed, out of control. "Enough of this, please," I stated firmly but gently. "Take it into the other room if you must continue. Look at your dad. He is lying here dying, for goodness sakes."

Maryanne burst into tears, apologising to her father. Charlie was a peaceful man, and always had been apparently. "He just hassles me all the damn time," she said of her brother. Maryanne had beautiful blue eyes and long black hair, someone who should be an artist's model I thought to myself. But her eyes were red from crying, and so sad.

Without pause, Greg retaliated in anger. "Well, I don't see why you should get as much as me in the will. You moved away. You've made less effort. I have worked harder, and been here for Dad the most since Mum died." My heart ached for Greg and this reasoning. It was just a fragile, wounded, little boy underneath these words. I could see their dad in both of them, but I think Greg must have looked like his mum, too. His hair was brown and his skin fairer than his sister's. He wasn't crying, though. He was fuming.

Looking at Charlie for direction, he just shrugged at me with a look of sadness from his own big blue eyes. Leading them out, I said, "I think it may be best if you both come out of the room now. This is not helping anyone, especially your father." With tea made, we sat in the kitchen and I listened to them talk. Maryanne didn't have so much to say, and when I asked her why, she said it wasn't worth the hassle. Underneath the hurtful words between them, though, I could still see love. Thinking back to how honesty had begun repairing my own family situation, I encouraged them to talk.

My relationship with my father, for example, had once been tumultuous and very painful for me. But with honesty, compassion, and time, it had healed beautifully. We were now enjoying a very respectful, humorous, and loving friendship. There was a time I would have never dreamed it possible, but any family relationship can be healed if love still remains and both parties are willing, as it was for us. It was obvious that love still existed between Greg and Maryanne, as did a yearning to be understood by each other. It was all just distorted by pain.

After they had both shared their grievances, I asked what they liked about each other. "Nothin'," Greg replied gruffly. I lightened the situation with humour, and before long he came up with a couple of things. Maryanne likewise named a few things. Their egos were battling with this, particularly Greg's, as he wanted to hate her. What drove me to suggest this, though, was that it had worked for me when thinking of some of my own family members. During those years when things became the most painful in my relationships with them, I tried to draw on things I liked or loved about them. I was the same as Greg at first, struggling to come up with anything. But it was only my pain talking, blinding me from seeing good things in them. When I let go of that, I saw that even though our lifestyle differences may never see us sharing especially close connections, they were all decent, good-hearted people.

I was able to recall things they had done with kind intentions in the past. While some of these were unfortunately used against me later, the initial intentions had been kind. There were also occasions I could recognise now when, in their own individual ways, they had tried to show me their love. But I had been so wounded myself that I had rebuked it, pushing it away. They were all beautiful people underneath any misunderstandings, though, as everyone is underneath the stuff that clouds one's best self. So today, it was just Greg and Maryanne's turn to work through some of their disagreements.

It turned out that Greg had carried resentment for his sister for decades, simply because she had had the courage to live the life she had been guided to, the life she wanted. It wasn't Maryanne who had stopped Greg doing this for himself also, though. It was Greg. A great deal of emotions came out that afternoon, and while they were certainly not best friends by the end of the day, they were much further along than at the start. Each of them then spent some individual time in with Charlie before they headed off. Then it was just Charlie and me again.

Walking back into his room after they had left, he looked at me, shaking his head and laughing gently. "Well, my dear girl. That one has been building for about twenty years now. I had always wondered when the volcano would blow," he chuckled. "I am glad it has happened now before I go. Maybe I will see them become friends after all."

Birds were singing in the native trees out the window, and an orange butterfly flew by. We both watched it, smiling, and then went back to chatting. Charlie told me how they had always been very close as children, Greg always looking out for his little sister, and her idolising him. When she became an independently thinking teenager, though, they had begun fighting and never found their closeness again.

"It's not Maryanne I worry about, though, Bronnie. She is relatively happy. It is Greg. He has never stopped trying to prove himself. When he says he always did more for me than Maryanne, he is right in some ways, although she has helped greatly in other less obvious ways. But he didn't have to. Most of the time, he was doing things I could still do myself, and would have actually liked to." Sighing, Charlie went on. "He works ridiculous hours in a job he hates, raising children who never see him, and I don't really know why."

"Does he know you love him, Charlie?" I asked with dare. He looked at me puzzled.

"Well, I suppose so. I always comment if he's done a good job here, around the house. He knows I am proud of him."

"How? Do you ever tell him directly that you are proud of who he is as a person, rather than of the job he's done?" I asked.

He paused for a moment. "Not directly, no. But he knows," Charlie replied.

"How?" I persisted.

Charlie laughed. "You damn women. You have to get to the

depth of it all, don't you?" Laughing, I then shared my thoughts with Charlie. He listened respectfully and openly. I wondered if what he had said about Greg always trying to prove himself was actually due to him seeking his dad's love and approval. The conversation continued as I showered Charlie and then wheeled him back to bed. He always preferred an afternoon shower, but it was starting to exhaust him and before long, it would be bed baths only. His breathing was poor and it took some time for him to get it regular again once back in bed. He was becoming a little frailer each day. So I left him to rest.

Poking my head back in a couple of hours later, he turned to me and smiled. So I sat beside the bed, assisted him to have a drink, and asked if he needed anything else. He shook his head, then continued to talk about his children. "All I want for them is to be happy. That's all any parent should want of their children. I wish Greg would stop working so hard by making his life simpler. He is a good man, but he is not happy in himself," he told me. "The simple life is the happy life. It is how their mother and I always lived. We didn't really have a choice, though. It was hard then. But simplicity is still possible today. It is a good choice."

A photo of Charlie as a dashing young man standing beside his bride sat in the centre position on the mantelpiece in his room. I thought of him and his wife raising Greg and Maryanne as infants. Charlie was a straight talker, and I liked that about him. There was something very old-fashioned about his honesty. He continued to share whatever came to mind as he thought out loud. "You know, I don't think he truly knows I love him. I've never said the words exactly."

"We are all different, Charlie," I said. "Some people know through actions, but most people need to actually hear it. Perhaps Greg is one of these kinds of people. What is it going to hurt anyway, by you telling him?"

He nodded. "I do need to tell him. What a terrible world we live in when a seventy-eight year old man is nervous about telling his son he loves him. I've had no practice in this, you know," he laughed. But seriousness came to his face. The look of a clear decision and determination became obvious. Charlie continued. "Do you think I might be able to convince him to live a simpler life if he is not trying to seek my approval anymore, if he knows I love him? And I do love him."

I said to Charlie that no one could determine how another will react. There were no guarantees this would change Greg's lifestyle. The important thing was that it was likely to bring him more peace by knowing he had his dad's love and approval.

The topic of living simply became more of an important issue for Charlie as his days wore on. He said people work too hard for all sorts of reasons. Often they think there is no choice, because they cannot get off the wheel of routine with bills and supporting their family. Charlie understood this. He agreed that survival is a genuine challenge for many people, but insisted there were always choices. "It is a matter of changing your perspective sometimes. Do we really need to live in a house this big? Do we need such a flashy car?" he asked. Sometimes, he said, it was more a matter of changing their thinking and finding a new solution, thinking hard about what they love and working as a family towards finding more balance.

Community was also a way towards simplicity, Charlie explained. If we work together more as a community, we don't need as many resources. There is less waste and we learn to help each other out. Ego and pride stop many communities from ever being born or developed, he said. But if we want to live more resourcefully and more simply, it is important to start understanding the huge importance and need of community in the area we live in. He was sad that times had become so fast and unbalanced that we had forgotten this.

Charlie acknowledged that it could be very difficult financially in these times. He said society had lost sight of true priorities, and it was society itself that needed a lesson in simplicity. But this only ever happens by individuals changing themselves first, one person at a time. Then eventually society will follow the way the majority thinks and lives, as it always does. He also believed those in power needed a good kick in the pants. There were some good people dotted throughout the political systems of the world. But they were too often restricted by red tape, and by others with more money and power. So to make a significant change, every single one of us had a job to do. Simplifying our lives was a very good place to start.

Charlie had raised a family of his own, so he fully understood the pressure of survival and supporting a family. But he was also dying and now saw things from a different perspective, wishing out loud that he had realised all of this sooner so he could have guided Greg differently. "Children are happier having more time with their parents than having more toys. They may complain at first. But the happiest children are those who get quality time with their parents, both parents if possible. Young boys, too, need more male influence. How can Greg's boys get that if he is working all of the time, trying to prove himself?" Charlie sat thoughtfully, as I saw new insights registering in him. "I do love my boy. I need to tell him, don't I?"

With happiness, I nodded. Then out of the blue, he asked, "Is your life simple?" to which I laughed gently.

"Yes, my physical life is quite simple, Charlie. And I am working on simplifying my emotional life, one step at a time," I replied honestly, still laughing a little as I thought about the complications of my emotional life in recent years, something that had been far from simple. "Meditation had helped me hugely to simplify my thinking. All of my life benefits from this in one way or another. It has truly transformed me, allowing me to move through a lot of stuff that used to hold me back. So my thinking is much, much simpler these days. And yes, my physical life is pretty simple, too."

Charlie was from a different lifestyle and generation, and didn't know anything about meditation, other than people overseas in orange robes sat with their eyes closed. He asked me what it was. I explained it as simply as possible, telling Charlie that by learning to focus the mind, we become better able to observe our own thinking. From this it becomes clear just how much of life is shaped by a mind running wild on its own, creating unnecessary suffering and fears. As these unhealthy thinking patterns grow and intensify, we become identified with this personality as being who we are and shaping our lives around that. When actually we are not this, but so much more.

We are wise, intuitive beings who have become blinded by the fears and misperceptions our minds have created over the years, through all of its reactions, both positive and negative. So by learning to focus our minds in meditation – say by observing our breath, for an easy example – we begin to take back ownership of our own thinking, thus giving ourselves the choice to consciously think better thoughts. And therefore, create happier lives.

Charlie sat speechless, staring at me. I smiled, waiting. "Wow," he finally said. "Why didn't I meet you fifty years ago?" Laughing, I hopped up and gave him another sip of his drink.

"Why didn't *I* meet me years ago, too, Charlie?" I laughed. "It would have saved me a lot of pain!"

The conversation continued and eventually turned to him asking me about the simplicity of my physical life, and what I had meant by that. After many years of moving, I told him, I had started to question the importance of belongings. With some moves, my furniture came with me. At other times, it was stored either for free on family farms, or in a shed I had to pay for. Whenever I was living a chapter free of those belongings, I was reminded of how much I didn't need any of it to be happy. I would question why I was keeping it at all.

So my furniture was sold, reducing my belongings to just household goods, enabling me to set up again somewhere else when the time came. And the time would come again, as I always loved my own kitchen space. Drifting suited me. There was a great freedom in it. But even freedom has its price. Everything has a price. Missing my own kitchen was what usually made me want to settle again for a time.

Yet after then settling for twelve to eighteen months, I would be missing the excitement of leaping out into the unknown all over again. Owning things would leave me feeling terribly weighed down. So recognising my own patterns, I came to accept that for these years in my life, I would actually be better off if I owned nothing much at all. Each time I had started again, furniture had come my way easily, through word-of-mouth, second hand shops, and yard sales. I loved that. Buying second hand things was also more conducive to my love of the Earth, as it asked no more if its diminishing resources. Our throw-away society seems to forget that everything new has to come from somewhere, and everything old has to end up somewhere. In most cases, it is the Earth that has to bear the burden at both ends. This comes at a dangerous price for the planet's survival and that of all of its creatures, we humans included.

As it was, they were always fascinating things I ended up with, creating a whole new home. It never occurred to me that the furniture would not come. So as a result, it always did and very easily. I've owned some gorgeous pieces over the years. If the furniture came my way so naturally each time I settled, then surely everything else would, too.

Having paid storage on my belongings for the previous twelve months, I decided this was a waste of money and an encumbrance I didn't need. So with the help of a beautiful and dependable friend, we set up a garage sale at his place. Cutlery, books, floor rugs, linen, ornaments, paintings – everything went. It was such a fun time, watching the excitement of people as my things became their new belongings and bargains. Whatever remained was taken to the charity shop that afternoon.

By now I was driving a car the size of a shoebox. The jeep had exited life in spectacular fashion a year or so earlier on a six-lane highway. The current car, while incredibly economical and nippy around the cities, was tiny. It was affectionately known as 'the rice bubble'. So the intention of the garage sale was to own no more afterwards than would fit inside the rice bubble.

A total of five boxes remained. Two boxes of my favourite books were included. I only kept those that I knew I would read again, or ones I would lend or give to others for inspiration. The rest of the books found themselves in new hands to be enjoyed again elsewhere. The remainder of the boxes contained CDs, journals, photo albums, a few small things of sentiment, the patchwork quilt my mother made me, and my clothing. Then with the rice bubble packed to the max and the stereo on, I headed off into another period of my life.

The music that accompanied me contained songs from Guy Clark, The Waifs, Ben Lee, David Hosking, Cyndi Boste, Shawn Mullins, Mary Chapin Carpenter, Fred Eaglesmith, Abba, The

Waterboys, JJ Cale, Sara Tindley, Karl Broadie, John Prine, Heather Nova, David Francey, Lucinda Williams, Yusuf, and The Ozark Mountain Daredevils. It was all brilliant music, each song proving to be a fabulous travelling companion. I sang happily and freely as the miles unfolded, knowing that all of my belongings in the world were there with me in the rice bubble. About a thousand kilometers away, I stopped at my folks' place and offloaded the boxes. After that, it was just my clothes and me.

Charlie listened with delight, rubbing his old, weathered hands together in joy at my story. I then shared how after that trip, I had drifted for a while. Now I was in Sydney, experiencing the life of a house-sitter extraordinaire, and indeed, my physical life was actually quite a simple one. He knew then that I understood what he was trying to say about the importance of simplicity. We agreed that it is not always obvious to people just how much having excess belongings can weigh them down, even if they have no intentions of moving on. Clearing out physical belongings always leaves a person feeling more spacious within as well.

Greg arrived the next day and spent the whole time in with his father. At Charlie's request, I had phoned Maryanne and asked her not to visit today. Tomorrow it would be the other way around. Maryanne would have her father all to herself and Greg would not be visiting. Charlie had asked me earlier to discreetly pop in now and then in case things were awkward between him and Greg, my presence hopefully altering this. But there was no need. The couple of times I did go in there, to deliver a pot of tea or pass on a message, it was obvious that an important personal discussion and sharing was underway.

Not long before Greg was due to leave so his dad could rest, they called me in. Greg's eyes were bloodshot from crying, and they were holding each other's hand. "Bronnie, I just want you to know, too," Charlie announced. "I love this man with all of my heart. He is a good son and a great man."

At this, of course, I almost cried. "My son is already enough," Charlie said. "There is nothing for him to prove. There is nothing he needs to do or to have, to become a better person. I love this man sitting here completely. And being his father has brought my life great joy."

Through my laughing smile, I said that Greg was blessed to have Charlie as his dad too. Greg agreed, using his whole sleeve to wipe his tears. "And Dad reckons I could learn a thing or two from you about simplicity," he announced.

Laughing, I replied that his dad still had enough time left to leave his own mark on Greg in that regard. He didn't need me to do the job for him. But as a departing remark, I said with a smile, "All I *will* add, though, is *keep it simple*."

Maryanne came around the next day. I heard her laughing and crying with her dad as well. There was a lot of love being shared in this household, and I couldn't help but be affected by it positively. During the next few weeks, the three of them spent a lot of time together and grew much closer. Never did I hear Charlie say goodbye without telling them both individually that he loved them, and they both said the same to him. The channel of communication had been opened in time for healing to happen, while Charlie was still alive.

On the day of his passing, Greg and Maryanne sat holding one of their dad's hands each. At their request, I also sat in the room as he slipped away peacefully, his breathing slowing until it ceased completely. It was a clear morning, and birds continued to sing outside his window as they always had. I thought how it added beauty to the occasion. They were singing him on.

Leaving Greg and Maryanne alone then, I sat out on the verandah for a while, enjoying my own memories of Charlie and sending him prayers and good wishes on the road ahead, wherever he now was. When I came inside again, Greg and Maryanne were sitting on the same side of the bed, holding hands as they looked at their dad, laughing and smiling through tears, speaking of him with joy.

About a year later I received an email from Greg. He and his family had sold their big home. He had taken a transfer with the company he was working for and was earning less money, but was now living in a small country town. He commuted to work the same distance as before. But it was now on a country road to a bigger country town and took him less than half the time of his previous commuting. This gave him an extra one and a half hours a day with his children. The cost of living was also less as their lives had become simpler. Yet their quality of life had improved enormously. His wife was happy, too, and they all loved their new friends and lifestyle. He thanked me for looking after their father and spoke lovingly of Maryanne, who apparently had just been there visiting.

Understandably, the email brought me much joy. It took me back to Charlie, his blue eyes, delightful smile, and the conversations we had shared. Knowing that his words had not only been heard, but also applied, was also a wonderful feeling.

The very best of the email though was how Greg had signed off. After wishing me well in my own life, he summed things up with three little words, leaving me with a huge smile across my face: *Keep it simple.*

Indeed, Greg and Charlie. Indeed.

REGRET 3:
I WISH I'D HAD THE COURAGE
TO EXPRESS MY FEELINGS

For a ninety-four year old man who was dying, Jozsef looked remarkably well when we first met. He was a gentle person with a lovely smile that made him look like a young boy at times. With his quiet but very quick sense of humour, I warmed to him straight away.

Jozsef's family had decided not to tell him he was dying. I found this difficult but tried to respect their decision, as much as possible. Over the next few weeks, however, his illness took a drastic turn downhill, which was impossible to ignore. Standing unaided became a thing of the past. With each new day, he depended on my strength more and more. His illness was not something that needed to be pointed out. It was obvious every time he tried to stand or sit, and it was something that was silently registered between us with each effort. So while the family continued the charade of not telling him he was dying, Jozsef's own realisation was setting in. He was indeed a very ill man.

Medications were used to compensate his pain as much as possible. But as was the case with many people, the side-effects of the medications were blocked up bowels. There are drugs to then compensate for that, but they were not working well in Jozsef's case. So I was required to assist with bowel discharge by inserting medication into his rectum, the poor old fellow. Once you are this ill, there is no privacy anymore. Certainly there was no dignity now, as Jozsef rolled onto his side for me to insert the small tube. I tried to keep the situation light, of course, and found myself speaking words I would hear me saying regularly to others later.

"It all starts off being about food and poo, Jozsef, and it all ends up being about food and poo," I gently joked with him. Working with the dying truly brought home to me the cycles of life. The things that keep a baby most comfortable at the very beginning are food and the release of their bowels and wind. At the end of life, the questions everyone asks of the dying person are if they are still eating and are their bowels working properly.

It is a relief to everyone when someone who is dying and is on strong painkillers finally manages a bowel movement, easing this other pain. So was the case for Jozsef and his family, when he made a dash to the toilet soon after and enjoyed an explosion from his bum. Of course this brought me relief, too, not only because my client was more comfortable, but also because I had succeeded in this procedure on my first ever attempt.

One of his sons lived in a nearby suburb and visited daily. Another lived interstate. His daughter lived overseas. Each day Jozsef and his son would chat for a little while, mostly about the business pages of the newspaper, until Jozsef became too tired. This was not long as his health was deteriorating so quickly. I liked his son but didn't feel a strong connection with him. I had no reason not to like him, though. When I mentioned to Jozsef later that his son was a nice man, he replied with, "He is only interested in my money." Preferring to take people as I find them, I tried to keep this comment from influencing my own opinion of his son.

Over the next few weeks my client shared many stories with me, mostly about the love of his work. He and his wife, Gizela, had been holocaust survivors, managing to find their way to Australia upon their release. Stories about his time in the camps came out in fragments. But I didn't push it. I was there to listen but not determine what he wanted to share. It was obvious that life was easier for both of them by not discussing it. Trying to empathise as much as possible with the situation, I hated to think how much pain they were each carrying, and my heart went out to them.

Jozsef and I fell into an easy association, and stories on other subjects flowed well. We had similar senses of humour and were both fairly quiet natured. So we liked each other. The generation gap made little difference as we came to share a strong conversational flow, one that strengthened daily. All the while, Gizela would come in with food, constantly encouraging Jozsef to eat. She was a great cook, but though he was hardly able to eat at all by now, she still cooked huge quantities. A part of this was possibly habit, but a part of it was denial.

The family had somehow also convinced Jozsef's doctor not to tell him that he was dying. It was a mass denial. But not only were they not telling him the truth about this condition and inevitable decline, the family were trying to convince him he was getting better. "Come on, Jozsef, eat up. You'll be getting better in no time," Gizela would say repeatedly. My heart felt for her, too. To be so scared of the truth must have been a huge burden to bear.

By this time, Jozsef was down to just a tub of yoghurt a day and was incredibly weak, no longer even able to walk to the lounge room with assistance, but they were still telling him he would be better in no time. I stayed silent on the topic until Jozsef brought it up with me directly.

Gizela had just left the room. Jozsef was sitting back, and I was giving him a foot massage, something he had never had in his life but had grown accustomed to with great delight over the previous weeks. I loved pampering my clients, and perhaps this is why we grew close. A lot of the conversations I had with them were while I was massaging feet, brushing hair, scratching backs, or filing nails.

"I *am* dying, aren't I, Bronnie?" he said when she was out of the room.

I looked at him with kindness and nodded. "Yes, Jozsef, you are."

He nodded with the relief of being told the truth. After my experience with Stella's family, there was no way I was going to be anything but honest from here on. He looked out the window for some time, and the foot massage continued in comfortable silence.

"Thank you. Thank you for telling me the truth," he finally replied in his thick accent. I smiled gently and nodded. Silence lingered for a moment or two. Then he spoke again. "They just can't handle it," he said of his family. "Gizela can't face the pain of talking with me about it. She will be OK. She just can't talk about it."

He was peaceful in knowing his situation, and I was peaceful in having been honest. He continued, "I don't have long left, do I?"

"I don't think so, Jozsef."

"Weeks, months?" he questioned.

"I really don't know. But I would guess it is only weeks or days. That's my feeling, but I really don't know," I told him honestly. He nodded and looked out the window again.

Very few people can truly predict *exactly* when someone is going to pass, unless the person is obviously in their last few days. But it was a question clients and families always asked, sometimes repeatedly. By now I was starting to gauge the decline of people, also seeing how quickly things could change. Often clients would appear to pick up again briefly, before the final turn home. The success of my role as a carer really came down to me working intuitively. It was on that basis I had answered Jozsef's question, even if somewhat reluctantly. I just didn't want to lie and say he had months left when there was no way he did.

The foot massage was finished, and I sat looking out the window, too. He broke the silence after a time. "I wish I hadn't worked so hard." Waiting, I let him continue. "I loved my work, I really loved it. That's why I worked so hard, that and to provide for my family and their family."

"Well, that's a beautiful thing then. So why regret it?"

He explained that his regrets were partly for his family, who had seen so little of him for most of their life in Australia. But it was mostly because he felt he had never given them a chance to know him. "I was too scared to let my feelings show. So I worked and worked and kept the family at a distance. They didn't deserve to be so alone. Now I wish they really knew me."

Joszef said he hadn't really known himself until recent years, so questioned how they could have stood a chance of knowing him anyway. His lovely eyes were sad as we talked about the patterns of relationships and how difficult it is to break those. We also discussed how necessary it is for a relationship to reach its greatest potential.

He also felt he had missed the opportunity to create loving warmth with his children. The only example he had ever set was how to earn and value money. "What is the point of that now?" he sighed.

"Well," I tried to reason. "You have done what you intended. You are leaving them with a comfortable life. You have provided for them as you wanted to."

A solitary tear ran down his cheek. "But they don't know me. They don't know me." I looked at him lovingly. "And I want them to," he said, as the tears started to flow. I sat in silence as he cried.

After a while I suggested that it wasn't too late. But he disagreed. He was too frail to speak for long periods now, so that alone would have made it difficult. He also admitted to not knowing how to talk with them about such depth of feelings. So I offered to go and get Gizela and his son, to include them in the current conversation, saying it may be easier with me there perhaps. But he shook his head and dried his tears. "No. It is too late. Let's not tell them I know. It is easier for them thinking the way they do. I know I am dying. It is OK."

Jozsef was near the age my own dear grandmother had been when she passed on. Although each of their lives had been vastly different, there was something about being with someone of this age I was comfortable with. My Gran and I used to be able to talk about death very easily, though. She said it was easier with me than with some of her own children.

She and her twin brother had been the eldest of eleven children. Gran was only thirteen when her mother died, and raised all of the other children herself. Her father was a 'hard man', as she put it. She also called him a 'mongrel' at other times. He provided food but little else, especially not love, she said.

A year or so after her mother had died, the youngest of her siblings also passed away, a little one called Charlotte. Then after raising all of those younger siblings, Gran went on to raise seven children of her own, my mother included. When I was born with a mass of dark curls and big inquisitive eyes, Gran saw a spitting image of Charlotte in me. As a result, we shared a close connection from my first day.

We would all be so excited when she came to visit us. Kids love visitors, and we were no different. Gran stood no taller than five feet but was a dynamic, amazing woman. She'd had to be with her upbringing. The love she gave me was unconditional and always totally accepting. A fine example of this, amongst many, was when my mother was overseas with her own twin sister, having a well-deserved holiday. My father worked away a few days a week, so Gran came to look after us.

I was twelve at the time, soon to be thirteen and in my first year of high school at the convent. The school was hidden behind ten-foot double-brick walls and run by nuns, some of whom were lovely women. The head mistress, though, was a tough cookie and not so affectionately known as 'Iron Face'. The older students had warned us off her from Day One. Although now, as a grown woman who is not influenced by such rumours, I admit she may possibly have been a lovely woman underneath that tough exterior. I want to believe that anyway. But she ran a tight ship, and in my years there, I must say that I didn't see her smile once.

In that first year of high school, there was obviously a part of me looking for something different, and I found myself hanging out with two of the toughest girls in the class for a short while. I was a pretty good kid and had been rarely noticed by the head mistress prior to this, which suited me just fine.

Climbing a tree and sneaking over the fence on our lunch break, we raced downtown and made our way into a store, where we each stole a pair of earrings with our initials on them. Gaining confidence from such easy success, we then ventured into the next store and shoplifted some lip-gloss. Rubbing my sweet tasting lips together and laughing at how good the stuff was, I felt a large hand on my shoulder with a voice saying, "I'll have that, thank you."

With legs almost paralysed in fear, I was led into the store manager's office with one of the other girls. The other had run off. They called the head mistress of the school, who was then waiting for us on our humble return. She tapped the ruler into her hand. "Into my office," she stated firmly.

"Yes, Sister," we said humbly in unison. If we had tails, they would have been between our legs by this time.

The deal the store did with the school was that no charges would be laid. But we had to go home and tell our parents ourselves what we had done. The parents were then required to call the head mistress and confirm we had told them. We were also banned from sport for a whole term, and being mad sports lovers, this devastated us both. Being hit across the backs of our legs with the ruler a dozen times was endured, too. She was a tough woman.

With Mum overseas and Dad home for the end of the week, I was terrified. Due to being a sensitive, gentle kid, I was already scared of anyone with a big voice. But Gran was there too, so I took her aside. With a big bottom lip trembling, I told her what I had done. She sat listening, not interrupting, not reacting. She waited until I was finished, by which time I was bawling my eyes out.

"Well, are you going to do it again?" she asked.

"No, Gran. I promise," I solemnly declared.

"Have you learnt your lesson here?"

I assured her, "Yes, Gran, I have. I won't do it again."

"OK," she finally said. "Well, let's not tell your father, and I will ring the school for you tomorrow." And that was it. Bless her. But the fear I had experienced from the incident itself was so enormous and enough that not only did I never shoplift again, I was never even capable of returning to that particular store.

Years later when high school was completed, I left the country town I grew up in. Not able to wait to spread my wings, I accepted the first job offered, a banking role near Gran's place in the city, five hours away. Living with my Gran and aunt was the most practical option.

At eighteen, fresh off the farm and out of convent schooling, it was not surprising that I was open to new opportunities. When my mother guessed later that year I was no longer a virgin, she was horrified and almost ready to disown me, unable to believe that I, a good girl with common sense, could be so easily swayed. It was Gran who fixed things again, telling my mum to lighten up, as times had changed and I was still a good girl in my own way. My connection with both of these wonderful women continued to strengthen from that point on.

When I discovered the world of alcohol and came home drunk to Gran's, it was she who left a bucket beside the bed, just in case. She was wise, accepting, and a hugely positive role in my life. She was also relieved when I announced at a reasonably young age that alcohol was just not for me.

Gran outlived all of her brothers and sisters, which was heartbreaking for her as they had been like her own children. We would write to each other from wherever I was living and share our lives as an open book. I shared her sadness of losing her last sister and her frustrations in growing older, gradually losing her independence. Seeing her slow down over the years was heartbreaking for me, too, as I had to face the fact that she wasn't going to be around forever.

I started to find it hard to hold back the tears whenever we would talk. So I openly told her how much I loved her and how much I was going to miss her when her time came. After that, we were able to speak about death with candid honesty. I am so glad we did. With no denial of what lay ahead, we savoured every conversation we had, and she was able to share her thoughts about passing with me. Gran was ready to go for years before she did.

Returning from a few years overseas, I couldn't wait to see her. The changes were huge. With hair now totally white, she walked with a stick and had shrunk even more. My Gran was now an old, old lady. She was in her nineties, but still the amazing woman I knew. Her mind was clear, and our conversations continued on with great satisfaction for another year or so.

The phone call came on a Monday while I was at work in one of my last bank jobs, managing the local branch. She had passed away the night before, dying in her sleep. My world fell out beneath me, and I shut the office door. With my head between my arms on the desk, I sobbed in farewell to my beloved, darling grandmother and for my loss. "Oh Gran, oh Gran, oh Gran," I cried into my own arms.

Leaving work early, bleary eyed and too sad to think clearly, I stopped at the mailbox. Flicking through the letters and bills half numb, I halted in amazement. There amongst them was a card from my little Gran. She had posted it Friday and had died naturally in her sleep on Sunday night. A torrent of tears flowed from both sorrow and joy as I held the card to my heart, sobbing but almost laughing at the same time.

I was so grateful for the connection we had shared and for having had the honesty to talk about death with her. There was nothing left unsaid. She knew I loved her, and I knew she loved me, even more so as I read the beautiful words she had written – *"I love you dearly, my Darling. You are so often in my thoughts. May sunshine follow you all the days of your life, Bron. Love, Gran."*

The thought of her dying may have brought me tears before her departure. I certainly cried after the event. But there was peace, too, knowing we had faced what inevitably happens to everyone with honesty and openness. That peace stays with me still. Her face smiles back at me from a photo frame on my desk. While there are days I miss her dearly these years on, I have no doubt that honesty gave us a relationship so special and positive that it continues to shape me in the best possible ways.

It wasn't so easy for my dear client Jozsef, though. The honesty was now too painful for him and his family. My heart went out to him as I felt his pain and frustration. What that dear man must have experienced in his life, I still hated to imagine. Gizela continued to come in with enormous meals, encouraging Jozsef to eat up. He would smile gently at her and decline the meal each time. Other carers came in of an evening, but I was the main day carer. We knew each other and it was comfortable and easy for him, especially now that he was able to open up, at least to me.

It was with surprise and sadness then when I learned I was being replaced. His son had been complaining of the costs of care. Explaining to his son that his father only had a matter of a week or two left, he chose to make other plans anyway, saying Jozsef could live on for ages. Finding an illegal worker willing to do the job for next to nothing was the solution.

Pleading with Gizela to convince their son otherwise, it was no use. Their minds were made up. There was other work waiting for me elsewhere. That wasn't the issue. It was that Jozsef had finally been able to talk, and he was comfortable with me. Surely his happiness should have been the priority for the last week or two of his life. I hated to think of how impersonal the alternative might be, especially as he was no longer able to speak a lot due to weakness and breathing difficulties. I felt for the new carer, too, and the language difficulties they would face together.

But it was out of my hands, and I had to trust that these events were also a part of Jozsef's life journey. How can any of us know what another is here to learn? We can't. So with a hug and a smile that said more than words were ever going to, we said our goodbye. Pausing at the doorway of his room one last time, I looked at him again. We each smiled the same way at each other, saying nothing but saying so much. Then it was time to go. Driving away from his home, knowing he would be staring out of the window in his own thoughts by now, my tears flowed. This role was exposing me to people I would have never met otherwise, and I loved what was shared and learned through each other, as hard as it sometimes was.

Jozsef's granddaughter called me about a week later to tell me he had died the night before. I was glad for him. His illness would never have allowed him any more quality of life anyway. It was for the best. Contemplating all that had unfolded, I found only blessings. Learning through these dear people before they died was a rare gift, and for that I was grateful. We will all die, but this work was reminding me we all have a choice, too, on how to live in the meantime.

Seeing the anguish Jozsef experienced in not being able to express his feelings left me determined to always try to be brave enough to share mine. My walls of privacy were being eroded, and I began to wonder why we are all so afraid of being open and honest. Of course, it is to avoid pain that may come as a result of our honesty. But those walls we create bring pain of their own, by stopping others from knowing who we truly are. Watching the tears fall down that lovely old man's face, as he longed to be known and understood, changed me forever.

After receiving the phone call about Jozsef's passing, I sat in a park near the beach just absorbing the surroundings. Children were playing everywhere, and I watched how naturally they all shared their feelings. If they liked someone, they said so. If they were sad, they cried, released it, and were then happy again. They didn't know how to suppress their feelings. It was beautiful to watch the honest expressions. It was also refreshing to see how they all played and worked on things together.

We have created a society where adults are now so insular and apart. Working together, expressing their feelings, and being joyous were the natural states of the children I watched. While it made me sad that as adults we have lost such ability to be so totally open, it also brought me hope. If we were once also like that, as we all would have been to varying degrees, then perhaps we could learn to be that way again.

I made a clear decision in the park there by the beach. I was not going to find myself ever regretting things as dear Jozsef had. It was time to be more courageous and to start expressing my feelings more.

The walls around my heart were of no use anymore. The process of dismantling them was, at last, now underway.

NO GUILT

The buzzer rang, bringing me out of a snug sleep in my latest abode. Slipping some cover on my feet and wrapping myself in a robe, I headed upstairs to attend to Jude. Words that may appear as a grunt to an untrained ear were uttered, indicating she needed repositioning, as her leg was in pain. Once Jude was comfortable and smiling again, I turned off her lamp, wished her sweet dreams again, and headed back down to the comfort of a beautiful bed.

Jude and I had been brought together through word of mouth. Someone in the songwriting circuit knew I worked as a carer and lived as a house-sitter, so passed my phone number on. The majority of my palliative clients so far had been elderly or past middle age, and most were dying of cancer related illnesses, but not all. Jude's illness, though, was a motor neurone disease, and she was only forty-four. Her husband and daughter – a delightful nine-year old with curly auburn hair and a precious smile – were loving and beautiful people, as was Jude.

By the time I came to be her carer, they were fed up entirely with agencies who sent different people all the time. Jude's needs were many and quite specific, particularly in understanding her comfort and her deteriorating speech. So the desire for one main carer became the priority. Other carers were employed to cover my time off, and thankfully I now had enough experience to train them. No longer able to support her own weight, we used a hydraulic hoist to move Jude to her wheelchair and bed. Each day I saw her abilities lessen and was glad to have arrived while she could still communicate reasonably well, as it enabled me to translate the grunts that were to come later.

Jude came from a very wealthy family and had extreme pressure on her as a young adult to marry well and live the life expected of her. Her first car was a luxury model, costing more than most people's annual salary. She had not stepped foot inside a regular department store until she was in her mid twenties. Designer clothes were all she knew. Her upbringing had guaranteed this.

Yet she had always been a creative and very down-to-earth person. The simple life was all she wanted, she told me. But her parents insisted she go to university, giving her the choice of studying economics or law. There was no other choice, despite her brief mention of wanting to study art. So under pressure and expectation, Jude chose law. Her choice was based on the idea that one day her parents would die and she may be able to then put her knowledge into a better cause, either the arts or community welfare. Things didn't work out that way, though. Her father had passed on by now, and it was most likely she would die before her mother. Regardless, she was no longer capable of working anyway.

Her love of the arts saw her falling in love with Edward, an artist himself. They both told of an instant attraction that had obviously not dwindled at all in the years since. Although both had been a little shy at first, the strength of their mutual attraction gave each of them the confidence to be brave.

In no time, they were in love, and the whole world fell away as they became each other's world. Jude's family was horrified by her choice, as Edward was raised in a lower-class family and was happy with a simple life, pursuing his art. He was actually quite a successful artist. But he was not a white-collar worker, and this was never going to be good enough for Jude's parents.

Sadly she was made to choose between her parents and Edward, so she chose Edward. Of course, she laughed. It was never a decision. She loved Edward with all of her heart, as he did her. Jude was then completely ostracised from her family. A few close friends remained from earlier years. But she was moving in a different, happier, and more accepting world now and enjoyed the new friendships that entered her life, too.

A few years later, Jude and Edward welcomed their little girl,

Layla, into the world. Every effort was made again to reconcile with her parents, as she wanted them to know their granddaughter. Jude's father finally conceded and came to enjoy a relationship of love and quality with his dear granddaughter before he passed. His relationship with Jude also improved. While he was polite to Edward, Jude's father still struggled with the knowledge that an artist had won his daughter's heart. So it was not a close relationship. However, it was as a result of his relationship with Layla that Jude's father purchased this harbour-side mansion for them all, much to her mother's disgust.

Things had been moving along well, they told me, until Jude had started to become clumsy, to the point it could not be ignored anymore. These stories were told in unison from Jude and Edward, and I suspected this would have been the case even if she were not struggling with the illness. They were just so close as a couple. Their love was both inspiring and heartbreaking for me to witness. These were people of my own generation.

Hours of deep and honest conversation unfolded between us all. The acceptance of death at such an age was one we spoke of, too. It is easy for us all to assume we will live forever. But life doesn't work that way. Through the storms of life, some young ones will always go. Like flowers blossoming, not yet ripened into fruit, they will be taken away before they can ever realise their full potential. Others will make it through to full maturity and go out at their best. Still others will live past their prime and slowly degenerate over the years.

While it is often referred to as dying before their time, it isn't really. We all go when it is our own time. Millions of people are not destined to live a long life. It is the assumption we will all live forever, or at least until a very advanced age, that brings so much shock and despair when someone young passes. But this is actually a natural part of life in all species. Some young ones die, some middle aged ones die, and others don't die until old age. Of course, it is heartbreaking to see young ones go when it appears they had their whole lives ahead of them. Some of my own friends have lost young children, and I have been there through their heartache, some of which has never left. But these children or young adults were not here for such a long life. They come in, shine bright, and are remembered with purity for all they gave during their brief time.

Even though Jude had made it all the way through to her forties with good health, it also would have been easy to think how wrong it was that such a good woman was now dying at only forty-four. But she and Edward had come to accept this, both just grateful they had met and known the love they did. They had also been blessed by bringing Layla into the world. In that regard Jude was peaceful in a way, knowing she'd had the honour of guiding this delightful little girl through her first nine years. Naturally, though, there was also heartache because she would not be around to watch her little girl become a woman, and for the pain Layla may suffer in losing her mum. But it helped Jude a lot knowing that her daughter had a loving dad to help her further on her way.

By now Jude had lost her independence and mobility completely, but her greatest frustration was that she was losing her speech. The thing she feared most, she told me one night as I repositioned her in bed, was when she would no longer be able to convey she was in pain and would have to lie there tolerating it. I thought about how difficult life can be and how different all of our lessons are. What an awful way to see your last weeks or months through, to have consciousness but no ability to communicate. On top of that, to be lying in pain but no one realising or knowing the exact way to ease it. This must happen the world over for sufferers of other diseases, too, like stroke or brain injuries. Gosh, what a way to be. It certainly put my own life back into perspective.

Each day I heard Jude's speech deteriorating a little more. Some days it was still reasonably good, quite audible. Other days, it was only because we knew each other and I worked intuitively that I was able to follow what she was saying. On days like this, Jude sometimes resorted to using a special computer program she had. Between the eyes of some glasses she wore, made especially for such use, there was a laser that would reach letters on the computer screen. Jude would pause on the letter long enough for it to type the letter, then move onto the next one. Then after a couple of letters were written, a choice of words would appear, and so on. It was a slow process for sure, but it at least enabled her to be heard. I silently thanked those who had created such an opportunity for her by developing this program. The time would come soon enough, though, when Jude would no longer be able to move her head to even do this.

So on the good days, I listened as much as possible while Jude talked. There was much she wanted to convey. Holding a juice to her lips I waited, as she took one slow sip at a time, enabling her to keep talking. One main point in particular she needed to make, and did so over and over. "We need to be brave enough to express our feelings," she said. Very fitting, I thought, considering my own journey so far.

Even though she had lost the relationship with her mother by choosing to be with Edward, she was happy knowing she'd at least been brave enough to make that choice, one she'd never regretted. She longed to share her feelings with her mother now, though, as her mum had never known Jude as a mother herself. Acknowledging that such an opportunity may never come, Jude had already written to her mother some time ago. The letter waited in Edward's office drawer. Jude's mum knew of the illness. But she was still in a place of stubbornness and un-forgiveness, unable to visit her dying daughter.

"We must learn to express our feelings *now*," Jude emphasised. "Not when it is too late. None of us ever knows when it will be too late. Tell people you love them. Tell them you appreciate them. If they can't accept your honesty or react in a different way to how you hoped, it doesn't matter. What matters is you have told them."

Jude said this was just as important for those who were passing as for those who would remain behind. Those passing need to know everything has been said. It brings peace, she said. If those who are left behind can muster the courage to express their feelings honestly, too, then they will not carry this regret to their own passing. Nor will they have to live with the guilt that is carried if someone they loved has passed and things have gone unsaid.

What had made getting this point across even more important for Jude was that she had lost a friend unexpectedly a year earlier. It had shaken her world up immensely. Tracey had been an effervescent woman, the life of any gathering. She was well loved by everyone due to her enormous heart, and held a total lack of judgment towards others.

"It is too easy to get caught up in life and not spend as much time with people you love, whether that be family or friends. But we really must get back to relationships and honesty. People don't realise how important this is, until they are dying themselves or living with the guilt after someone else has died," Jude told me.

She said how there is no need for guilt at all if we have truly made our best efforts to express our feelings and to spend time with those we love. But we need to stop thinking that hose we love will be around forever. It is over in a flash, she reminded me. Jude was grateful she'd had time to say her own goodbyes, but emphasised that not everyone receives the blessing of time to express these feelings at the end. In fact millions don't, as they depart suddenly and unexpectedly.

Even though expressing her feelings about the love she felt for Edward had ruined her relationship with her mother, Jude was glad she'd had the courage to be honest. Not only did it allow her to know the fullness of love she and Edward still shared, she was peaceful knowing she had been true to her own heart. It also showed her how much she was under the control of her parents until then, particularly her mother. If a relationship is based on control, she said, how can the other person ever know a truly healthy relationship with that person anyway? If this was the only kind of relationship on offer, she decided she was better off without it.

But having tried to communicate with her mother, Jude said she would be dying free of guilt. She'd had the courage to express herself. Thankfully, the same had been the case for her with her friend Tracey. Jude had always been very honest, and though the shock of losing Tracey had been enormous, she was again guilt-free. Only a few days before losing her friend, they'd had lunch together. When they hugged goodbye, Jude had told Tracey how much she loved her and valued their friendship.

It was not the case for most of her friend's family or other friends though. Tracey had been such a bright person that it was hard to ever imagine she would not be around. Then her life was taken suddenly in a car crash. The ripples of shock and guilt still continued just as strongly in Jude's circle of friends, a year later.

"She had changed people's lives, but they had never told her so. Tracey wasn't the sort to need the confirmation, no. But people have to live with their own lack of effort afterwards, and I have seen this guilt turn toxic in people since, as they battle with how differently they could have done things." I could understand this, of course. "Also," Jude said, "although Tracey didn't need the validation, she would have loved to have heard that encouragement from others. She was so open and beautiful. And now she is gone."

I naturally agreed with her that sharing feelings and honesty was important. Life was certainly throwing those lessons at me already, even more so now as Jude and I talked. She was a beautiful woman, still naturally elegant, despite not being able to hold herself well anymore. Her mouth drooled at times, and her clothing had to be more practical than stylish. But her spirit and remnants of who she once was still remained with its own radiance. Smiling at her and in agreement with her opinion, I shared my thoughts. "Yes. So much is held back by pride, apathy, or fear of reprisal or humiliation. But it also takes a lot of courage sometimes, Jude, and we are not always strong enough to do this."

"Yes, it takes courage, Bronnie," Jude continued. "That's the point I am trying to make. It takes courage to express your feelings, particularly if you are not doing OK and need assistance, or if you've never expressed honest feelings to someone you love and don't know how it will be received. But the more you practice sharing your feelings, whatever they are, the better things become. Pride is such a waste of time. Honestly, look at me now. I can't even wipe my own bum. What does it matter? We are all human. We are allowed to be vulnerable, too. It is a part of the process."

Leading up to the time at Jude and Edward's, life had been particularly hard for me. I decided to share some of this with Jude, as it was relevant to how hard it can be at times to share our feelings.

The palliative work had slowed down for a while. It often came in those waves of all or nothing. This didn't bother me, as my creative work benefitted then instead. After almost two months of hardly any work, though, things were starting to get a bit difficult and there was no work on the horizon. Any money I earned was usually invested back into my creative work in some way, so there was not a lot to fall back on. But having survived it before, I was never too perturbed about this.

House-sits likewise came and went. Sometimes I would have very little notice of where I was going next, only knowing when the owners were due to return. Usually, though, a house would present itself at the last minute. During stronger times, I did enjoy this risk and excitement to a degree. The adrenaline certainly flowed. It would happen relatively often, where someone would call me in a panic and ask if I could look after their home – starting tomorrow, for example, as they had just been called away suddenly. The relief that came from those calls always brought huge sighs and smiles. Such occasions would save us both.

Sometimes clients worked in with other friends in the house-sit network to ensure they wouldn't miss out on me being available. So they would plan to go on holidays the same day their friends were coming back, knowing I would then be free. On these occasions, I was sometimes booked for months in advance. Naturally, I liked this. It made life much easier.

There were times, though, when I was unable to find anywhere to look after for a few days, or a week or two, in between scheduled house-sits. So I would leave town and visit someone in the country, enjoying the break. Or if I had a specific client whom I didn't want to leave, I would crash out in a friend's spare room or on their couch temporarily. Initially this was easy enough. But after a few years of this pattern, I began to dread asking and felt like I was wearing out my welcome. My friends said I wasn't. They supported me and understood me well enough to know it wasn't forever. When I had settled home bases years earlier, my homes always had visitors, but for me, learning to receive was so much harder than giving.

Having to ask friends repeatedly if I could stay left me feeling absolutely hopeless. While I had worked through a lot of my past wounds, enabling me to have compassion for others, it was still taking me a lot of work and pain to transform my thoughts towards myself. Decades of negative patterns were being undone, and it was a slow process to change my thinking completely. New and positive seeds had been planted and, in many ways, were sprouting in my life. But I was yet to eradicate all of the old seeds, so they would still sometimes surface.

On this particular occasion the work had stopped ages ago, the money had pretty much run out, and I was feeling hopeless all over again. I rang my closest friend and asked if I could stay. But she was going through something herself and it was just not possible. This wasn't about me at all. It was her stuff and her life. But because of my thinking and emotional state at the time, I took it as a total rejection and felt even worse for having put her in the position of having to say no. I reluctantly called a few other friends but sorry, full house with interstate visitors, another away, and another consumed in a work project that needed total concentration. I didn't have the money to leave town and get back without having to borrow some, which would have just left me feeling more hopeless anyway. So I accepted I would be sleeping in my car.

This wasn't an issue years earlier when I had the jeep and was on the road travelling. In fact, there was nowhere I would have preferred sleeping than in the back of that old car, on the comfy bed in there. But not in the rice bubble, a car so small I couldn't even straighten out my legs when I tried to lie down. It was also without curtains or privacy and was the middle of winter. I couldn't think of anyone I could call, though, without feeling even worse by asking. As much as I was a little scared to be sleeping on the city streets so exposed, I was sort of resigned to it, that this is what a hopeless person has to do sometimes.

Driving around before dark, I checked out a few options of places that looked relatively safe and suitable. I also needed to consider I might need to go to the toilet. Freaking people out by piddling on their front lawn in the middle of the night was not the kind of attention I needed, on top of my existing emotions.

The days are long when you are homeless and trying to stay out of visibility. You have to be up and out of the way at sunrise and cannot settle in until everyone else has gone home and settled in themselves. In the meantime, of course, you are homeless so you can't go home and wait. Yes, these were long days, and the nights were very uncomfortable, achingly cold, and lonely.

One night I went to a café where I heard some music, staying as late as possible on my one cup of tea. I felt like the old man in the Ralph McTell song, 'Streets of London', trying to keep his one cup of tea going all night to enable him to stay indoors. How ironic, I thought, that this had been one of the very first songs I ever learned on the guitar.

Turning up at the council toilets near the beach at sunrise, I would wait for them to open. Then I would have a wash, clean my teeth, and use the toilet, all the while enduring the scowls of the council worker who had unlocked the door. I think he saw me as a camper, freeloading, or something. But there was nothing he could have thought of me that was any worse than what I was already thinking of myself. So I really didn't care. And one of the blessings already in place from my time with the dying was that by now, I genuinely didn't care what others thought of me anymore. As it was, I had enough to deal with just with own head.

Another night I went to the Hare Krishnas' 'Feed the Hungry' program. Whenever I had money, I was always generous with it. Queuing up now, I found more irony in my situation as I had often thrown ten or twenty dollars into their bucket for this very program, if I ever saw them trying to raise funds. I liked the Hare Krishnas. They were vegetarians, played happy music, and fed hungry people. That was enough for me. But now I was a recipient of their goodwill, and it was rather humbling.

Then one morning, I sat on a rock by the harbour, praying for strength, endurance, and a miracle. Just then a pod of dolphins came by and one flipped itself out of the water in play. My life felt so serious until that moment, so it gave me a little bit of hope again. I then thought of some friends who lived farther out and decided to call them and ask if I could stay. They were always lovely people. But my sense of unworthiness and hopelessness had not enabled me to ask any more people for help, or even think of anyone else I could ask. I had not had the courage to express my feelings, even though I could have very honestly just said to these sweet people, "Look, I'm feeling crap. But may I please come and stay for a little while?"

So with a brighter resolve, I went for a walk around the harbour. Before I had the opportunity to call my friends, my phone rang and it was Edward, asking if I was free to come and be Jude's carer and could I please begin immediately? There was also a beautiful apartment on the property available for me if I needed. That night I lay with legs fully outstretched again, no longer aching with cramps and cold. A snug duvet kept me warm after my nurturing bath. I'd eaten a healthy meal with three delightful people, and I was earning money again. How quickly life can change!

I could look at this time and say it was because the work dried up, or the house-sits did. That's what happened physically anyway. But it was a situation I had created through my own lack of self-worth and by nurturing old seeds that no longer served me. Obviously there were new seeds being sewn, too, as at other times I was starting to live an abundant, amazing lifestyle. Learning to undo these old patterns in my head was taking time, though, and I had made it harder on myself by not being able to ask for help.

When another lull in house-sitting appeared at a later date, the first thing I did was to phone the friends I had thought of that morning with the dolphins. They welcomed me into their spare room with loving joy and excitement. Allowing goodness in was possible for me again. I was still learning how to express my feelings, but I was getting there.

I told Jude how openness was a learning curve for me, as I had become so shut down in the past. So I appreciated her opinion and the opportunity to discuss this all so honestly. "We all need the reminder, Bronnie. Everyone holds things in that need to be said, whether it is what people want to hear or not. We must express our feelings in order to grow. It helps everyone in one way or another, even if they don't realise it. Above all else, honesty works."

Smiling, I looked out at the boats on the harbour as the full moon shone beautifully on the water. It was a magnificent setting. Jude returned to the subject of guilt and how we have a choice to not create it by honestly expressing our feelings as they surface. Then it is never too late, especially if someone we love passes unexpectedly. It also enables us to be free of constraints, as we once were as children. We should never feel guilty for expressing our feelings, and we should never make someone else feel guilty if they have found the courage to do so.

After a couple of months with Jude, her deterioration became so severe she was admitted into a palliative care hospice. Work was flowing for me again back at the agency, and a decent length house-sit had presented itself. I dropped into the hospice to see Jude, pleased to be able to catch up with Edward and Layla at the same time. Sitting on the other side of the bed was a lady I'd never met, but it took no time to see the likeness between Jude and her mother.

Edward had taken it on his own initiative to deliver Jude's letter to her mother, before his beloved Jude passed over. By now she was unable to talk, but it had all been said in the letter. Jude had told her mother she had loved her, and still did. She wrote of happy memories she held dear and of the positive things she had learned from her mum. The letter contained nothing negative, as Jude hated guilt and wanted her mother to know she was loved, despite the sadness of their relationship. Jude's mother had turned up unexpectedly a few days later and had been back every day since, holding Jude's hand, watching as her daughter's life was coming to an end.

Kissing Jude on the cheek after talking to her for a while, I said my final goodbye and thanked her for everything. "See you when I get there, Jude," I said through tears and a smile. She grunted back and her eyes smiled, even though her mouth no longer could.

Edward and Layla walked me out to the rice bubble, both of them holding one of my hands each. We were all tearful. But love flowed so honestly that tears didn't matter. Edward told me that Jude's mum had been talking a lot to her and tears had fallen down Jude's cheeks, particularly when she heard her mother say she loved her. Her mother apologised for having been so judgmental. She admitted to being secretly jealous of her daughter, and of Jude's courage to step out of the opinions of society, something that had robbed herself of true happiness.

After hugging both Edward and Layla goodbye, I wished them all the very best in life ahead. I thought of beautiful Jude lying there with her mother sitting at her side, and how powerful the force of love really is. My heart was aching, but it was also joyful.

An email came a couple of years later from Edward, which was a lovely surprise. Layla and her grandmother had enjoyed some cheerful months of getting to know each other before the older lady had died. He said she was a different woman by then and reminded him of his beautiful Jude at times. When the estates were settled, Edward and Layla decided to leave the city and move up to the mountains, closer to his father and where the air was cleaner. He had met a new lady about a year ago, and Layla now had a little sister on the way.

My reply included my best of wishes to them all. I was also happy to share with him the things I remembered about Jude: her smile, her patience with the illness, her acceptance, and her determination to get her points across. Guilt is toxic. Expressing our feelings is a necessity for a happy life.

I can still remember sitting beside her bed as the full moon shone on the water, with Jude determined to be heard for as long as her voice would allow.

She'd made her point, and I now know the joy of expressing my feelings, as honestly as that dolphin showed its joy when it flipped up out of the water.

GIFTS IN DISGUISE

⚜

A few temporary shifts in nursing homes had seen me working with clients suffering from Alzheimer's. But Nanci was my first private home, palliative client with this disease. She had been a gentle woman, the mother of three children and ten grandchildren. Her husband was still about, but rarely came into her room. In fact, it would have been easy to forget he actually lived in the house at all.

Nanci's three sisters and two brothers would come and visit on alternate days, as would a few of her friends initially, though I did observe these visitations slow down in time. Looking after Nanci was hard, exhausting work. She was restless and very hard to monitor, never wanting to stay in one place for more than one minute, and very distressed much of the time. Moments of peace were few and far between for her – and as a result, for me, too.

Eventually her anguish became so concerning to everyone, especially her family, that the dosage of her medications was increased. Nanci then slept some of the day. When she was alert, her words and sentences made no sense at all, as is typical of those with Alzheimer's. Parts of one word were mingled with parts of others. You could recognise it as an English dialect at times, but nothing structured, formal, or coherent. Still, I treated Nanci as I did all of my clients, with love and gentleness, chatting to her as I did my job. Sometimes she acknowledged I was in the room, sometimes she was miles away and I could have had ten heads without her noticing.

Occasionally I would shower her myself when I arrived at eight in the morning, but this was usually the night carer's role. Washing her fell to me if it had been a particularly troublesome night and Nanci was still sleeping when I arrived, which was fine. More often than not, though, the showering would be happening when I arrived around eight. Nanci would sometimes smile at me as she sat on the shower chair, while the night carer washed her. Yet one particular carer had significantly different methods of care than the rest of us, and she insisted that was the way things were done where she came from.

The first incident happened one very cold winter morning. Arriving in Nanci's room, I found her lying naked on her bed, shivering cold and fully exposed. She had just been showered and while there, her bowels had opened, leaving a huge pile of faeces under the shower chair. This was nothing new. Clients often experienced this when their backsides were hanging through the opening of the chair, as their bowels recognised it as a toilet seat. These chairs were also used to sit over a toilet, if clients needed an elevated seat. So it was not entirely surprising that sometimes these things happened in the shower.

Nanci was a modest woman, from a modest family. So lying there naked without any covering would have been traumatic enough for her, but she was also shivering cold and looked like a fragile little child. The minute I walked in and saw her like that, I finished drying her off and covered her with a warm blanket as soon as possible. The other carer was found in the bathroom, cleaning up the mess. It was impossible for me not to comment, although I did so diplomatically, saying I could have cleaned it up later. The priority needed to be the client's comfort rather than a clean bathroom floor. The night carer's only response was a shrug.

The other incident came while crossing over shifts with the same carer a few weeks later. Generally I don't like to wear a watch and avoid having to be structured by a clock at all if I can help it. But rather than causing stress by having to rush, if I must work in to a strictly regulated timetable, I usually tend to leave myself excess time to get to places. This allows me to enjoy the journey more, however long or brief, and to be more present along the way. On this particular morning, however, the traffic had been flowing particularly well. So I arrived earlier than expected.

Following the other incident, the night carer had now taken to showering Nanci even earlier. So I saw none of her procedures. The carer and I actually got along quite well. We always had, as we had shared a few clients and had often seen each other at handover of shifts during the past years. The lack of empathy I had witnessed from her with Nanci and previous clients, though, did leave me struggling to continue regarding her as a caring professional. This increased even more when I walked into the bathroom to say good morning and found dear little Nanci sitting on the shower chair, shivering cold, absolutely freezing, with her teeth chattering.

Asking what was happening, the carer explained that where she was from this is how they showered people. Freezing cold water blasted all over the body for a couple of minutes, followed by a couple of minutes of lovely warm water, followed by another couple of minutes of cold, then warm, but always finishing off with cold. It gets the circulation going, she said, which could be right. I wouldn't know and I didn't care, though I did accept that swimming in cold water had often left me feeling very invigorated.

The problem was that it was the middle of winter. Winds howled outside, windows shook, and even indoors, decent layers of clothing were required. This little lady was so ill she was dying. She hardly needed invigoration to go running around the block. Nanci was too frail to do anything by now and just needed to be warm and comfortable. Our job was to attend to her wellbeing, which included this comfort, not having her sit on a shower chair looking completely terrified, so cold her teeth were chattering. In my opinion, the poor darling just needed to be snug and lovingly cared for.

Never having been terribly forceful, I *can* draw on my strength when required, though. What triggers this forcefulness is injustice or cruelty. Speaking gently but honestly to the other carer, my message was received, and she accepted that just warm water would be used for the rest of the shower.

The days continued to unfold in a series of routines. This particular night carer was heading off on holidays and would not be back for a long while. Her replacement was another carer I had often met in passing, Linda. It was always refreshing to come onto a shift after her, as she was pleasant to chat with and her work ethic was of a high quality. Relieved for our client, I sent out a prayer of thanks.

Nanci continued to speak as incoherently as always. When she was out of bed, she was still restless and agitated most of the time. But due to the increase in her medication, these occasions were not for so long. The sides on her bed were supposed to be up the whole time. But if things were calm, I would lower the railings to remove the barrier between us. Sometimes Nanci would respond well to some pampering, like when I rubbed cream into her legs or things like that. But even during the calmer moments, if Nanci did speak it was always in the language only Alzheimer's sufferers would understand. There was no clarity or structure, just mumbled syllables that didn't work together. Her speech had already been like this for several months by the time I met her.

After assisting her to the toilet one day, she shuffled back towards the bed holding one of my hands. A tube of something in my other hand slipped to the floor and I laughed, bending down to pick it up. I always treated Nanci the way I would any client, even if she was miles away. So I stood up again, still talking to her and laughing. Then as clear as day, looking me straight in the eye, Nanci said, "I think you're lovely."

A huge smile broke onto my face, and we stood smiling at each other for a minute. I was looking at a totally sane and present woman. At that moment, she knew completely what was going on. So I replied truthfully, "I think you are, too, Nanci." Her smile grew wider and we hugged, after which we both smiled at each other again. It was beautiful.

Her balance wasn't great by now, though, so we continued to shuffle back to the bed holding hands. As I sat her on the side and bent to lift her legs up, Nanci came out with a jumbled sentence of Alzheimer's language, one that had no chance of being understood by anyone. She was gone again, but she had been there with me briefly, as clear as anything.

No one will ever convince me otherwise. Alzheimer's sufferers may not know what is going on most of the time, but just because they cannot convey their thoughts clearly and are often very confused, this does not mean they do not absorb some of what is going on. Seeing this first hand changed my whole perspective of the illness and others.

A few weeks later I mentioned the incident to Linda, the other carer, who agreed it was a special thing to have happened. A short time later, Linda then experienced further clarity from Nanci, though perhaps not so endearing. It was a part of her night shift duties to roll Nanci over every four hours, to avoid bedsores. Often Nanci would be in a deep sleep but it had to be done, doctor's orders. On this particular night, though, as Linda went to roll her over at about four in the morning, Nanci very firmly and clearly said to her, "Don't you dare move me."

"No worries, Nanci," Linda replied, startled. "Sweet dreams." Linda was amazed but went back to her duties.

The family came and relieved me for half an hour each day. They were long and exhausting shifts, and I welcomed the break. Nanci's home was in a beach suburb, so I would head straight down the hill and stand on a rock shelf looking out to sea. The rocks were partially covered with barnacles and puddles of ocean water, but there were plenty of places to step, allowing me to access the edge of the shelf safely. Breathing in the ocean air, I'd delight in the fresh breeze and the vastness of the ocean.

Occasionally there would be another person farther along the rocks, farther out, right on the point. He would be playing a saxophone. It was magical to observe and to hear, such perfect tunes floating across with the rhythm of the ocean. I would stand there spellbound, absorbing it for every possible moment before reluctantly heading back up the hill. The music would sustain me for the rest of the shift, every time without fail.

Naturally I would tell Nanci about it, even if she were completely off in another world. It didn't bother me. My intention was to try and keep her world a little stimulated if I could, by bringing in conversation from the outside world. Nanci's whole world by now was just her bedroom, en-suite, and sitting room.

For a couple of months the saxophone man was mentioned to her, with no response or sign of interest reflected back. Then one day when I returned elated, and tried to describe the tune he had played that day (like you can ever truly describe music through words), Nanci looked me in the eyes and smiled. As I put some washing away a few minutes later, she started humming a tune. This was usually the time of day she was most agitated, but instead she hummed for ages. As quickly as it had started, though, it stopped and she was miles away again, uttering incomprehensible syllables.

These glimpses of clarity made me so grateful to have kept talking to Nanci all this time, regardless that I was usually not getting the responses I may have liked. But just because someone doesn't respond the way you wish, doesn't mean you should regret the attempt to having expressed yourself.

The reaction of others is their choice, just as our own reactions are no one else's responsibility. As my walls were being eroded one brick at a time, I was finding the need to express myself increasing. To express who I am now became more important. But in other ways it also became less important, as I was also becoming less bothered by how I was perceived. In the end, I guess it was mostly about how I perceived myself. I wanted to be courageous and honest from here on, regardless. Learning to be open was also starting to feel good, very good in fact.

Yet I also knew that just because I was changing in many positive ways, it didn't mean others in my life would embrace this. New patterns were being created, releasing me slowly from my past, beginning to empower me. This was not always well received by others, but I had to be who I was now and not who people had come to expect me to be. There was a new person being born from within me and she wanted to come out, to share her new self.

One particular friendship in my life was feeling terribly unbalanced and had been for a few years. Obviously it was a lesson in boundaries for me, and one I was learning. Then with all of the changes happening within, including the satisfaction of honest expression, it came to the point where I finally needed to say how I was feeling. So, with honesty, I explained my thoughts in the hope they would be understood. It wasn't an attack on the friend, merely just me sharing what I was feeling about the expectation on me to make all of the effort for our visits and the imbalance I felt was happening.

We had been friends for a long time and I felt honesty would get us through. What it did, though, was show me how it was only history and habit that had been holding us together recently. My friend lashed out at me with anger I had no idea she owned. It was fear and hurt that triggered this in her. I understood that, but the level of anger that came at me was overwhelming. I realised I didn't actually know this person at all. There was nastiness in her I had never even glimpsed or suspected. So when she then severed our connection completely, I accepted her decision and peacefully obliged. It was time to move on.

Either way, I still reflected on our friendship as a beautiful gift for the years it had existed, and still do. In the end, only happy memories remain, but letting go of the friendship was relatively painless, as I could see no point in having a relationship that did not allow for honesty or balance. None of us are perfect, myself included. I'd also contributed to the breakdown of that friendship, whether consciously or not, but to be in any sort of relationship where you do not express yourself, simply to keep the peace, is a relationship ruled by one person and will never be balanced or healthy.

At the other end of the scale, honesty enhanced a different friendship a couple of years later. Life was changing a lot for me. So I would sometimes call to bounce things off someone who knew me well, but this friend was rarely available until she needed me again. This all came to a head one day and through my weariness, I expressed very honestly how I really needed to lean on her for a while. That truthfulness brought us closer ten-fold and opened up a beautiful conversation. She shared a lot with me, too, and our friendship benefitted from mutual respect and emotional maturity. In the end, she was not the kind of person who could be totally reliable ,and we both came to acknowledge and accept this.

Instead, I came to lean on myself more and rely upon longer-term friends. While this released my need of the friendship a little, my friend also had to adjust to me not always being available for her. I wasn't always strong enough to be, nor did I feel the need to play that role anymore. The acceptance of each other's frailties and the courage to be honest with each other brought us even closer on many other levels. These days, the friendship is without pressure from either side. It is mature, very honest, and always fun.

We don't catch up as often as we used to, and our lives are not so entwined as they once were. All relationships go through changes, though, friendships included. Despite all that unfolded, we are closer friends than ever now. We are honest and totally accepting of each other for who we really are, not who we wanted each other to be. When we do manage to catch up, we both savour the gift of time and understanding we are blessed with.

So while expressing feelings may come at a price, as it did with the first friendship, I know that any remaining relationships in my life are now of mature honesty and true quality. Expressing who I am is one of my core driving forces these days. Being honest and opening up also gets easier all the time. It took a long time to get to this place, but it is immensely freeing. It also enables me to recognise the struggle others go through in trying to do so. When I look at the rewards that come from honest expression, I can only hope others will find that place in themselves one day, too.

Nanci's brief response to me amidst the jumbled language she lived with was one of the most beautiful moments ever. Had I not expressed myself to her prior, regardless of expecting a reaction or not, I would never have received such a reward as that moment.

Assuming others know how you feel or will always be there are high risks to take when they could be dead in an hour. So could any of us. Taking people for granted is a high price to pay. Not every day is going to be a happy one. We are all growing and all have hard days, but there are beautiful thoughts to be shared as well. This is why it is imperative to share your feelings honestly and listen to others on a regular basis. It is too easy to get caught up in your own little world and forget.

There is a song by a well-known and loved Australian songwriter and performer, Mick Thomas, that perfectly conveys taking people for granted. It is about getting caught up in life, so much that the guy in the song wouldn't even notice if his woman has changed the colour of her hair or other attributes. The main message and line in the song is, "He forgot she was beautiful."

While the song applies to a guy taking his woman for granted, it can be applied to anyone in our lives. Women take their men for granted, too, no longer seeing their inner or outer beauty. Women also don't always recognise that a man shows his love in different ways, like doing things for his partner. Kids take their parents for granted. Parents take their children for granted sometimes. Friends, cousins, brothers, sisters, workmates, grandparents, and members of the community are all taken for granted.

It is easy to focus on what we don't like about a person, which is really only a partial reflection of ourselves anyway. But even the things we love about others are too often not acknowledged. Yes, it takes courage sometimes to speak honestly, and we cannot control the reaction of those with whom we share this openness with. We must be sensitive to their needs as well.

I have found that honesty is rewarded, though, even if it may not be in the way we anticipate. It may come as self-respect, living without guilt when someone has passed on, richer relationships, unhealthy relationships being relinquished from your life, or in any number of unimagined forms. The main point is that by having the courage to express your feelings, you are bringing gifts to yourself and others. The longer you delay this expression, the longer you are carrying things that need to be said.

No more words of clarity flowed from Nanci again, but it didn't matter. The blessing I had received that day was more than enough of a reward. Her grandson also noticed another moment of clarity when he sang to her one afternoon. Nanci didn't speak, but she looked her grandson in the eye and smiled lovingly at him – not in an Alzheimer's way, but as a grandmother smiling proudly at her grandson, peaceful with the expression he had chosen that day, through singing.

We can never know the gifts that will flow to us until they arrive, but of one thing I am certain. Courage and honesty are *always* rewarded.

REGRET 4:
I WISH I HAD STAYED IN TOUCH
WITH MY FRIENDS

⊘

Occasional shifts were done in nursing homes, in between regular clients in their private houses. They were not common shifts, to which I was grateful as I found these places absolutely awful. The clients attended to in these situations were not always palliative either. They were just people in some need of help, and sometimes I was employed simply to be an extra staff member in an existing team, rather than looking after any one particular client.

If ever one wants to live in denial about the state of our society, avoid nursing homes. If ever you feel strong enough to look at life honestly, spend some time in one. There are a lot of lonely people in them – a lot. Any of us could become a patient at any time.

Being exposed to the staff on these occasions was both devastating and inspiring. Some of those I worked with briefly over the years were beautiful, goodhearted people who were obviously working in the right field. Their spirits were bright, their hearts kind. Thank goodness for these people. But as most nursing homes were understaffed, they were constantly challenged to spread their good cheer around.

At the other end of the scale were those who had either grown weary and despondent working in the field, or had never had the enthusiasm in the first place. Empathy goes a long way in life and was lacking terribly in the team I was placed with on the night I met Doris.

The residents shuffled into the communal dining room on their walking sticks and frames. They were people from relatively decent means, as it was a private and so-called 'luxurious' nursing home. The décor was lovely, the gardens well maintained, the communal areas clean. But the meals were awful. Everything was pre-cooked outside of the home and reheated in the microwave, without taste or enticing aroma. There was nothing nutritious or fresh about any food I saw there. Residents placed their orders at the end of the previous week and usually had a plate of something slid in front of them, with no greeting or kindness from the staff.

Seeing a cheerful face, they would touch my hand to keep me at the table talking with them. These were regular people whose minds were clear and who loved social interaction. Their bodies were ageing and becoming frail, but that was all. A year or two earlier these same charming, delightful people were living completely independent lives of their own. As I returned to the kitchen for another tray of plates, scowls from some of the staff awaited me. I had merely chatted and laughed with some of the residents briefly on my rounds and this was met with disapproval. I just ignored it.

Returning a plate of lamb, I told the head person in a friendly manner, "Bernie ordered chicken, not lamb."

She half laughed, replying, "He'll get what he's bloody-well given."

"Come on," I said, not intimidated by the nonsense. "Surely we can give him a chicken dish."

"He'll get lamb or he'll starve," she said bitterly. I looked at her with compassion for her obvious unhappiness, but with no respect for her manner in the role she was playing.

A lovely staff member fell into step with me as I returned the lamb to Bernie. "Don't worry about her, Bronnie. She's always like that," Rebecca said.

I smiled, glad for a genuine heart. "I'm not worried about her at all. It's the residents I care about who have to live with this treatment day in and day out."

Rebecca agreed, "It used to affect me a lot when I first started here. But now I just do what I can to give them all the kindest treatment possible, within my limitations."

"Good on you," I replied with a smile.

She rubbed my back as she walked off in another direction. "There *are* a few of us who care – not enough, but there are a few."

When the meals were served and somehow eaten, and the kitchen was clean, some of the staff members went outside for a smoke. A few of us stayed inside and chatted to the departing residents. It was jovial, as a dozen or so people gathered around to share a laugh with us. Their wit and cheerful spirits amazed me as I marvelled at the resilience of these people, having adapted so well to their new conditions.

Each of the residents had their own room and bathroom. As I did the nightly round of helping people to get dressed for bed, each room revealed some personality of its resident. Photos of smiling families, paintings, crocheted rugs, and favourite teacups dotted each room. Some balconies had potted plants on them.

Doris was already dressed in her pink nightdress when I breezed in cheerfully, introducing myself. But she just smiled without saying anything, then looked away. Asking if she was OK, I was then met with a flood of tears. Immediately sitting beside her on the bed, I held her in my arms. No words were spoken while she sobbed, holding onto me desperately. I prayed for strength and waited.

When the tears stopped, it was as quickly as they had started, and she reached for her handkerchief. "Oh silly me," she said wiping her eyes. "Forgive me, Sweetheart. I'm just being a silly old woman."

"What's going on with you?" I asked gently.

Doris sighed, then shared how she had been there for four months and had hardly seen a cheerful face since. She said my smile had set her tears off, which almost made me want to cry. Her one daughter now lived in Japan, and while she was in touch fairly often, they were no longer terribly close.

"You never think as a mother nursing your beautiful little girl that anything could ever take away your closeness. But it has. Life has. Not through an argument, mind. Just life and its busyness," she shared. "She has her own life now, and I learned over the years you just have to let go. I brought her into the world, but we do not own our children. We are just blessed with the role of guiding them until they can fly on their own, and that's what she is doing now."

I warmed to this dear lady instantly and promised to return in half an hour for a longer chat, if she could stay awake long enough for me to finish my shift. She said she would love that.

Later then, Doris sat up in bed talking away. In a chair beside her, I listened. She held my hand the whole time, now and then playing with my fingers or the ring I was wearing, without realising she was doing so. "I have been dying of loneliness in here, Sweetheart. I had heard it was possible, and it is. Loneliness can surely kill you. I get so starved for human touch at times," she said sadly. My hug had been the first she had had in four months.

She didn't want to burden me with it, but I insisted on her continuing. I was genuinely interested in knowing her, so she went on. "I am missing my friends most of all. Some have died. Some are in situations like me. Some I have lost touch with. I wish I hadn't lost touch with them. You imagine your friends will always be there. But life moves on, and suddenly you find yourself with no one in the world who understands you or who knows anything about your history." I suggested we try to reach some of them. She shook her head, saying, "I wouldn't know where to start."

"I can help," I offered, as I went on to explain about the Internet to her. It was all very foreign to Doris, but she did well to understand it to a degree. At first she declined, worried about my time. Finally, though, I convinced her I would love to. Investigative skills were something I enjoyed. During my years in banking, I had worked for a short time in frauds and forgeries and had loved it. She laughed at the comparison. "Please allow me," I requested. So she agreed with a hopeful, wistful smile.

I wanted to help Doris for a few reasons. I had liked her from that first moment *and* I could help her. I had the skills to try to find her friends, but I also wanted to help because I knew how she felt. I had also known the crippling pain of long-term loneliness and the longing for understanding.

In previous times, the pain of my past had worn me down to such a place that I had withdrawn a long way into myself. It was the misled belief many people experience, that if you keep people out, you keep the pain out. You stop yourself from being hurt even more. If no one can get close, then no one can hurt you anymore either. Of course the only real way to heal is to let love flow in and through again, not to block it out, but reaching that point can take a long time.

On the surface I was a friendly person to those I came across, but the pain I was carrying from my difficult past was still weighing me down. I had definitely grown into a place of compassion by now for those who had previously thrown their negativity my way. That wasn't the problem. It was my thoughts of myself that were still taking some time to be transformed. Decades of negative thinking were being undone, and at times the pain was unbearable. Although I knew intellectually that I was worth more than what I had been conditioned to believe, emotionally the healing still had distance to go.

"Sunday morning coming down" became my theme song. Having always loved Kris Kristofferson's music and being quite influenced by him in my own writing, I found that song to be the best expression of my loneliness. Sundays were always the worst. Lucinda Williams wrote a good song about this, too, singing "I can't seem to make it through Sundays."

It wasn't just Sundays, though. Loneliness leaves emptiness in the heart that can physically kill you. The ache is unbearable, and the longer it hangs around, the more despair adds to it. Miles of city streets, country roads, and everything in between were walked during those years. Loneliness isn't a lack of people. It is a lack of understanding and acceptance. Huge amounts of people the world over have experienced loneliness in crowded rooms. In fact, being alone in crowded rooms often highlights and exacerbates loneliness.

It doesn't matter how many people are around you. If there is no one available who understands you, or accepts you as who you are, loneliness can very readily present its agonising self. It is very different than being alone, as I had loved this often in the past. Being alone can mean you are lonely *or* you are happy. Loneliness is a longing for the company of one who understands you. Sometimes being alone and loneliness are related, but very often they are not.

The loneliness became so unbearable, the ache in my heart so constant, suicide became an occasional accompanying thought. I didn't want to die at all, of course. I wanted to live. But realising my own worth, not what I had been led to believe, and breaking free of the pain sometimes took incredible strength to master. Allowing love and happiness to flow back through my life, to even accept that I deserved it, was so unbearably difficult at times that the option of suicide felt more appealing.

As the pain and loneliness finally became too much to bear, when I had reached the most painful place so far, my prayers were answered via an act of kindness and understanding. A friend rang at the perfect time. He knew I was going through some hard stuff but didn't know at that very moment I was writing my exit letter through slow, heartbroken tears. I was ready to go. I just couldn't live with the constant ache in my heart anymore.

He insisted I didn't have to say a word. I just had to listen. So via my exhaustion and tears, I reluctantly agreed. Through the phone I heard him begin to play his guitar, then the words "Starry, starry night" from Don McLean's song "Vincent" started to reach my ears as he sang to me, replacing Vincent with Bronnie. My tears just fell harder as I related to the song, its tragedy and pain, the gentle melody telling the story of Vincent Van Gogh's own suffering. When he had finished, I continued to sob. There was nothing else I *could* do. He sat patiently in silence, and then I thanked him and hung up the phone still crying. I wasn't capable of more words at the time.

Falling asleep that night, I was totally drained and emotionally exhausted. I acknowledged, though, that through my friend's understanding and kind intentions, a small pilot light of hope had at least been reignited. The following evening a friend from England rang out of the blue. We talked long and honestly, and my strength slowly started to return, little by little.

On another very difficult occasion, though (sometime later but during those same lonesome years), I was pleading and praying for help, trying so hard to be strong. At the time I was driving into town and I hit a bird. It had been of a decent size, and the noise on the windscreen was enough to wake me up. Of course being an animal lover, this made me feel even more abysmal in a way but it was a good wake-up call. Life can be over as quick as that, and did I *really* want mine to be so?

I thanked the bird for the role it had played in my evolution and drove on with more mindfulness. Just then a piece of classical music came onto the radio, lifting me into the most beautiful place. The incredibly delicate sounds soothed me, gently wiping away my heartache. Instead, I was blessed with a beautiful and inspiring moment as the music soared. I decided then that this is what life was about: Beautiful moments of purity. That's it, as simple as that. Beautiful moments. And I wanted to live, to experience and acknowledge more of them.

Having previously been to this level of sadness and loneliness, though, I now understood that the pain Doris was experiencing was real and tangible for her. She was around people at meal times, and here and there during the day. But she was longing for understanding and acceptance, missing her friends because they were the people who truly understood her. If I could help to ease that pain, then why wouldn't I?

The following week I dropped in to find a list of names waiting for me in the dear lady's lovely handwriting. Doris told me what she could about the four friends and where they had been living when she had last made contact. We drank tea as she shared their stories with me.

One of the women was easy to locate, but she had suffered a stroke and could no longer talk. With news of this, Doris dictated a brief message that her friend's son would read on to her. While she was saddened to hear of her friend's state, she was peaceful knowing a message could at least be passed on.

Dear Elsie. I am sorry to hear you are not well. Years have flown by. Alison is still living in Japan. I sold the house and am in a nursing home. A young lady is writing this for me. I love you, Elsie.
Yours sincerely,
Doris.

It was simple, but said everything she wanted to. I called Elsie's son that night and passed the words on. He called me back later telling me how Elsie had smiled in delight. I passed this on to Doris, which then left her with a smile of content.

Over the next few weeks, I managed to find out about another two of her friends. Sadly, they had both already passed over. Doris nodded in acceptance of this. Sighing, she said, "Well, it was probably to be expected, Sweetheart."

The pressure to find the last friend left me very determined. Scanning the Internet and making numerous phone calls, things were not looking good. People were lovely and helpful when I called but, "Sorry. Right name. Wrong family," became a familiar reply.

In the meantime, I still visited Doris twice a week. She would always hold one of my hands as soon as I sat down, and for the duration of our conversations. Sometimes insisting I must have better things to do, she would try to rush me off or convince me not to come. When I assured her I was gaining great pleasure from our time as well, which I was, I would see the relief on her face and the eagerness for each new visit. There is much to learn from older people, so much history is carried forward with them. How could I not enjoy our delightful conversations? They were fascinating.

A breakthrough finally came while looking for the last friend. I received a phone call from an elderly man who said he had once been Lorraine's neighbour. He told me what suburb the family had moved on to, and I was successful in tracking her down. In fact, it was Lorraine herself who answered the phone in her elderly but friendly voice. Explaining who I was and my intention, she gasped in joy and wholeheartedly agreed for me to give Doris her number.

Naturally, I took it straight in to her. Hugging Doris as I grinned, I then handed her the piece of paper with Lorraine's name and number on it. She grabbed me again and hugged me full of excitement. It was precious. Signalling for me to bring the phone, I couldn't get it fast enough for her. Before the number was dialled, though, I said I would leave her to her phone call rather than just sit in on them both. She protested mildly, but I could see she really didn't mind. She was too excited. Asking me to stay until the call went through, though, I agreed. So we exchanged a warm and loving hug goodbye before I dialled Lorraine's number for her. My heart was beating fast with excitement.

As she held the receiver, Doris's face lit up in joy at the sound of her friend's voice. While Doris's own voice was old – and I knew Lorraine's was, too – the spirit in that phone call was instantly like two young women. They were laughing in no time and chatting non-stop. I tidied the room up a bit, pottering around, unable to extract myself from this incredible happiness. Eventually, though, I did leave. At the door, I quietly waved goodbye to Doris, who was radiant. She stopped talking for a moment, asking Lorraine to wait and said to me, "Thank you, Sweetheart. Thank you." I nodded while smiling so much my face ached. Walking down the corridor ,I could still hear Doris laughing until the door had closed properly. The smile didn't leave my face all the way home.

It was a glorious day, and a swim was beckoning. The high stayed with me while I enjoyed the water flowing around me, as I dipped and swam for a couple of hours. At home, just after sunset, I received a phone call from Rebecca, the lovely staff member I had met the night I worked there and had first met Doris.

Dear Doris had passed away later that afternoon in her sleep.

Tears of sadness fell instantly, but there was joy, too. After all, she had died happy, the dear lady.

It is amazing how a little bit of time can change a person's life. When I think about the lonely woman I met that first night to the person I hugged goodbye to on her last day, no amount of money could substitute the satisfaction this gave me.

There are thousands of beautiful but very lonely people in nursing homes all over the world. There are also many young people whose lives are now confined to nursing homes. Young or old, though, a couple of hours a week of a new friendship can make all the difference to these people and to their final chapter. Of course, keeping people out of nursing homes in the first place is preferred, though sadly not always possible. There are many people in homes who shouldn't be there; people just disposed of, in a way. It is awful to witness. Yet a bit of time given has the potential to change these people's lives immensely.

For me, the timing of Doris's departure was perfect. Simply, it was her time to go, and she had been happy. We had played the role we were meant to in each other's lives, and for that, I will always be grateful. She was a darling woman. Lorraine and I met soon after. The phone call between them had gone on for ages, she said. Both had parted with great happiness. We sat under trees at a café, talking happily about Doris and life in general, until it was time to drive Lorraine home. It was lovely to have been able to meet her friend. Certainly, it had been beautiful to know Doris, too.

And hopefully, of course, our dear friend was able to meet up with her other friends when she reached the other side.

TRUE FRIENDS

❦

The hectic pace of Sydney was wearing me down a bit. No house-sits were on the horizon to keep me there, so I moved down south to experience another chapter in Melbourne. It had been several years since I had left, so it was lovely to be back enjoying the delights of such a wonderfully creative city and to see old friends. My house-sitting reputation also arrived before I did, so my calendar had bookings again in no time.

The first house I lived in was the holiday house of Marie, my boss at the pre-natal centre back in Sydney. It was about an hour south of Melbourne, on the lovely Mornington Peninsula, and it had her energy all through it, making me feel at home instantly. It was autumn when I arrived and the first couple of weeks were spent walking rugged cliffs as the water lapped below me. Walking long distances while being rugged up in a big coat and hat, with cold ocean winds gusting by, left me feeling very alive. I enjoyed walking like this and did it while I could. Then snug inside, sitting by an open fire, my cosy evenings were spent writing and playing guitar.

As much as I could have done this forever, income was needed, too, which is what brought me to caring for Elizabeth. In some ways, her situation was heartbreaking to me, but I was learning to accept that we all have different lessons to learn. What may appear as tragic situations to others were also great opportunities for growth and learning for the person involved.

Working through my own stuff was teaching me to find the gifts in the learning, and I was coming to find a lot of blessings through my past. Many good things were discovered, gifts that could not have come to me had I been raised in a perfect home situation, if such a thing really existed. Strength, forgiveness, compassion, kindness, and many other lessons had been offered to me through my circumstances, all of which I was not only grateful for but were shaping me into a better person every day.

So I had to detach a little with the clients and accept that I did not know what they were here to learn. For whatever reasons they had attracted the life they had, it wasn't up to me to save them. I was there to bring them loving care, friendship, acceptance, and gentleness in their final weeks. If this helped them to find their peace, as it sometimes did, then it made my work even more satisfying. As they say, it is in giving we receive, and I was definitely receiving many blessings in this field.

Working with the dying was an honour, too. Through all of their reminiscing and stories, my own life was being transformed. To be exposed at such an age to the insights they discovered about themselves was an incredible gift. I was already implementing much of the learning from my clients into my own life by now, without having to wait until I too was on my deathbed and then regretting the same things. Arriving at each new client's home, I was stepping into a whole fresh world of learning for myself, all over again. Each home was a different classroom, with either new lessons on offer or similar lessons from different perspectives. Either way, I was absorbing a great deal.

Elizabeth was not an elderly woman, only about fifty-five. She had been an alcoholic for the past fifteen years and was now dying from an associated illness. While she was still resting on the morning I arrived, her son gave me the run-down of the home and of her condition. He also explained how the family had decided not to tell her she was dying. "Oh boy," I thought, "here I go again".

Through my desire for self-improvement and inner peace, I always tried to live as much as possible in the present moment. In the case of Elizabeth, I realised this was going to be the only way through. If she asked me if she was dying, I would deal with it at the time, rather than wonder how to deal with it in the meantime, accepting that she may never ask – but I wasn't going to lie to her.

Confusion and despair surrounded Elizabeth. The family had

removed all of the alcohol from inside of the home, locking it in a cupboard in the garage, which they helped themselves to whenever they wished. As she was ill and dying, they decided to remove it from her access completely. This was one of the things I found heartbreaking. She was dying anyway, so why put her through the pain of withdrawing on top of things? But again, it wasn't my life, nor was it my decision.

Alcoholism in others was something I had been exposed to at too young an age. Then later, working in the hospitality industry, on the island, and while travelling, I was exposed to it even more. Alcohol doesn't bring out the best in anyone and not only ruins the goodness of the alcoholic, it ruins families, friendships, careers, and the innocence of children exposed to it. This is the case with other drug addictions too. The only true thing that brings out the best in anyone is love.

Alcoholism is also an illness, though. And while it is one that can be treated, the sufferer needs ongoing and loving support to break the patterns, and to start believing in themselves and their potential for a better life. Taking a chronic alcoholic off their addiction, with no loving support or explanation, appeared to be a pretty awful thing to me.

All Elizabeth knew was that she was ill. Her energy was exhausted. She needed assistance with almost everything, and her appetite was fading. She was also desperately missing the alcohol. The family had only told her that the doctor said to take her off the drink 'for a while'. It took some strength for me not to judge them, particularly when I saw them sneaking alcohol into their own bodies regularly while denying a dying woman of it. Who was I to say, though, what her lessons in life were to be?

Her general physical weakness would not have allowed Elizabeth to be out and about anymore. The family had also banned some of her friends from visiting, as they were drinkers. It was not surprising then to see Elizabeth experiencing despair and confusion, having had all of her pleasures removed from her.

She accepted the ban of her drinking friends with quiet resignation, though it had removed more than that from her.

Elizabeth had been on the boards of a couple of charitable societies before becoming so ill. These friends were her link to the outside world and to her former life.

After six or seven weeks together, her strength was disappearing even more significantly, while her need for rest increased. Elizabeth was quite funny, in an unobtrusive way. Very dry humour came out of her at some of the most unexpected moments. Sometimes one of her remarks would come to mind at home after a shift, and I would find myself smiling as I thought of her. We had grown to like each other and had established workable routines within the restraints of her illness. One of those was our cup of tea every morning in the sunroom. It was the nicest room in the house by far, and at this time of year, the sun shining in was glorious. It was while in the sunroom one morning that things moved to a new level between us.

"Bronnie, why do you think I am not getting better? I am not drinking, but I am still getting weaker by the day. What do you think?" Elizabeth asked.

Looking at her directly and lovingly, I replied tenderly with a couple of questions. "What do *you* think is the reason? I am sure you've thought about it a bit before now?" I was very gentle with her, but needed to know her line of thinking first.

"I dare not say what I am thinking," she sighed. "It is too big to grasp. Yet deep down I know the answer anyway."

We sat in silence for a while, watching the birds out of the window, the sun warm on us both. "If I ask you, will you tell me? I really need some honesty here," she admitted. Lovingly, I nodded.

"Is it what I think?" she asked, but with the question almost unfinished. I waited, sending her love, seeing if she wanted to go on. She did. "Oh God, it is," she said, answering herself with a sigh. "I am dying aren't I? Kicking the proverbial bucket. Flying with the angels. Passing on or over or whatever it is. Dying! I am dying. I'm right, aren't I?" With a heart tangled up in the bitter-sweetness of her now knowing, I slowly nodded.

Silently we both sat watching the birds until Elizabeth was ready to talk again. It was a while before that happened, but I had grown used to comfortable silences with my clients. They had so much to think about and to absorb that sometimes conversation could just get in the way. There was no need to fill the silence at such a time. They would talk when they were ready. After some time, Elizabeth did.

She said she had suspected this for a while now and how she was frustrated with her family's lack of honesty. Taking her friends and social life away was cruel she said, to which I somewhat agreed. Elizabeth understood she wasn't strong enough to go out of the house, but said she would have liked to seen her friends from time to time. Acquaintances dropped in sometimes, people the family approved of and trusted to come without alcohol. They were pleasant people, she said, but there was no closeness.

Once we reached this level of honesty, our conversations flowed unhindered. There was no time for holding back. So Elizabeth and I found ourselves enjoying each other's company more each day. After years of being so withdrawn, I often surprised myself now, by how easily I expressed personal thoughts. With death on her doorstep, Elizabeth too enjoyed the openness of our constant exchanges. Her initial reaction was anger that her family had not told her she was dying. Eventually, it shifted to acceptance. She expressed that the controlling behaviour from her family had possibly been fear based. For that, she was able to forgive them.

However, she was unable to pretend that she didn't know she was dying, and addressed this with them on one of my days off. It brought them all closer, with the family feeling relief that none of them had had to tell her the big news. It was good for me to hear this and not to be under anyone's wrath for my honesty, but they remained fixed. Her drinking friends could only contact her by phone.

Elizabeth was evolving enormously, though, and became accepting of this, now without resignation. She admitted to me, though wouldn't admit to her family, it was probably only drinking that had truly held that circle of friends together anyway. Drawing on my own experiences, I told Elizabeth how several years earlier my friendships had changed immensely when I began extracting my life from the pot-smoking world. It had sorted out who my friends truly were and who were mates simply because we shared a smoke together. Some people who I thought were quite good friends were actually not comfortable around me at all if I was not stoned with them. It didn't make anyone a bad person. But when I stopped moving in that world, I saw it was only the smoke that had kept some links joined. Without that, there was no longer a common denominator to hold our friendships together. So we had drifted off naturally, in entirely different directions.

"I wish I'd stayed in touch with my friends, my real friends," she said, as I recognised the words from previous people. "My drinking moved me out of those circles, and now fifteen years later, there is little to connect on with my old friends. They have all moved away anyway."

While discussing the acquaintances who were allowed to visit, Elizabeth said she wouldn't really call them 'friends'. We spoke about how loosely that word is used at times and how there are so many different levels of friends. I had begun to think of some of my own 'friends' more as warm acquaintances lately. It didn't mean I thought less of them. They were still a blessing in my life but having been to some pretty dark places in myself by now, I understood what a real friend was. It is easy to have a lot of acquaintances, and I did love those people for the enjoyable role we played in each other's lives. When it comes to the crunch, though, not many people can hang around through the very worst of the pain with someone else. Those who do are truly friends.

"It is about having the right friends for the right occasion, I suppose," Elizabeth pondered. "I simply don't have the right friends for this occasion, for my departure. Do you know what I mean?"

Agreeing, I shared with her that while it was not at all such a serious scenario as her situation, I held a very clear memory of such an occasion for me, of missing the right friends for the right occasion. Because of this memory, I could definitely understand that there are different levels of friendships and associations, and sometimes it is a specific quality of friendship we yearn for, rather than just anyone.

Following the years on the island, I worked for a short time in a printing company in Europe. My co-workers were nice people and I appreciated the opportunities that were presented to me, opening my world up even more. The island community had been like a family, though. Whenever any of us went away – on a holiday to the mainland, for instance – we would all say how beautiful it was to come home to our family on the island.

New friends were made in Europe, though in hindsight I would now call them pleasant acquaintances. Through these people, I ended up on a trip across a couple of countries, to the Italian Alps with three others around my age. We had rented a cabin high up in the Alps, with no electricity or running water. It was gorgeous and unlike any terrain of my beloved Australia, which has its own magnificence, but is hugely different. So I found the Alps overwhelmingly beautiful.

Bathing was done in a flow of water running down the mountain. Though it was summer, the water was freezing. It was really just melting snow forming a downhill stream. As the water rushed down all around me I sat in its flow, gasping for breath. All the while, I was still enjoying the magnificent views and feeling invigorated. But the water was *absolutely* freezing, biting as it hit me, rushing past.

Whenever I had found the courage to swim in a freezing river or ocean, I'd always felt a bit playful after, a bit like a dog after they've had a bath. They rush around like mad, all crazy and energetic, regardless of whether they've enjoyed the bath or not. That's sort of what bathing in this freezing mountain stream did to me. It left me feeling ridiculously silly afterwards.

So I was a bit off my head with excitement and playfulness after drying off, getting dressed, and returning to the cabin. Carrying on with good-natured humour, entertaining myself immensely, and sharing silly anecdotes with my new friends, I realised every single one of my jokes was totally lost on them. The worried smiles that said, "*What* is she on about?" told me so in a second. Their puzzled faces sort of just cracked me up even more. At least *I* was enjoying the jokes anyway. They were happy and lovely people. It was just that the humour of our cultures was so different. In an instant, I missed my old friends with painful longing. They would not only have related to the silliness but would have been cracking up with me by now, adding their own jokes, and turning it all into an even greater laugh.

That evening, after a massive afternoon hike to the top of a mountain, we all sat by the light of lanterns as we ate and chatted a while. It was nice. Not long after, though, everyone retired for the night – everyone except for me. The hike had been amazing, and I was still in a jubilant mood. Really, all I wanted to be doing was sitting around with friends and just generally having a laugh, to wind up a fantastic day. Certainly I didn't want to be going to bed yet anyway.

But all was now quiet in the hut as my friends slept. Carrying a lantern into my little room, I placed it on the table and spent the next two hours writing. In the distance I heard bells ringing as cows moved about in the night. I smiled in bliss that here I was, in a gorgeous little cabin, writing by lantern light high up in the Alps, and listening to sound of distant cow bells. It was a world away from my own world, and while I was overwhelmed by the peace of the moment, it made me miss my old friends terribly.

It was a perfect night but with the wrong people. There were plenty of reasons to like each of my friends on this trip, and I did. I was experiencing a very special moment in myself, though, and I wanted to be sharing it with the right people, with friends who truly knew me. Of course, this was never going to happen. So I savoured the blessing of the moment all to myself instead.

I knew what Elizabeth was now talking about when she said she wished she had the right friends around. Sometimes there are just particular people who understand you, no matter what – and these are old friends. It was like that for me that night in the Alps, and it was like that now for Elizabeth as she began accepting that her life was coming to a close.

When her doctor came to visit, I asked him privately if it would make any difference to Elizabeth's condition if she were still drinking. He shook his head. "No, she's on the home straight now regardless. I told her family if she wants a little brandy in the evening to allow it. Are they not?" he asked me. I shook my head. He restated it would make little difference now.

Later I spoke to her family quietly about it. But again, it had been a family decision and no, they would definitely not be giving her any drink. They then went on to explain why. It seems that the Elizabeth I was spending time with and the Elizabeth they knew when she had been drinking were two entirely different personalities. In fact, they couldn't believe what a pleasant person she was again now, as they hadn't seen this side of her for at least fifteen years.

Over the next couple of weeks, I asked her more about her drinking habit, if she brought it up. Elizabeth said that as much as she was still craving it now, she was kind of glad, too, to be able to remember who she was before alcohol had taken over her life. It had begun easily enough. She'd always had a few wines with the family at dinner and had done so for years with no problem.

Then she became active socially, being on the boards of various charities. She admitted that many people she met through these scenes did not drink excessively at all, but she had been drawn to those who did. She didn't feel noticed at home anymore, but felt like her presence mattered to these new friends. Now that she was feeling clearer, she realised they were all just as needy as her, all needing validation through this circle of friends and their drinking.

Elizabeth said alcohol gave her confidence – or when she was drunk, she thought it did – but she became outspoken, loud, and eventually quite bitter and nasty to others. This is what had made her lose her original circle of old friends. They had tried to reach her with love and support, trying to help her see her own demise, something they were watching with heartache. But she was arrogant with them all, eventually pushing every last one of them away.

This only validated to her drunken mind just how loyal her new friends were, who didn't judge her for her drinking habit. Of course this was because they were drinking. The other reasoning for her drinking that she had justified to herself during these years, was that at least now her family noticed her. While it may not have been in a positive way, at least she didn't feel ignored like she used to, before she had started drinking excessively. Her loss of control ensured they had to start paying attention.

The more Elizabeth's capabilities declined due to alcoholism, the more her family had to help her and the worse she eventually began to feel. It had begun with her enjoying their attention. But in the end, she was incapable of helping herself, and this lack of control left her feeling even more insecure and negative about who she now was. So while in the early days she could see she was hurt about her family not valuing her presence or opinion, in the end she came to truly depend on them and hated herself for it. This just perpetuated the cycle of low self-esteem even more.

"You know, not everyone *wants* to get well either, Bronnie. And for a long time I didn't. The role of the sick person gave me an identity. Obviously I was holding myself back from being a better person this way. But I was getting attention, and trying to fool myself of this made me happier than being courageous and well." This admission from Elizabeth was the hindsight of a woman who was now on a fast track to wisdom. Being dry for almost three months and facing the fact that she was dying was changing her enormously.

Knowing Elizabeth's full and honest story about her addiction also helped me to understand her and her family more. In the end, their severe actions had actually helped her to become a better person again. While I may not have done it in such a closed and secretive fashion, I came to respect that they were really trying to help her and themselves. And they were successful in doing so. Part of their success, too, was Elizabeth herself. Facing her death had made her look at life very differently, and she had courageously embraced her learning.

During her last two weeks, I watched some extraordinary healing unfold between Elizabeth and her family. One of the most beautiful things I was learning through palliative care was to never underestimate anyone's capacity for learning. The peace I witnessed Elizabeth find was something I had also seen in previous clients. It was a very gratifying thing.

About a week before she died, I spoke with her husband and one of her sons about Elizabeth's regret of losing her old friends and wondered if it might not be too late to reach some of them, even if they could just speak on the phone. By now, there was no concern about friends sneaking alcohol into Elizabeth. It was the least of everyone's concerns. Her comfort was all that mattered, and as the family had healed so much, they immediately jumped to the idea.

A couple of days later, two beautiful, healthy, and lovely women came in to Elizabeth's room, just after I had sat her up comfortably and offered her some tea. One of them was now living in the mountains outside of the city, about an hour away. The other had flown to Melbourne from the Sunshine Coast in Queensland as soon as she had heard the news. Now they sat around Elizabeth's bed, talking with her, holding hands, and smiling.

Leaving them to their privacy and me to a quiet tear of joy, I left the room. As I was doing so, though, I heard Elizabeth apologise to them both and their instant forgiveness returned. It was past. It didn't matter, they said. Her husband, Roger, and I sat out in the kitchen, both of us teary but delighted.

The friends stayed for a couple of hours, by which time Elizabeth was both exhilarated and completely exhausted. She fell into a deep sleep instantly, so I had no chance to chat with her before going home. When I returned a couple of days later, she was very weak but wanted to talk.

"Wasn't that wonderful? Oh, to see their faces again," she smiled with delight. Unable to lift her head off the pillows now, she looked across to me sitting beside her.

"It was beautiful," I told her.

"Don't lose touch with the friends you value most, Bronnie. Those who accept you as who you are, and who know you very well, are worth more than anything in the end. This is a woman speaking from experience," she insisted lightly, smiling at me through her illness. "Don't let life get in the way. Just always know where to find them and let them know you appreciate them in the meantime. Don't be afraid to be vulnerable either. I wasted some time in not being able to let them all know what a mess I was." Elizabeth had forgiven herself and was able to let go of her own judgment. She had found her peace and she had found her friends.

When her last morning came, I was adding some moisture to her lips. Her mouth was no longer producing saliva properly and she was struggling to speak, not that she had the energy to anyway. As I finished, she looked to me smiling, then mouthed the words "Thank you." Looking at her, I returned the same gratitude with a smile. Then I kissed her on the forehead and held her hand for a moment, which she squeezed.

Her room was full of people who loved her. All of her family was there, as were the two delightful ladies I had met a few days earlier. I stepped back and allowed her to be surrounded by those she had loved the most.

Just in time, Elizabeth had let love back into her life and appreciated the value of her family and true friends. She departed this Earth surrounded by love, knowing her presence had been valued enormously and that her friends knew she loved them, too.

ALLOW YOURSELF

‿⊙⌒‿

As far as work went, looking after Harry was the easiest time I ever had. Not only was he a wonderful person, but his family insisted on doing everything. Three of Harry's five daughters lived in the same suburb and would bring his main meals over most days, and one of his sons insisted on caring for his dad himself. Questioning the need for me to be there at all, the daughters and other sons assured me they definitely wanted me there.

It meant, however, that much of my time was spent reading or writing. There is only so much housework to be done in an already clean and tidy home, with its only tenant bedridden. I did create a couple of delicious soup recipes in his kitchen, though.

Harry had bushy eyebrows, hairy ears, a red face, and an honest laugh. We liked each other immediately. Within the first minute of meeting, we had both cracked a joke with each other. So it was an easy, natural association from the start.

His son Brian was a different story, though. He was very highly strung. Harry and Brian had fallen out years ago, and while contact had remained between them, their bond was never quite the same. The rest of the family explained it as being Brian's fault. I wasn't there all those years ago, nor had I walked in either Harry or Brian's shoes, so I don't know. It didn't matter to me either way. But it *was* obvious that Brian was now trying to make up for lost time by insisting he be his father's primary carer.

Brian interrupted any attempt I made to help Harry. By now, I was very good at finding the right position for a client's comfort. It was an intuitive thing, and one many clients commented on. But family often rearranged pillows and supports out of kindness, not realising how sensitive a person's body is at this time, and how the slightest adjustment can undo the only tiny bit of comfort they have.

When his son reluctantly went off to work every day for a few hours, the first thing I would do was to get Harry comfortable again. If there was a tiny moment of time during the day when I could attend to him without being hounded out by his son, literally, the first thing Harry would ask was for me to quickly adjust his pillows.

Each afternoon, we had those few hours together before the family arrived back en-masse for dinner, even though by now their dad was hardly eating. These hours were wonderful and what Harry affectionately called 'the peace hours'. While I attended to his physical needs, we would chat and laugh. This was usually followed by a cup of tea and some more chat.

Harry had lost his wife twenty years earlier but had come to continue living his life well. He had enjoyed his work, though became even busier on retiring, joining a couple of sporting and social clubs. While his illness was terminal, prior to this he had experienced amazing health for his whole life.

"I respected the gift of health I was given," Harry told me, "by staying active and not believing some quota of years saying I should be acting this way or that. People make themselves old before their time, you know." Despite being a dying person, Harry was the healthiest man of eighty years I had ever seen. The illness was certainly starting to wear him down, but evidence of his prior fitness was still apparent. Massaging his legs, for example, muscle tone from all of his walking could still be seen.

"When you're retired and your children are raising their own children, the need for friends is even more important," Harry said. "So when my wife died, God rest her soul, I joined the rowing club. Then I joined a bushwalking club. I don't know how I ever had time to work!"

Harry very much believed in the importance of extended family, that grandparents are an integral part of children's lives and should be given plenty of opportunity to spend time with them. It was obvious in his relationships with his grandchildren, who visited him daily, that he had a very positive and loving influence on them all.

"My family comes first, but you need people your own age, too.

If it weren't for the friends I've made through the clubs, I would have been a very lonely old person. I wouldn't have been lonely for company, as I have my children and grandchildren, but lonely for like-minded company of people my own age."

Hours were spent chatting in his room, until the late afternoon sun would warn us of the peace hours being almost over. The family would soon be descending on us again, but Harry always talked for as long as he could. He said he didn't understand why people left it too late to realise the importance of friends. Also, while it was beautiful when elderly people still managed to hold a loving and respected position within their family, he grew frustrated that so many of them hadn't left time for friendship along the way, too.

"They'll realise it too late," he insisted. "But it's not just my generation. I look at the younger ones as well, who get so caught up and busy, not taking just a little bit of time out for themselves now and then to do things that make them happy on an individual basis. They lose who they really are completely. A little time with friends reminds them of who they are when they are not Mum, Dad, Grandma, or Grandfather. Do you understand what I am saying?"

Agreeing that I had seen plenty of people go down that road, I also said I had seen others who had maintained just a slight bit of time out for themselves and were much happier people. They were also much better company to be around.

"Exactly!" He laughed, slapping the bed in agreement. "Good friendships stimulate us. The beauty of friendship is that these people take us as we are, on the things we have in common. Friendship is about being accepted as who you are, not as who someone else wants you to be, like a partner or family. We must maintain our friendships, my dear girl."

By the stream of visitors that came to visit Harry regularly, it was obvious this man walked his talk. His friends were all happy, jovial people and brought great joy with them. Equally respectful of his illness, though, they accepted that sometimes he was resting and could not be disturbed.

On another afternoon, Harry asked me about my own friendships. So I filled him in on my close friends and explained how some of my other friendships were changing lately, as was I.

"Well, that's natural, too," he said. "Friends will come and go throughout life. That's why we should value them while they are here. Sometimes you simply finish learning or sharing what you were meant to through each other. But others will stay the distance, and that history and understanding is a comforting thing when you're at the end of the road."

During these talks we both agreed that women approach friendships much differently than men. Women value friendships in a stronger way emotionally; that is, the friendships grow closer with a lot of talk about emotional things. Men need friendships for talking, too, he said. But they do this best when they are doing things together, like playing tennis, cycling, or doing something active. Men enjoy friendships where they can work things out, resolve problems, whether physical or emotional – and this often happens best when they are active.

"Like building a fence around a paddock together," I suggested.

Harry cracked up laughing. "My, my. You can take the girl out of the country, but you can't take the country out of the girl. Yes, a very rural example, Bronnie, but exactly. Building a fence or doing something manual together is a bonding thing for men."

He carried on laughing, and said if I ever wanted to bond with a good-looking man, all I had to do was to help him to build a fence. I told him I'd keep it in mind.

Sharing some of his favourite stories about mate-ship with me, Harry reinforced the blessings of the friendships still existing. Every day lovely friends visited him. They were now operating a roster amongst themselves, though, so as to not exhaust him. This way, everyone still had a chance to spend time with Harry. It was loyal and wonderful.

We both admitted that through these peace hours, we were each receiving a new friendship into our lives, too – each other. It frustrated him, he said, to know I was out in another part of the house for the rest of the day, just reading or writing, when I could be in his room chatting. In total agreement, I laughed. But he understood, as did I, Brian's need to make amends and the desire to assist his father. Harry didn't want Brian to be carrying any guilt, though he was sure he still would, unfortunately. So he was happy to go with it and allow his son to feel needed during their last weeks together. "Even if he can't arrange the pillows well," he sighed.

Harry was philosophical about his illness and what was to come. He had lived his life to the fullest, he said, and was ready to see what lay beyond. While we did speak about his approaching passing sometimes, he still steered many of the conversations to the subject of friends: the memories, the value of them, and the necessity of them for happiness and acceptance. He also encouraged me to share some of my favourite memories with him about my friendships so far. "Start with one from your childhood. Let's hear where you're coming from," he said, then laughed in delight when my story began in a rural setting, a paddock of wheat.

By the time I was twelve, we had moved from a cattle and lucerne growing farm to a sheep and wheat farm. It was miles from town, under a magnificently huge sky. About a year later my first dog disappeared suddenly, when she was seven. We think it may have been a snake's bite, as we never found her. This wasn't surprising, as the farm was so large. It was devastating for me, though. A few months later my folks bought me a new dog. She was a little white Maltese Terrier, who neglected to realise that she was supposed to be a housedog. Instead, she spent her days chasing the sheep dogs, the border collies and kelpies, over paddocks near and far.

My closest friend through my high school years and for a long time after was Fiona. Although she lived in town, much of our time was spent out at the farm. I stayed in town at her parents' place a bit, too, particularly as we grew a little older and there were boys to be kissed. One of the main things that linked Fiona and me over the years, though, was our love of walking. I cannot think how many miles we ended up walking together over the decades of our friendship: beaches, rainforests, city streets, foreign countries, bush tracks, you name it. It all started with walking those paddocks of wheat.

As usual, my dog and a couple of the other dogs came along with us. It was not particularly strange to turn around and see a cat or two also following. While we girls stuck to the track that led to the furthest paddocks away, the dogs would run through the wheat. This was fine while the wheat was low, but as it grew, my little dog became invisible. Fiona and I were given the most beautiful comedy sketch this day.

Following the big dogs, which we could see clearly above the tallest sections of crop, was a trail of movement in the wheat behind as my little dog ran blindly after the big dogs. Then every now and then the movement would stop. A little white head would pop up and look around like a submarine telescope coming out of the water, until it spotted the other dogs. It then disappeared below again into the wheat, blazing another trail of movement in the new direction. Then the movement would stop, up would pop the little white head, spot the target again, disappear below and run on. This went on for ages and by the end of it, every time we saw the little white head pop up and look around, Fiona and I would break into hysterical teenage giggling all over again. Our cheeks ached from laughing and as tears ran down our faces, we leaned on each other, holding the other up before spotting the dog popping up yet again, and doubling over in laughter even more. In the end, we could hardly even stand up.

Sharing this simple but precious memory took me back to the value of friendship in an instant. Harry and I laughed together, as I missed that innocence of youth and the carefree, uninhibited laughter I used to share with Fiona. "Where is she now?" Harry asked. I went on to explain that she was living in another country and we had lost touch. Life had moved on, I said, and there were now others in my life whom I was closer to. Other factors had also affected our friendship – other people, yes, but also other tastes and gradual differences in lifestyles. Harry agreed that you can't go back, but maybe life would bring our paths around again. Having already observed many cycles in life, I agreed it was possible. But either way it didn't matter. I valued the memories and wished Fiona well; silently thanking her for the learning and friendship we had once shared.

Many of my best memories of friendships were of walking, talking, and laughing. Over the next week or two, I shared with Harry stories from some of these other friendships. He had also been a keen walker and shared some of his own with me, of places he'd walked and of friends with whom he had shared the experiences with. I could imagine any group being brightened by Harry's laughter as they walked. It made me smile at the thought, and when he asked what I was smiling at, I was happy to tell him. Harry agreed they had always shared some great laughs while walking.

As it was, I was to leave Harry the following week to go on a long walk myself. I hadn't been sure if he would still be alive when I had booked into it. So while I was looking very forward to getting out of the city, I was also a little sad to be leaving him, not sure if he would still be here when I returned. When I told Harry what I was doing, though, he wholeheartedly agreed with enthusiasm and said he would be there with me in spirit whether he was alive or not.

The walk was in a remote area and was held each year, always ending at the same lake. Each time a different tributary was followed; this particular year it was starting on some farms where the very mouth of a river began. We would follow that river, much of it now just dry riverbeds, and eventually end up at the lake.

The concept of the walk was to give the participants the opportunity to heal with the Earth, as we walked the paths trodden by ancient civilisations. Rivers were like highways then, thoroughfares at least, where tribes would live and walk along its banks, from one place to the next. An Aboriginal Elder blessed us as we all partook in a cleansing smoke ceremony, then off we went, walking for six days.

We all fell into our own rhythm. There were about a dozen of us. Some walked in groups and talked all the way. Others meandered in and out of conversation. Some stopped and took photos of everything, and some of us walked more alone. Each night, a couple of volunteers would turn up with the trailer carrying our gear and we'd establish a camp. Then around a peaceful campfire a communal dinner was prepared, while beautiful friendships formed under a magnificent blanket of stars.

With every footstep, the connection with the Earth increased. While I enjoyed conversations when we stopped for a break, I found more enjoyment in walking alone, and my pace ensured this anyway. Having done so much walking in the past, my natural rhythm carried me ahead of the main group. One other walker, the wise and loving soul who originally started these walks, was always ahead of me, also walking to his own rhythm.

The time alone, just walking and walking, was also great for finding clarity within myself again. During this time I realised I didn't want to keep house-sitting for much longer. Something in me was starting to think about having my own kitchen again. All of the moving I had once loved was starting to exhaust me. A new seed was planted, not with big fanfare, just a quiet acceptance within that some things were changing. I walked on peacefully.

It is rare to be able to walk so far in modern times as land is now separated by ownership. Thankfully, this was all approved of beforehand so we walked across farm after farm without any problem. In the modern rush of life, it is very easy to not be aware of the Earth beneath our feet. Sure, most of us feel a connection with the Earth when we stop and absorb the beauty of nature. To be able to walk for six days unhindered, though, left me feeling a connection with the Earth I hadn't known was missing, despite all of my time previously spent in blissful appreciation of the planet.

Along the way, we discovered carvings from ancient people and marvelled at magnificent red gums, trees hundreds of years old. There were intricate carvings, as well as indentations where canoes had been crafted from their bark. This evidence of past people, whose tribes were now long lost, was heartbreaking and inspiring at the same time. The energy in certain places was incredibly strong, too, and I understood why it was a walk intended for healing.

On top of this, much of the farmland we crossed reminded me of where I had grown up. Even the smell of sheep poo brought a flood of memories rushing back, and I loved being in the dry, dusty climate again, even if only temporarily. With every footstep my fitness improved, and I dreamed of returning to a world where walking was the main means of transport. It just made more sense to me than all of the rush and bustle of modern life.

Finding a cooling waterhole to have a swim in was a welcome relief one day, when I had somehow lost the group briefly. Stripping off and swimming in this clean, refreshing water was rejuvenating, as the water cleansed my spirit as much as it did my body. Every moment of this week was a spiritual blessing, as the connection with nature grew more enhanced.

The landscape changed constantly as we walked from about

eight in the morning until five or so each afternoon, then set up camp. Other signs of previous life dotted our path as well. An old cart that had once become bogged in the river was now a part of the dry landscape and possibly had been for over a hundred years. A stone cabin with no roof told of river dwellers in other times, too. The best, though, was when we saw the carvings and realised what a unique history lesson we were all blessed with, confirming the lives of those ancient people whose footsteps we were now following.

After six full days of walking and about eighty kilometres covered, we arrived weary but exhilarated. It was with great sadness that I said farewell to the other walkers, but with even greater sadness that the walk had finished. The following day I walked for another five hours, around the dry lake itself, as I just couldn't get out of walking mode. A small music festival followed a few days later, which was organised with equal reverence as the walk. So I hung around for that and then headed back to Melbourne.

Thankfully Harry had not yet passed, so I was able to spend a little more time with him. During the ten days I was away, though, the disease had taken over his body, and I found him looking quite emaciated. All of his tone had left his once muscular legs, and his big round face was now gaunt with loose skin. Yet he was still Harry, still a delightful, beautiful man.

The intensity of Brian's desperation to look after his father had increased enormously. He was even more controlling than ever and would only leave the house for an hour maximum each afternoon. I was grateful that both Harry and I had already appreciated those peace hours before I went away, as they were hardly on offer now. In addition to Brian's obsessive behaviour, Harry was sleeping much more anyway.

As life would have it, though, Brian was called away unexpectedly one morning and had to reluctantly hand the care over to me. And it was when Harry was at his brightest – not that his brightest was bright anymore. But he was awake and capable of talking a little at least.

At his request, I told him all about the walk and the insights I'd had into myself while I was away. He asked about the other walkers as well and any positive changes they'd noticed in themselves or that I had noticed. There was much to share.

"And what are you doing this week in regards to friends, Bronnie?" he enquired in his weakening voice. "What time are you giving of your week to spend with good quality friends? That's what I want to know." I laughed at his persistence on the subject, and said there would be plenty of time to catch up with other friends later. Right now I wanted to enjoy my time with him, Harry, who was also my friend.

"It's not enough, my dear girl. You are doing what others do. Surely you have learned by now that you must take time out for you, too. Find some balance and make time for your friends regularly. Do it for yourself even more than for them. We need our friends." Harry looked at me sternly with a look of warning. But we both knew there was love behind his insistence.

He was right. I needed to maintain some time out with friends regularly, rather than be working all of these twelve-hour shifts and catching up with them all later. As much as I loved this work and sometimes shared some wonderful laughter with the clients and their families, it was a pretty serious world I was living in. Being around dying people and the sadness of their families needed to be balanced with some lightness that only friends could provide. Joy was missing from my life, and it was only now I was able to truly acknowledge this to myself.

"You're right, Harry," I admitted. He smiled and put his arms up for a hug. I leant down on the bed and embraced him, smiling.

"It's not just about staying in touch with your friends, my dear girl. It is about giving yourself the gift of their company, too. You understand this, don't you?" he asked with both words and eyes.

Nodding with conviction, I replied, "Yes, Harry, I do." Leaving him to his rest a little while later, I appreciated the point he had made and the direct honesty shared.

Harry was blessed with a smooth passing. He died in his sleep a few nights later. Calling to let me know, his daughter thanked me sincerely. But as I said to her, Harry gave a lot to me, too. It had been my pleasure to know him.

"Allow yourself time with your friends," I still hear him say. The words of that dear man with the bushy eyebrows, red face, and big smile live on still.

REGRET 5:
I WISH I HAD LET MYSELF
BE HAPPIER

Being an executive in a global corporation, Rosemary was a woman ahead of her time. She had moved up the ranks long before women were ever seen in these types of roles. Prior to this, though, she had lived according to society's expectations in those days, and had married young. Unfortunately, with her marriage came physical and mental abuse. When she was left almost dying after one particular beating, it was time to escape for good.

Despite it being a very valid reason to leave a marriage, divorce was still a scandal in those days. So to uphold the family reputation in a town where their name was well known, Rosemary had moved to the city and started afresh.

Life had hardened her heart and her way of thinking. Self-validation and family approval were now found through her success in a male-dominated world. Consideration of another relationship never crossed her mind again. Instead, Rosemary moved up the ranks with fierce determination, a high IQ, and a lot of hard work, until she was the first woman in her state to hold the high level of management she did.

Used to telling people what to do, Rosemary enjoyed the power her intimidating manner gave her. This behaviour then carried over to her treatment of the carers. She was going through one after another, never happy with any of them, until I arrived. She liked me because I had a banking background, which in her eyes exempted me from being a fool. This way of thinking was certainly not one I resonated with, but I had nothing to prove anymore either way, so I figured she could judge me in whatever way made her happy. After all, she was in her eighties and dying. Rosemary then insisted on keeping me as her primary carer.

The mornings were particularly bad with bossy moods and nastiness. Having a strong sense of my own self by now, I tolerated it to a point but knew there would be a limit. When her mood turned especially nasty and personal one day, I gave Rosemary the ultimatum: Be kinder or I was out of there. To this she screamed for me to go, to get out of her house, saying even nastier things than before, while sitting on the side of her bed.

While she was screaming at me, I just went and sat next to her. "Go then! Get out!" she kept yelling, pointing to the door. I just sat there looking at her, sending her loving kindness, waiting for her outburst to subside. Silence followed. We both sat there for another minute or so, saying nothing, but sitting close enough to be leaning on each other. "Finished?" I asked, smiling gently.

"For now," she huffed. I nodded, saying nothing. Silence continued. Finally, I just put my arm around her, kissed her on the cheek and went out the kitchen, returning a few minutes later with a pot of tea. Rosemary was still sitting in the same position, looking like a lost little girl.

Helping her up off the bed, we moved across to the settee in her room. The tea was waiting on the table beside it. Rosemary sat, looking up at me smiling as I placed a lovely rug over her legs, then I sat myself down, too. "I'm so scared and lonely. Please don't leave me," she said. "I feel safe with you."

"I'm not going anywhere. It's OK. As long as you treat me respectfully, I'm here for you," I told her sincerely.

Rosemary smiled like a little girl in need of love. "Stay then, please. I want you to stay." Nodding, I kissed her on the cheek again, which made her smile hugely.

From this point, things turned better between us immediately. She spoke of her past, which helped me to understand her more, and of how she had always pushed people away. Having known that pattern in myself for a long time, and the benefits of breaking free of it, I explained how it wasn't too late to let people in. Rosemary said she didn't know how, but she wanted to try and be nicer.

Her illness was slow to take hold, but there were definitely signs of it spreading daily, particularly with her increasing weakness. It was a slow change at first, and while I could see it, Rosemary was still in occasional denial. Making plans for me to do her books and get all of her investment portfolios in order, she would talk in detail about this and that. I just listened, knowing that it would never happen. Rosemary explained how she was going to spend a few hours with me to get started on it all when she had the energy. I had seen this before, where people continued to make plans towards their future, while in the meantime their strength was disappearing more each day.

She also insisted on me making her appointments around town, ensuring I made the calls from her bedroom phone, where she could listen to every word I said and butt in constantly, controlling the whole conversation. I'd then have to reschedule them, not cancel them, one at a time. There was no denying Rosemary had a controlling personality. While I was happy to do certain unnecessary things for her, I refused outright at other times; like being unwilling to waste my time and energy looking for things we had already looked for in every single inch of the home.

Each day saw her emotional walls breaking down more and our closeness increasing. Rosemary's relatives lived away, though did telephone regularly. Quite a few friends were frequent visitors, as were former business associates. Mostly, though, it was a pretty quiet home with a lovely garden we would enjoy together.

While watching me from her wheelchair nearby as I put some linen away one afternoon, Rosemary told me to stop humming. "I hate that you're happy all the time and always humming," she declared miserably. I finished what I was doing, closed the linen cupboard door, turned around and looked at her with amusement. "Well, it's true. You're always humming and you're always happy. I wish you'd just be miserable sometimes."

This was such a typical viewpoint from Rosemary that I wasn't surprised by it at all. I wasn't always happy, but when I was it gave her something to moan about. Instead of responding verbally, though, I just looked at her, then did a pirouette, poked my tongue out at her, and left the room laughing. She loved me for this, as when I came back into the room shortly after, she was smiling with mischief and acceptance. Never did she condemn my positive moods again in such a way.

"Why are you happy?" Rosemary asked one morning soon after. "I mean, not just today, but in general. Why are you happy?" I smiled at the question, thinking how far I had come in myself to even be asked such a question. Considering what I had been going through in my own life while caring for Rosemary, it was a rather poignant question.

"Because happiness is a choice, Rosemary, and one I try to make every day. Some days I can't. Like you, I've had a hard life, in different ways but still hard. But rather than dwelling on what's wrong and how hard I've done it, I am trying to find the blessings in each day and appreciating the moment I am in, as much as I can," I told her honestly. "We have the freedom to choose what we focus on. I try to choose the positive stuff, like getting to know you, like doing work I love, not being under pressure to reach sales targets, and appreciating my health and every day of being alive." Rosemary smiled, looking at me intensely as she absorbed my words.

What she didn't know, though, was that while I was caring for her I had also been dealing with illness of my own. Some time prior, I had had a minor operation. When the specialist called me with the results, he told me they were open to doubt and a larger operation had to be done immediately. I told him I would think about it.

"There is nothing to think about," he had stated adamantly. "You *must* have this operation or you could be dead in a year." Again, I told him I would think about it. I had already done some big learning through my body, which isn't surprising since the body is where our past is stored. All of our pain and joy manifests within the body in one way or another. Having managed to relieve myself of smaller ailments previously by healing various painful emotions, I decided a huge gift of healing was now on offer to me. So I would approach my illness from that perspective.

Having enough of my own fear to deal with, though, I was only able to share the situation with one or two people. It was going to take all of my strength to get through it and to stay focused on what I wanted, which was health. So I couldn't risk taking on other people's opinions or fears. These may have been intended with love, but there was not one inch of space for anyone else's fear on this healing journey. Having the courage to express myself emotionally, to release things from some very deep levels, became even more important and things certainly turned dark for a while. A lot of past stuff surfaced from the depths.

At one stage, it became so difficult and emotionally painful that I ended up welcoming the thought of dying, and asked the illness to take me away. When I had to seriously contemplate my whole life and accept that despite my efforts, I *may* actually pass on from this illness and not live through to an old age, I reached a point where an amazing peace was found. Realising I had already lived an incredible life and had the courage to honour my own heart and calling allowed me to look my death in the face and accept either outcome. The peace that followed this acceptance was beautiful.

While continuing with my usual meditation practice, though, I also worked through various healing books and visualisation techniques, in addition to releasing the emotions that wanted out. Various shifts started to occur within me. Eventually, I reached a stage where I felt the worst was behind me, and that I was on the road to wellness.

A lovely house-sit was offered in a rambling little cottage, covered in vines and hidden away behind a high fence. It was in a fairly affluent suburb, but was almost invisible and I loved it. Soaking in a bath had always been a bit of a lifesaver for me, too, and this house had an enormous one. Being in such a congenial environment, I decided to do a juice fast, as I had numerous times before, and a couple of days of silence and meditation.

My body had always been a great indicator of where my emotions had been. If a minor ailment would present itself, I could recognise where my thoughts or activities had been in the days or weeks leading up to this. As a result, over time I had come to enjoy a very clear and honest communication channel from my body, always now listening to what it was saying and doing my best to adhere to methods of improvement. Often clients or friends would admit to knowing there was something wrong in their body, long before they did anything about it. But having seen the lack of quality that life offers once health is gone, I had learned to act on any signs from my body as soon and as best as I could. Health offers amazing freedom that once gone, is often gone forever.

One of the meditations I did while in the cottage was guidance from a book I had recently bought. There were many stages leading up to this point, though, and much work had already been done. This particular book was looking at the intelligence of our cells, how they worked together, and offered guidance in asking them to eradicate the illness from the body. It was healing at a cell level. So mid-morning, I sat myself down on my meditation cushion and slipped into a deep, peaceful place within. Following through with the visualisations and requests, I asked my cells to free me from the last of the illness, if by now any of it remained in me.

The next thing I knew, I was running to the toilet and projectile vomiting. It came from the deepest parts of my body and I continued to vomit for ages, until I felt that there was absolutely nothing left inside of me. Sitting on the floor totally drained, leaning against the bath, I waited in a daze in case there was more. It came, and then even more came, until eventually it all ceased. I stood up using the bath as support, due to exhaustion from my efforts. My stomach was also aching from the repeated heaving. Walking back slowly to the meditation room, feeling very shifted, I lay down on the soft carpet, pulled a big blanket over me, curled up into a foetal position and slept for six hours straight.

The late afternoon light shone into the room, and the beginnings of the evening chill woke me gently. Lying there still snug under the blanket, looking at the beautiful light shining in, I felt like I was in a new life. Sending out a prayer of gratitude for the guidance and courage that had brought me to this point of healing, I smiled to myself. My body was still a little weak from the day's events. But as I became more mobile, getting up and on with the evening, euphoria washed through me. Preparing a gentle meal after the fast, my face ached in happiness. It was over.

My body had healed, and no sign of the illness has resurfaced in the years since. While I am very respectful of everyone choosing their own method of healing, whether that is through surgical operations, natural therapies, eastern traditions, or western pharmaceuticals, I had chosen the right method for myself. It had taken everything I had ever learned to get myself through this time, but I had done it.

It never felt appropriate to share this story with my clients, though, as the methods I used took almost four decades of preparation through my own life experiences, and many months of healing. It would not have been kind to offer false hope to them. By the time I knew all of these people, they were already too close to the very end of the illness and their life.

Through this experience, I appreciated the gift of my life much more and found choosing happiness was a daily thing, a new habit to integrate into my thinking. There were days when I couldn't be happy, but I think that accepting this leads to a more peaceful existence anyway. It allows for acceptance of the harder days, knowing they bring gifts of their own and will pass, with happiness waiting again on the other side. Yet consciously choosing to focus on happiness and blessings when I could was certainly creating positive changes within me.

So when Rosemary asked me why I was always humming and happy, it was because I had just experienced a self-made miracle and was feeling very empowered and blessed.

Rosemary wanted to be happy, she said to me later that day, but didn't know how. "Well, just pretend to be, for half an hour. Maybe you'll enjoy it enough to actually be happy. The physical act of smiling changes your emotions anyway, Rosemary. So I dare you to not frown, complain, or say anything negative for half an hour. Instead, say nice stuff, focus on the garden if you must, but remember to smile," I directed her. Reminding Rosemary that I didn't know her in the past, it allowed her to be whoever she wanted to be right now. Sometimes happiness takes a conscious effort.

"I don't think I ever felt like I deserved to be happy, you know.

My marriage breakup tarnished the family name and reputation. How do I *be* happy?" she asked with sincerity that broke my heart.

"You allow yourself to be. You are a beautiful woman, and you deserve to know happiness. Allow yourself and choose to be." Rosemary's hindrances were ones that I myself had known too well in the past. So reminding her that her family's opinion or reputation could only rob her of happiness if she allowed it to, I lightened the mood with some humour, assisting happiness to flow.

Although a little hesitant at first, Rosemary began to give herself permission to be happy, letting her guard down more each day, sharing a smile often, which eventually turned into occasional laughter. Whenever one of her old moods would strike, where she would rudely order me to do something, I would just laugh and say, "I don't think so!" Instead of becoming even ruder, she would laugh and then ask in a kinder manner, to which I would happily oblige with no fuss.

Each day her health faded, though, and was now at the point where she was noticing it as well. While continuing to speak about how she was going to show me what to do with her books, she no longer looked so puzzled when I didn't join in with encouraging conversation about it. Rosemary's time out of bed was also becoming less and less. She had to accept being washed in bed now, as it was too much of a risk on her health and my back to try moving her into the shower.

If I spent too much time out in the rest of the house doing things, she would call me back in for company. As Rosemary was now in a hospital bed in her bedroom, her own bed was vacant beside her. The hospital bed was necessary as she was no longer able to assist with any transfers out of bed. The hydraulics of the hospital bed also allowed her to sit up without breaking my back, or the night carer's back. So when there were no other duties to do, other than to keep her company, I took to lying on her old bed while we talked. Rosemary was most comfortable resting on her side, so this allowed her less effort and was rather snug for me, too.

Before long we fell into the habit of having an afternoon nap each. Her street was peaceful at that time of day, and I was right there if she needed anything. So I slept well, getting myself all snuggly under the blankets. We would wake and share any dreams we'd had and continue lying there talking to each other until I had to get up and attend to things. They were special, tender times for us both.

One afternoon, while we were lying down talking, Rosemary asked me what death is like, the actual dying part. Other clients had asked this, too. I guess it is just like when people ask others of their experience in various things, like pregnant women ask other women what childbirth is like. Or people who have travelled will ask other travellers what a particular country is like. But in this case, a dying person cannot ask someone who has died what it is like, as they are rarely around anymore to tell them. So they often asked me of my opinions and of what I had experienced. With honesty, I always told them about Stella going out smiling. I also shared how all of the transitions I had witnessed were over in a short time. Stella's story always brought them peace, just as it had for me in being there.

In modern society, such little emphasis is put on spiritual and emotional wellbeing in the treatment of dying people, or in the treatment of anyone who is ill. Unless dying people are blessed to be in a centre that embraces these aspects of life, they are usually left to wonder about these things. This is very frightening for them, as well as isolating. There is an enormous gap between treating physical health and even *acknowledging* the *link* of spiritual or emotional health in modern society. By uniting these needs and treating all aspects of someone's journey, the dying person would be able to reconcile a great deal more within themselves prior to their last weeks or days.

This area is one of the obvious failings we have by hiding death from society's eyes. Dying people have so many questions, things that could have been asked much earlier in their life had they considered that they would one day die, as we all will. If asked earlier, these questions about matters much deeper would allow people to find their answers and their own peace sooner. They would then not have to live in denial about their approaching death out of pure fear and terror, as was often the case.

It came a time, though, when Rosemary could no longer deny her approaching death. There were times when she wanted to be alone, 'much to contemplate,' she would say.

As I came back into her room early one evening, she declared, "I wish I'd let myself be happier. What a miserable person I have been. I just didn't think I deserved to be. But I do. I know that now. Laughing with you this morning I realised that there was no need at all to feel guilty for being happy." Sitting down on the side of her bed, I listened as she went on.

"It really is our own choice, isn't it? We can stop ourselves from being happy because we think we don't deserve it, or because we allow the opinions of others to become a part of who we are. But it is not who we are, is it? We can be whoever we allow ourselves to be. My God, why didn't I work this out sooner? What a waste!"

Lovingly, I smiled at her. "Well, I've been in that place, too, Rosemary. But being gentle and compassionate is a healthier way to treat yourself. At any rate, you've worked it out now, by allowing at least some happiness into your life recently. We've had some beautiful times." Recalling things we had laughed at, Rosemary agreed, and found herself in a happy mood again.

"I am starting to like who I am these days, Bronnie, this lighter side of me." Smiling, I said I liked this side of her, too. "Oh, wasn't I a tyrant?" she chuckled, thinking back to our first weeks together.

It wasn't all laughter between us, though. There were moments shared that were sad and tender, too, when we held hands and cried together, knowing what awaited her. At least Rosemary had experienced some happiness in her final months. She had such a beautiful smile. I can still see it.

On her last afternoon, pneumonia had taken over, and her throat was very thick with mucus. A few relatives had arrived by now, as well as a couple of lovely friends. While her departure was not entirely the smoothest I'd seen, it was incredibly brief. The dear woman had moved on elsewhere.

Due that afternoon was the community nurse, who arrived about ten minutes later. While Rosemary's relatives and friends were out chatting in the kitchen, the nurse and I cleaned her and then dressed her in a fresh nightdress. The nurse was one who hadn't met Rosemary, and as we were attending to her body, she asked me what she had been like as a person.

Looking at the body of my lovely friend, and at the peaceful face that now lay sleeping forever, I smiled. Memories of our afternoons lying in accompanying beds came flooding back. Images of Rosemary laughing, giving me cheek, also flashed by.

"She was happy," I replied truthfully. "Yes. She was a happy woman."

HAPPINESS IS NOW

Of all of my clients, Cath was by far the philosopher of them all. She had an opinion on everything. But it wasn't blind opinion, rather very informed. As a lover of knowledge and philosophy, she had absorbed a huge amount of learning in her fifty-one years. Cath also still lived in the house she was born in. "My mother was born and died here. I am going to do the same," she stated with determination.

She was also a lover of baths, so the best conversations we had in our first couple of months together were usually with her in the bath and me sitting on a stool beside it. With my own love and appreciation of a good soak, I was determined to help Cath use her tub for as long as possible. After a while, though, she had grown weaker and wasn't going to be strong enough to get in or out anymore, even with my assistance. The risk of a fall was also too high.

When she knew it was to be her last ever soak in the bath, Cath started to cry, her tears falling into the water surrounding her. "It's all going. It's the bath now," she cried. "Then it will be my walking. Then I won't even be able to stand, then me, myself, gone. It's all going. My life is winding down." Her crying soon became sobbing, raw and uninhibited. As much as my heart felt for her, and my own tears were very near the surface, it was also good to see someone able to release their emotions with such honesty.

From the depths of her soul, Cath cried a river of tears. When it seemed there was nothing left to come out, she sat in the bath quietly, exhausted from her sobbing, staring at the water or drawing patterns on the surface. Then it would start again, each sob coming from a place even deeper and more primal than before. She cried for every sad memory ever held within her, for all of the people she had lost, for all of those she would lose by going. But especially, Cath cried for herself.

Any time I would attempt to leave, to give her some privacy, she would shake her head and ask me to stay. So I sat on the stool, sending her love, saying nothing, just being there while she sobbed. It was heartbreaking but healthy at the same time, knowing she was letting go from such a deep place.

When another half an hour had passed and the water was losing its heat, I offered to top it up with some more. Cath shook her head. "No, it's OK. It's time," and with that, pulled the plug and looked to me for assistance in getting out. Taking her in her wheelchair out into the sun soon after, wrapped in her pale blue dressing gown and fiery red slippers, she seemed peaceful.

"Listen to the bird," she smiled. We both sat quietly, delighting in its song, smiling even more when we heard its mate reply from a tree farther up the street. "Every day is a gift now, you know. Every day was always a gift, but it's only now I have slowed down enough that I am truly seeing the huge amount of beauty each day offers to us. We can take so much for granted. Listen." Different songs rang out from a few nearby trees.

Cath said how she had come to see what a powerful force gratitude is. It is too easy to always want more from life, she said, and that's fine to a degree, since expanding who we are is a part of dreaming and growing. But as we will never have everything we want and will always be growing, appreciating what we already have along the way is the most important thing. Life goes so fast, she stated, whether you live until your twenties, forties, or eighties. She was right. Every day in itself is a gift and a blessing. It is all we ever have anyway, the moment we are in.

For the past twenty years I had kept a gratitude journal, where I wrote a few things down at the end of the day for which I was grateful. Often there were lots of things to be grateful for. But occasionally, through the darkest times, I struggled to come up with any. Emotional exhaustion had worn me out to such a point that even finding a few blessings was an effort. Yet I always persisted. Even then I would manage to come up with things I was grateful for, like clean water, somewhere to sleep, food in my belly, a smile from a stranger, or a bird singing.

But, as I explained to Cath, while I was appreciating things at the end of the night when I was writing them down, it had still taken some training to get into the habit of always appreciating things as they were happening as well, particularly intricate things. At the very least, it was a new habit to create by saying a silent prayer of thanks at the very time each of the gifts was given.

Nature had always received thanks in the moment, definitely. An example I gave was if a soft breeze kissed my face, I was grateful for being healthy enough to be outside to feel it. But I wanted to be more grateful for other things along the way, too. Although writing in the journal had certainly opened me up to a much better level of gratitude, it was the success of living more presently that had finally brought gratitude into my every day living situations. There is something to say thank you for every hour, I decided, and that was how my habit was formed.

"Then I'm sure you receive many blessings, if you are grateful along the way?" Cath enquired.

"When I allow it, Cath, when I remember my own worth and let it flow, yes. I've definitely had some great blessings in my life. Sometimes I just have to get out of my own way first. Like everyone, blessings come to me more when I am in a place of gratitude and flow."

Cath laughed at my theory and agreed. "Yes, it wants to flow to us. But without gratitude and allowing it through, we block it, I think. Most people just don't realise how good they have it. I didn't for a long time either. But thankfully I had started working it out before this illness struck, so I was able to live from a better place in myself then."

After some lovely time in the sun, Cath needed her lunch and a rest. Lunch was ice cream and stewed fruit. That was all she could handle eating now. Everything else took too much effort to chew, she told me, and tasted lifeless. Afterwards, I lifted her legs up onto the bed and moved her into a comfortable position, then drew the curtains closed. Her painkillers had recently been increased, which left her more comfortable but exhausted. So in no time, she was in a deep sleep.

In the early evening, Cath's ex-girlfriend dropped by to say hello. There were no hard feelings between them. They had remained good friends after their breakup more than a decade ago. It was a kind and respectful friendship. Other visitors were regular as well, such as Cath's older brother and his wife and children, and her younger brother. Some neighbours dropped in daily, and friends and work colleagues also came by every chance they could. She was a well-loved woman.

From the various stories shared by her visitors, Cath had been very driven in her work but usually with positive energy for everyone. Now, as with any dying person, she loved her visitors to bring her up to date on their lives and what was happening in the world outside her fence. When dying people can no longer live in that world themselves, they seem to savour every morsel of news from outside. Often friends and relatives don't know what to say. Hearing about life outside keeps a person in the swing of things, and this is positive for them, not negative.

Such was definitely the case for Cath. She wanted to hear about happy things as much she could. It was hard for the visitors, though, as they were often heartbroken at the impending loss of someone they loved. Because of our easy connection, I was able to speak openly with Cath about anything. So at the request of her friend Sue, I touched on the emotions of her visitors one day.

Sue was battling every day to stay positive for her friend, when all she wanted to do was to sob her eyes out every time she visited. Sue told me how she would sit in her car outside, psyching herself into being strong and happy before each visit. Then she'd sit out there again afterwards, crying her heart out. "I sort of see that," Cath admitted later. "I just don't know if I can deal with Sue's sadness on top of my own. I can't carry that, too."

"But you don't have to carry it," I said. "Just allow her to express herself honestly by not changing the subject when she shares her feelings. She needs to say stuff, and all you need to do is allow her to. You don't have to carry it as well. She's not asking you to do that. She just needs to tell you how much she loves you, and she can't do it without crying or without you letting her."

Cath understood where I was coming from and said she felt slack for creating so much sadness for everyone. It almost embarrassed her. "Gosh, Cath, at this time in your life, does pride really matter?" I asked directly, but kindly. She laughed in reply. "Just bring it out into the open and allow others to tell you how much they love you," I said.

Cath smiled at me and sat silent for a moment before responding. "Some time ago, when I was realising the seriousness of my disease, I learned to accept my feelings and not reject them. They come up, and I allow them to now. That's how I was so free sobbing in front of you that day in the bath. I've learned to accept my feelings as what they are in the moment, without rejecting them by trying to block them out. They are really just a by-product of my thoughts and mind anyway. I know it is possible to create new feelings by focusing on better things. But those within me already are a part of the current me, and are best released, not carried forward. Yet here I am, not respecting the feelings of others by rejecting and blocking their honest expression." Cath shook her head at herself and sighed. Then after a moment's thought, she looked at me smiling, and said, "I guess it is time for me to be brave and let their tears flow, too."

Nodding in agreement, I suggested that things could still possibly be light on occasions following. But the current build-up of emotions from her friends and relatives needed to be shared. They loved her, and they needed to be able to say and show this, even if it meant through tears sometimes.

Soon after, there were many tearful conversations between Cath and her visitors, but the love that flowed was inspiring. Hearts were opened – and though they were breaking in some ways, they were healing, too, through the expression of love now flowing.

On one particularly tearful day, the last friend had just left. She was laughing through tears of both sadness and joy as her and Cath cracked jokes with each other until she was out of sight. When she was gone, Cath looked at me with love. "Yes, it is important to let feelings come out, to accept them. And it is healthy for my friends as well," she said. "These will also be better memories for them. They won't be blocked by carrying things they don't need to."

Enjoying her analysis, I nodded in understanding. In my darker days, I'd finally been able to separate myself from my feelings, realising they were just an emotional expression of my pain, or joy, and were not who I truly was. Like everyone, I carried the wisdom of my soul within me. But to know my true self, that divine wisdom residing within, I had to allow my feelings out. If not, they would always block me from reaching the potential of who I was truly here to be. So I loved to hear of Cath coming to similar conclusions, but expressing it in her own words.

Already being a thin build, it took very little time for her to start looking ill as the weight continued to fall off. "My time is winding up. I can't ignore the signs, that's for sure," she declared one morning, while sitting on the commode. So many conversations with clients happened as they sat doing their morning business on the portable toilet, while I sat nearby. The fact that they were having a bowel movement never really came into it. It was just a part of the routine, and there was no point in letting such business get in the way of a good yarn. As I helped Cath back to bed after, I agreed that indeed, the signs were pointing to her time winding up.

Once settled back into bed, she said, "I am not sorry for how I have lived, because I have learned through most of what I have done. But if I was to do anything differently, given the chance to again, I would have allowed more happiness in." I was a little puzzled to hear these words from her. By now I had heard them from other clients, of course, but Cath appeared as a happy person. Well, as happy as one can be when you are dying and feeling absolutely awful in your body in the process. So I questioned her on this.

Explaining that she had loved her work, she then told me of how she had put too much emphasis on the results. Cath had worked on projects for troubled youths and believed that making a contribution was vital for a satisfying life. "We all have talents to share, every single one of us. It doesn't matter what your job is. What matters is that you are trying to make a conscious contribution, hoping to create a better world," Cath elaborated. "The only way things are going to improve is for us all to realise the inter-connectedness we share. Nothing good can be done alone. If only we could learn to work together for the good of all, instead of against each other in competition and fear."

Despite being exhausted and spending her time now mostly confined to bed, Cath still had a lot to say. The philosopher would be the last part of her to go, I suspected (which suited me just fine). I rubbed cream into her arms and hands as she went on. "We all have a positive contribution to make. I've made mine. But while I was searching for my purpose in life, I forgot to enjoy myself along the way. It was all about the result of finding what I was looking for. Then when I did find work I loved, work I could do with the heartfelt intention of contributing, I was still results-based."

This was something I had seen often. They were also familiar words from other clients. While working towards goals, the present moment is too often neglected along the way. This is what Cath was talking about. Her happiness was based on the end result, and was not enjoyed during the process of getting there. I commented that none of us were immune from doing that at times, myself included.

She continued. "Yes, but this way, I have robbed myself of potential happiness. That's what I mean when I say I would do it differently. It is important, sure, to work towards finding your purpose and contributing to the world, in any capacity. But depending on the end result for your happiness is not the way to do it. Gratitude for every day along the way is the key to acknowledging and enjoying happiness now. Not when the results come in or when you retire, or when this or that happens." Cath sighed, exhausted from her fervent outburst but with a need to be heard, as was so often the case.

After listening and then sharing my understanding of her thoughts, I adjusted her blankets and headed out to the kitchen to make us some tea. Cutting some fresh lemongrass from the garden, I thought about Cath's words. Very similar words from other dying people came to mind, too. As a bird sang and the scent of lemongrass, now in the teapot, wafted through the kitchen, it was very easy to feel completely present and grateful.

Wanting to relax and listen now, Cath asked me where I lived. Laughing a little, I explained how this was the first question any of my friends asked me whenever they called. "Where are you these days?" were words my ears knew well. So I told Cath all about my earlier years of drifting, followed by the recent years of house-sitting, and how recently, my energy for such a transient existence was beginning to wane. House-sits were not as forthcoming or consistent for me in Melbourne as they had been in Sydney. Not knowing where I'd be living next was starting to leave me weary, as was the whole moving process. Something I had once thrived on and loved was now beginning to exhaust me.

After staying with a few friends in between house-sits, I had recently rented the spare room of a house belonging to a woman I knew a little. Although I was hugely grateful for her kindness and to not be moving every few weeks, it was still very much her domain. So it never truly felt like home and was not ideal for the long-term.

Yet it was all meant to be, as the situation served to intensify the longing for my own space again. It had been almost a decade since I'd had my own kitchen and home space. The desire for this continued to increase daily. Cath said how she couldn't even imagine such a life when she had lived in the same house for fifty-one years. I said I couldn't imagine her life either and that even though I was starting to long for my own space again, a part of me would always love to roam a little. Now, though, I was thinking in terms of having a settled base and travelling from there, rather than moving my whole home base every time itchy feet kicked in.

The years of roaming, which had been a part of me for my whole adult life, were a big part of who I used to be. But changes were happening within me, and I no longer had the desire or energy to maintain the life I had before. All I really wanted was my own kitchen again and the privacy to be in my own space.

Agreeing that change is a guaranteed part of life, Cath laughed and said I helped the law of averages out by changing my life so often. Replying that people like me were needed to balance out people like her who lived in the same house for half a century, we both giggled. Our lives were so different, yet we shared a very strong connection. It was due to our shared love of philosophy.

Wanting to know how I ended up in this field of palliative care, Cath was astonished when I spoke of all of my years in the banking industry. "Oh, I cannot imagine it at all," she said surprised.

"Me either, thank goodness," I laughed. It amazed me thinking back to then, just how much can be fit into one lifetime, and how it was difficult to even imagine myself being in that world, let alone for so long. "Stockings, high heels, and corporate uniforms just never sat right for me Cath, nor did the structured life."

"I'm not surprised, considering the life you have chosen since," she chuckled, before turning more serious and asking how long I was going to do this work for and if I had any other career aspirations. There was no point holding back. I had already learned the importance of honesty and it felt marvellous to be able to talk so freely on this topic. Many things had been on my mind in this regard recently, and talking them out with Cath gave me some clarity.

Somewhere along the way in the last twelve months or so, the idea of teaching songwriting in a jail had come to mind. The prison system was something I knew nothing about, yet the idea had stuck with me. Over this time the seed had continued to grow slowly. I had recently made some contact with a great woman who had taken me under her wing, guiding me through the possibilities of finding funding.

"Yes, get back to the living, Bronnie. It is beautiful work you do here and obviously a part of your purpose this time around. But it must wear you down sometimes," Cath insisted. Telling her how it had now been almost eight years since I first began working in this field, I felt something shift within, an acknowledgment that I was indeed close to hitting the wall if I continued. I was starting to burn out.

Seeing people find their peace and being a witness to their growth in the sunset of their life was an incredible honour. It brought me many, many rewards of satisfaction and fulfillment.

There was no denying that I had loved this work and still did. But I also wanted to work where there might perhaps be a little bit of hope, around people who had a chance to grow and change their lives considerably before they were dying. The desire for working entirely in a creative field had also been building, as had the hope of being able to work more from home, once I did find my own space to live in again.

Hearing myself speaking all of these thoughts out loud to Cath gave tangible energy to the process. Before I knew it, ideas about teaching in a jail were occupying my thoughts more and more. My time in care work was coming to an end. It needed to. I'd given almost all I could to it.

Not long before passing on, Cath got a second wind and appeared to be getting better for a couple of days. I'd seen this before and telephoned all of her regular visitors to come and spend some brief time with her, as she was about to turn onto the final, downward slope. Some of them questioned me after their visit, as she looked so great and her energy had improved. It seems to be a blessing we are occasionally given after someone has been ill for so long. It helps us to remember them with a bit of their old spark, before the illness had taken over. Laughter rang out from Cath's room for two days while she cracked witty jokes and enjoyed beautiful clarity with friends and family.

When I arrived the following day, though, I was looking at a dying woman, hardly able to even respond to me verbally. Cath was limp with no strength at all and remained this way for another three days. She mostly slept, but when she was awake she smiled at me, as I changed her pads and washed her. Even the luxury of urinating on a commode was now in the past.

Friends returned and left solemnly, knowing they had just said their final goodbye to their dear Cath. At the end of the third day, it was obvious she would not make it through the night. So when my shift was finished, I stayed on there with Cath's brother and sister-in-law. The night carer had never seen a dead body and was hugely relieved I was staying. Thinking back to when I had been in that position all of those years ago myself, I saw how far I had come.

Little did I know just how many beautiful people I would meet, in such a personal way, nor the unforeseeable blessings of learning that would flow to me.

Cath's painkillers had been given to her intravenously for the last few days, as she could no longer swallow solid tablets. The palliative care nurse arrived in the evening to dispense some more. Cath was no longer awake or coherent. "This will be the last," she told Cath's brother and me. "She won't make it through the night anyway." We thanked her gently, and I walked her out. "She'll be gone within the hour," the nurse told me as I said goodbye at the gate. There was so much joy and sadness in this role: Sadness in saying goodbye and letting go. Happiness for the end of their suffering and for the love we shared. It was bittersweet and some tears slowly fell.

Cath didn't wait another hour. She passed away as I was walking back to her room. Her breathing had simply slowed down and then stopped. Looking at her lying there, that beautiful spirit now elsewhere, I smiled through my tears, still hearing her voice in my head. "Don't hang around with dying people forever – let some joy back in," she had said to me in a dying whisper the previous morning.

My tears burst forth, and I let them flow, as I stood beside her bed. "Happy travels, my friend," I said silently from my heart. Her brother and sister-in-law came around to the side of the bed, each giving me a loving hug, through their own tears. Formalities were then to be attended, which her family wanted to do. So I looked back at Cath's body one last time, a body I had washed and massaged so many times. But Cath wasn't in there anymore. Her spirit had moved on. She was still in my heart, though, and smiling softly, I said my final goodbyes to her and her family. The night carer also said goodnight, before she headed off down the road. Then walking out of Cath's home for the last time, the streetlights shining bright in the quiet suburban street, I pulled the gate closed behind me.

The world always felt surreal after I had experienced a passing. My senses were heightened, and I felt like I was observing the world from somewhere else. As I walked up the stairs of the tram, I was hardly aware of others around me. The world went by outside as I sat thinking about Cath and the beautiful time we had shared.

When the tram stopped at a red light, I watched laughing people walking into a restaurant. It was a balmy evening and everyone I saw coming and going was jovial. My tired, weary eyes smiled, viewing signs of such happiness. Sounds from inside the tram then came to my ears, after having been zoned out for some time. All I heard from there were happy conversations as well. It was just one of those nights, where happiness was in the air. Although there had been certainly been sadness in my night, there was happiness, too, for having known Cath.

The sounds of laughter from others danced with me, bringing me happiness of my own. As the tram moved on again, I looked out the window and thought about the good hearts of people everywhere and of those who were in my view. Gratitude warmed my own heart, and I couldn't help but smile.

I wasn't thinking of the past or the future. Happiness is now. And that is where I was.

A MATTER OF PERSPECTIVE

ﾞﾟﾟﾟﾟﾟﾟﾟﾟﾟﾟﾟﾟﾟﾟﾟﾟﾟﾟﾟﾟﾟﾟﾟﾟﾟﾟﾟﾟﾟﾟﾟﾟﾟﾟﾟﾟﾟﾟ

One of my final clients and one who had a beautiful and lasting impression on me was a dear man who was in a nursing home. It was still with reluctance that I ever took any of these shifts. They always brought me down the moment I walked through the door, leaving me feeling heartbroken from seeing the situations of these people. So it was only when there was absolutely no work on the horizon with private home clients that I accepted the work. In this case, I was very glad I did.

Lenny was already close to passing when we met. His daughter had employed me as an extra, knowing that regular staff members at the nursing home were all too busy to give him the care she wanted him to have. He slept much of the day, accepting cups of tea but declining all food. When he awoke, he would pat the side of the bed for me to sit close to him, as he didn't have the energy to speak loudly. "It has been a good life," he would say regularly. "Yes, a good life."

This was certainly a matter of perspective and reinforced how happiness is based on choice far more than circumstances. Lenny's life had not been easy at all. Both of his parents had died before he was fourteen, his siblings either dying or dispersing over the following years until he had lost contact with them all. He met Rita, the love of his life, when he was twenty-two and married her in a whirlwind, as he put it.

Four children came from the marriage. Their oldest son had died in the Vietnam War, something he still shook his head about. Lenny spoke fiercely of war and the insanity of it. He said he would never understand how anyone could possibly think that war would ever bring lasting peace. His thoughts about the madness and sadness of the current world situation were shared. I soon valued this lovely man's intelligence and philosophies.

Staff members would drop by now and then offering food, which he always declined with a smile and a shake of his head, resting against the pillow. The busy activity in the halls seemed to fade away after a while, as if we were in our own dimension, totally unaffected by the noise nearby.

Their eldest daughter had married a Canadian man and moved there. She died six months later, after losing control of her car in a snowstorm. "A shining star," he said of her. "She was always a shining star, and now she is one forever."

Working in this field I had long ago given up the effort of trying to hold back my tears. The more I evolved, the more naturally my emotions were expressed anyway, without thought. So much effort in society is put into keeping up appearances, but it all comes at too high a price.

The honesty of my own emotions also helped the families at times, as it gave them permission to let their own tears flow. Some people had not allowed themselves to cry for their whole adult life. More and more I had become an advocate for honesty. So it was that an occasional tear fell as Lenny shared his stories with me. There was just something about the beauty of this man and the way he told his story that triggered it, I think.

Lenny's youngest son had been too sensitive for the world and spiralled into mental illness. In those days, the support systems were not in place for this, and if the family could not cope completely, patients were admitted to mental asylums. Lenny and Rita wanted to keep Alistair at home in a loving environment, but were not allowed to by doctors. Alistair spent the rest of his years in a drugged haze, and Lenny never saw him smile again.

Their remaining daughter now lived in Dubai, where her husband had a construction contract. She phoned the nursing home while I was working and spoke with me. She was a nice person to speak with, but unable to get home to her father.

His love, Rita, had died in her late forties, only a few years after they had lost Alistair to the mental health system. From Rita's diagnosis to her departure, it was only a matter of weeks. Yet here was this lovely man telling me he had had a good life. Through tears, I asked how he saw it that way. "I have known love, and it is love that has not lessened for one day in all of these years," he told me.

I found myself not wanting to go home at the end of the shift, but Lenny needed his rest anyway. As I returned each day, I prayed he would still be there. It was a difficult thing in a way. I knew he wanted to go, to be with Rita again and to the children he had lost. In that regard, I wished for him a speedy departure. But for my own growth and connection with him, I wanted to hold on as long as I could.

He had worked hard, too hard, he said. But it had numbed his pain initially, and he didn't know any other way to deal with his losses. In later years, on the recommendation of Rose, his daughter in Dubai, he had sought counselling and had learned to speak of it all. Talking of his losses had healed him well and he was now able to speak about his life freely. I told him I was grateful he could.

He asked me about my life and found it fascinating how a young woman would sell all of her belongings, pack up her car, and head off into a new life, with no idea at all of where she would end up. And that she had done this quite often.

I explained how much my first serious relationship had affected my life. There were parts of me back then yet to be discovered (as there always will be). The suppression experienced at the time, though, seemed to create a tantalising invitation from the unknown life. When the relationship was finally over, I felt a sense of freedom I had never known. I had met him when I very young, so had never truly known the freedom of adult life. By the end of the relationship, I was twenty-three and starting to do what all twenty-three year olds should be doing – having fun.

Driving six hours to a friend's wedding a few months later, I discovered a part of myself that was like coming home. Simply, a part of me belonged on the road and always would. It was the most natural thing in the world for me to be driving long distances. Since then, my freedom had become one of the biggest driving forces of who I was. Most of my decisions were based on how they would affect my freedom, and I shaped my life accordingly. Of course freedom can be obtained in a regular life, too. It is a state of mind more than anything. The freedom to be you is the greatest freedom of all, regardless of the town or suburb you live in.

Lenny said that many partners think they own each other. While there was definitely a need for compromise and commitment in any relationship, especially so if children are involved, it is up to each individual to maintain a sense of his or her own self. He questioned me more about my life with genuine curiosity, and listened when I told him I was thinking about moving on from this work. "Yes," he said. "There is a good life waiting for you, Bronnie, without having to spend all of your time around death. Get back amongst the living." He was a dear man, and I smiled at his blessing.

The nursing home was run by a Christian denomination. Lenny had stopped going to church after Rita died. Not because he didn't believe anymore, but because it was too painful for him to be there without hearing his beautiful wife's voice singing in the pew beside him. Lenny said he didn't care whether it was a Christian nursing home, one run by any other religion, or one run by no religion at all. He would have made the best of any situation. Either way, he was going home to Rita soon and that's all he cared about. But Christian it was, and there were many volunteers there as well as staff.

One of these was a man named Roy who would do the rounds, reading to the residents from the Bible each day. He had offered his services to Lenny months earlier, which Lenny had politely declined. Roy had persisted and offered them again on numerous occasions since, each time, Lenny again politely declined.

Now that Lenny was in his last days, with no strength to resist, Roy brought it upon himself to come in every afternoon and read passages from the Bible to him. He read for a long time. Even a well person, and one who was totally devoted to Bible study, would have grown a little weary by the end of his monotone delivery every day. Through politeness I also did my best to stay attentive as Roy read on. But sometimes I too nodded off without meaning to. Like I say, he read for a *long* time with no expression, a very long time.

Even worse was that Roy would then want to discuss the passage he had read with Lenny. As Lenny's carer, my priority was the well being of the client. So I gently explained that Lenny was only able to speak when he had the energy to, which was true, and should not be forced.

"I know you're a lovely lady, Bronnie," Lenny said to me quietly one day, after Roy had moved onto another room. "And I know you like to think well of people. But if that bloke comes back in here again, I am going to boot his butt from here to Timbuktu." We both laughed aloud, knowing full well that Roy would be back at the same time tomorrow.

"If I am not going to heaven by now, then what's the point of all of this religious stuff anyway?" he chuckled. "I can't concentrate on what he is saying regardless. I don't have the energy."

"His intention is kind, Lenny. That is the main thing surely," I replied. We both laughed gently about the situation. Roy was a sweet man, and although it was obvious he meant kindly, it *was* becoming a bit of a comedy sketch. Each afternoon when he arrived, we both knew what we were in for. He was really not doing the wise words of the Bible any justice through his monotonous, lifeless delivery. "You can sleep through it at least," I laughed. Lenny nodded to me, smiling.

The days were wearing on and other work had been offered to me, but I declined. I wanted to see this beautiful man out, if it worked out that way. I was feeling a loyalty to his daughter Rose, too. It would be awful to think that her dad is dying in another country and he has a new person to deal with every day. I also knew I would miss our quiet talks soon enough and didn't want to give them up any sooner than I had to. As it turned out, that time came around very quickly anyway.

It was a busy Thursday afternoon in the busy suburb. Everything was busy – the roads, the shops, and then the nursing home when I arrived. Staff members with food trolleys were buzzing about the corridors. Doctors were doing their rounds. Nurses rushed about with more work than they could handle. Patients were wheeled about in their big chairs, some of them drooling out the sides of their mouth, staring vacantly into space. Nursing homes were such tragically sad scenes, and today was no different.

As I walked past, office girls were moaning to each other about another office girl. I wondered how they could be so surrounded by death and yet still put their energy into complaining about trivial things. But by then, I'd already had the blessings of learning from many beautiful clients and from my own life. The things most people give their energy to are so irrelevant in the long run.

As usual, from the moment I walked into Lenny's room, it was like being in a different world. The peace in this slightly darkened room was felt the moment you entered. It had been this way from the start, and I had commented on it the first day to Lenny. He had smiled. "Ah yes, it is a peaceful space. But it takes a certain person to recognise it. So many of the staff here come in with all of their busyness and miss the feel of the room completely." I observed this afterwards. A few of his visitors were peaceful people, though, and they felt it immediately as well, which was nice.

Dragging the chair closer to Lenny as he lay sleeping, I read a book for a while. But my mind was on him. He stirred after some time and saw I was there. Patting his hand on the bed for my hand, I gave it to him. Smiling, he drifted back to sleep and the hours went by. Every now and then he would stir, and I would give him a sip of drink or just kiss his hand.

"It's been a good life," he said quietly from the silence as he woke. "It's been a good life." He drifted off again as I watched lovingly. My heart was aching and a few tears started falling. I wondered why I couldn't have settled for an easier job with no emotional attachment. It was just too painful at times. Yet I knew that other jobs didn't come with the gifts I also received in knowing my clients.

"Mmm. A good life," he repeated, opening his weary eyes again and smiling at me. Seeing my tears, he squeezed my hand. "Don't you worry, my girl, I'm ready." His voice was almost a whisper. "Promise me something."

I wanted to sob, but I just smiled through my tears. It was one of those smiles that aren't really smiles, just a sign of someone trying to be brave but not succeeding. "Of course, Len."

"Don't worry about the little stuff. None of it matters. Only love matters. If you remember this, that love is always present; it will be a good life." His breathing was changing and it was getting harder for him to talk.

"Thanks for everything, Len," I managed through my tears. "I'm so glad we met." They seemed like such childish words in a way, as there was so much more I could have said and wanted to. But in the end, they conveyed my feelings in the simplest way. Leaning over and kissing his forehead, I saw that he was drifting off again.

I sat there allowing my tears to flow freely. Sometimes it takes just loosening the tap on tears to find there is a whole collection of them waiting to pour out. You don't even know what they are all for. I had loosened the tap and cried and cried. But Lenny continued to sleep through the next few hours. It was possible he would never wake again. When my tears were drained, I sat quietly, looking at him with tenderness. Then, of course, in walked Roy.

I wanted to laugh, knowing Lenny would see the humour of the situation if he had been awake. But he wasn't awake, and my gentle smile to Roy, through eyes bloodshot and tired from buckets of tears, told him the full picture. Lenny may not wake up again.

A few slow tears of love fell again. But it was no longer a torrent of sorrow, and they eased off before long. I think it was seeing Roy's sweet face and knowing his kind intentions that had set me off, even if a part of me knew that Lenny didn't particularly want him there.

Roy sat on the other side of the bed. He opened his Bible to start reading but looked to me for approval. I just pulled a face that said, "Well, it's up to you, but I think he'd like the peace." He nodded. The Bible stayed open in his hands, but he didn't read. I loved him then for respecting the reverence of the moment. It's not that him reading the Bible would not have been a reverent intention. But it wasn't necessary in the already existing sacredness of the moment.

Lenny reached for my hand with his eyes still closed. I stood up and gave it to him. His breathing was rattling and irregular. I could smell what had now become too familiar to me, but which is impossible to describe. It was the smell of death.

Then opening his eyes, Lenny looked straight at me and smiled.

But it wasn't my mate Lenny whom I had come to know. It was Lenny and the full glory of his soul. There was no illness in his smile. It was one of a soul now free of ego and personality.

It was *pure* love, completely free of everything else, radiant, glowing, and joyous.

I smiled back with honesty as my heart burst open. Both of us smiled joyfully, knowing it is all just love in the end. I'd never known such absolutely uninhibited smiling, given or received. There was *nothing* in the way. It was just pure joy. As we both smiled into each other beaming, time was frozen.

After a while, Lenny closed his eyes and a peaceful smile remained on his lips. My own smile remained, as my heart was just too open to stop smiling.

A couple of minutes later, Lenny passed on.

Watching from the other side of the bed, Roy's life was transformed. Closing his Bible, he said quietly that he now understood what God's love looked like and felt he had experienced a miracle seeing Lenny's peace before passing. I agreed that God works in mysterious ways.

Roy and I sat in the silence for a while longer. I knew the moment would be gone as soon as I notified the staff, which I needed to do before long. When we said goodbye, Roy held my hand for a long time, trying to find the right words, unsure what to say or how to articulate what had happened. He seemed hesitant to let me go, as if it would pop his balloon if he didn't have me there to share the story.

"We've been blessed, Roy. That's all we need to know," I said to him gently. He grabbed me and hugged me tightly, like a frightened child, not wanting to be alone with it. "You're going to be alright, Roy."

"How do I explain this to anyone?" he pleaded with me.

"Perhaps you don't," I smiled. "Or perhaps you do. Either way, the same force that just gave us that miracle will be there for you again to help you say the right words if you need to share them."

Shaking his head, but with a smile of joy he said, "My life will never be the same." I smiled lovingly at him, and we hugged again.

When all of the paperwork was done, I left the nursing home. There was too much activity now around Lenny's body, and we'd had our time. Peak hour traffic had gone, and the late afternoon light shone spectacularly on the tree-lined avenue I walked. My heart was open and smiling. I was in love with everything and everyone.

Yes, the job had had its ups and downs. But no amount of planning or qualifications could have ever given me the gifts that this role had bestowed upon me time after time.

Still euphoric from the gift of love I had been given, tears of joy and gratitude fell as I walked with a huge smile.

Yes. It is a good life, Lenny. It is a good life indeed.

CHANGING TIMES

❦

Caring for so many dying people had left me both elated and exhausted. Countless positive changes had unfolded in my life as a result, but I was definitely ready for a change and pursued the idea of teaching songwriting in the women's prison system.

There was a lot of red tape and much to learn about the private philanthropic sector – which foundations had funding guidelines available that my project would fit into, and how to make the applications. Some of my guidance came from a group of women who had been doing theatre workshops in jails for several years. As it turned out, I had been living right next door to them during my first Melbourne chapter almost a decade ago. Back then, though, I hadn't even written my first song. So I was hardly in the position to set up a songwriting program, but it was strangely delightful to walk down that street again to their place, all the while gauging the changes in my life and self since living there.

My initial efforts brought no success in any jails in Victoria, so I decided to try for New South Wales. Also, I was conducting a long-distance relationship with a man in New South Wales. I didn't think the relationship was going to work, but it had a better chance if we were closer together rather than being separated by a thousand kilometres. A delightful cousin also lived in the area chosen and offered to put me up while I found somewhere to live.

Liz, who had taken me under her wing months earlier, was my greatest help through the whole establishment process for the jail program. Her insistence that anything can be done by using networks of people and linking the right ones up kept me encouraged. I was also reminded of words from many clients, in that nothing good can be done alone. We need to work together. Liz also educated me on the need to find an auspice for the funding. Most philanthropic foundations required a charity to receive the funds on my behalf, enabling the foundation to enjoy the tax concessions that come with donating to charity groups. I would then invoice the charity for the full amount and draw on that as my wage as a self-employed person. Finding an organisation willing to channel these funds was somewhat challenging initially. As life would have it, though, I was reminded again of the cycles of life and how often we do a full circle.

Prior to moving to the country town I grew up in, my family had lived on the outskirts of Sydney. In those days (in the seventies), it was a rural area. My first year of schooling was undertaken there. Now, after numerous phone calls and emails, the auspice door finally opened to me, via the church connected with my very first school. Thirty-five years had passed and there I was, sitting in an office overlooking the playground I knew as a little girl in kindergarten. It added such beautiful sentimentality to the jail process for me.

The enthusiasm from the Senior Education Officer at the women's jail I chose also kept me hanging in there when funding applications became challenging. She was a progressive, enthusiastic woman and marketed my proposal to her regional management with complete belief in my vision. I had contacted two women's jails initially, but the differences of support offered were enormous. One said they would not even supply pens and notebooks. I would have to do that myself. The other offered not only those, but also guitars and anything else they could assist with. As I became more involved in the process, it became obvious that dealing with one jail and one class would be more than enough anyway. The choice of which of those jails to go with was very clear.

For ages things seemed like they weren't moving, but when it finally fell into place, it moved like lightning, and I was on the road north within a couple of days. For a month or so I lived with my cousin and her huge family. It was strange but wonderful to be around so many people again, after the quietness of my work and previous home situation. The house was pretty crazy with three generations living there, as well as seven cats and three dogs, but the longing for my own kitchen could not be ignored. Despite hearing that rentals were hard to get, I found a cottage the day after I decided it was time. It was up in the lower Blue Mountains, with a creek and bush land across the road and was as cute as a button.

With no belongings at all to live with, I wasn't fazed. It felt right, and the cottage had come my way so easily that my faith was strong. Everything I needed would come, and come it did. It poured forth in a torrent. The owners of a storage shed business offered me some things they had been asked to clear out, a lounge from one shed, some linen supplies from another. My cousin had lived in the area for decades and had an established community of friends. Through that, a washing machine came my way from under someone's house. Then a fridge arrived, as did bookshelves, kitchen things, curtains, and an antique desk. A huge network of people pitched in with excitement, giving me whatever they could, fascinated by my situation, and just being good-hearted people. It was beautiful.

I bought a van as soon as I arrived in New South Wales. Although I wanted to somewhat settle, I was also going to quite a few folk festivals and had been missing owning a bed on wheels. It was more my style than pitching a tent at festivals and helped me maintain a sense of freedom, knowing I could still go away whenever I wanted and to anywhere. My timing for the van purchase and the move into the cottage was also spot-on. I moved in the same month as the annual council cleanup was on in the neighbourhood.

Furniture that people no longer wanted was left out on sidewalks, to be thrown out or collected by whoever would like it before the council's rubbish truck arrived. People waved to me from their verandahs as I collected small things from their piles, smiling and encouraging me to take whatever I wanted – a cane washing basket, a narrow cupboard for my pantry, an outside table. I also picked up quite a few classic pieces of furniture. Previous owners even helped me to load some of the things into my van themselves, including an old but great lounge for my verandah.

I also attended lots of bargain filled garage sales and had

immense fun in the process. The only thing I cared about getting new was a mattress. I wanted one that was good for my back and one that no one else had slept on, with just my energy on it. A beautiful woman I knew a little gave me a housewarming present, because she was excited that I was settling down after so many years. The gift was exactly the cost of a mattress. So within three weeks, I went from having six boxes that fitted into a small car to having a fully furnished two-bedroom cottage that looked like I had lived in it for years. It was a fantastic time.

The first night there, I lay in the middle of the living room floor with my arms outstretched and smiled hugely. My own space! At last, I had my own space again. The relief, gratitude, and joy were so overwhelming that hardly anyone saw me for a month. I just couldn't bear to leave the house except for work. When I'd return home, I'd look at my place and be smiling all over again.

While I was not successful in getting the full amount of funds I had applied for, I was able to get the prison program started with what I did receive, thinking I would look at applying for further funding as time unfolded, through other foundations. Even receiving the funds I did, though, was a very exciting achievement, to have watched this idea turn into a reality. As the funding was provided through the private philanthropic sector and the prison system did not have to pay me, I was a volunteer in their eyes. My course outline had been approved. I demonstrated what I hoped to teach and achieve. Because my program was not an accredited one, I was not required to have teaching qualifications. The staff in the Education Department simply believed in my ideas and ability as I did, and were able to gain approval based on that, which in hindsight is rather fantastic really! At the time, though, I didn't see it as particularly unusual, as I was just going along with each step as it unfolded until I finally found myself standing in front of a room full of convicted criminals, teaching them songwriting!

Having never taught in any classroom environment in my life, to now be standing there with dozens of eyes on me, many unfriendly, was pretty interesting. It may have been daunting if I stopped to think about it, but I didn't. I just got on with the job.

Until I'd started liaising with the department, I had never been inside a jail either. So with lesson one prepared and a lot of guts, I began the class. It took some pretty dry humour to get any reaction at first as everyone just sat there stone faced, checking me out, and needing to stay cool in front of each other. But after a while, the women realised I was OK.

We were doing rhyming exercises and instead of using some of the examples I had intended from my lesson plan, I began improvising and making the rhymes funnier and more relevant to the situation, laughing at myself with them.

> *"I'm sitting here in my greens hoping for some tunes,*
> *Is she just going to talk rhyming words all damn afternoon?*
> *I want to learn to play guitar and be like Emmylou*
> *So I'll stick it out with her a while, what else can I do?"*

Some of the women then started to giggle and contribute to the class, adding more jokes, which enabled the rest of the inmates to relax and have a say, too.

> *"So come on, Miss, get on with it and teach us what to do*
> *'Cos for rhyming we don't give a shit, and we wish you*
> *wouldn't, too."*

Laughter broke the ice forever. Also, once we found a shared theme, in this case the music of Emmylou Harris, we were well and truly off and running.

> *"OK, OK, I hear you all, but there are things you must learn*
> *So humour me and do these rhymes, guitars then you will earn*
> *You will soon be playing songs from your own heart*
> *But the longer you put off this stuff, the later you will start."*

In reply I received:

> *"OK, Miss, if we must, we will write these silly rhymes*

But don't linger with this stuff too long, I want a guitar that's mine."

The banter continued in rhymes, and by the end of that first class, laughter was flowing freely. Most of the women were contributing well. It turned out to be great fun.

All of the people in the Education Department were good-hearted, and it was nice to be working in a team environment again after so much one-on-one work with clients in their homes. They warned me, though, to not get too close to the inmates and I understood this for security and privacy reasons. But I could only be myself and saw the students not as inmates, but as women learning to play the guitar and write songs. I was street-wise enough to remember I was in a jail, but I also lived by honesty, so I could still only be myself.

As a result of my sincerity and belief in each of them, barriers between us were dismantled over time as trust was established and strengthened. We chatted as women, and my encouragement for them to show their softer sides through songwriting allowed them to gradually remove the emotional walls they had built to protect themselves. The class became a very personal and healing space for the students. It was from this healing perspective I continued to design the curriculum.

Using various writing exercises, the women learned to release their emotions and eventually to write with hope. Songs of anger and hurt were written, certainly. There were songs of dreams and aspirations, too, though. When asked if they could do anything, if there were no limits on them in any way – no financial, geographical, skills-based limits – what would they do, they began dreaming and listening to their hearts for the first time in years. One wanted the freedom to live with her children without answering to government departments, another said she would be in a music video, one would have a tummy-tuck, another wanted to know life without domestic violence (which she had *never* known), one wished she could be free of her drug addictions forever, and another wanted to visit heaven and tell her mum she loved her.

As the honesty continued to flow, very few classes went by where tears were not shed. But we had made a pact that it was to be a supportive environment, no matter what. So women who once did not get along became tolerant and eventually supportive of each other in class. One woman was not even going to join the class due to another's presence. She did, though, and within about four classes, they were giving each other genuine encouragement for their songs and getting along well out in the yard, too. This was the nature of the class. The courage it took to express themselves so honestly gained the respect of the others, as they empathised and listened with genuine interest as each of their songs evolved.

It was also hugely confronting for them to learn to perform in front of the class. They encouraged each other, though, feeling the pain of their song's messages. One student, Sandy, wrote about how hard it had been as a half Aboriginal, half white woman, who didn't quite fit into either part of the town she lived in. Others in the class knew the same feeling and kept her encouraged, reinforcing the need for these things to be expressed.

Another, Daisy, had been in and out of jail so many times, mostly due to violence, that she didn't even know how long she was in for this time. She said she would go numb and tune out whenever she was in a courtroom, as it just overwhelmed her. (She was going to find out the length of her sentence soon after.) So she wrote about those feelings and how much she hated that her life was now a part of the system and never felt like her own anymore. Another student, Lisa, wrote a song for her son telling him how proud she was of him. She choked up with emotions every time she played it, but was very proud of herself, too.

Performing these songs in class was cathartic for them, as it allowed full expression, not just written expression, despite how it would challenge their nerves. But having been in this place emotionally myself years earlier, just as shy and nervous, I encouraged them gently, and the emotional walls of fear slowly crumbled. A few months later when one of my students, who had initially been very timid, played one of her new original songs solo in front of over a hundred inmates and visitors, it was me who was crying, joyfully.

The class numbers were not huge, but this suited everyone. The first few classes were overflowing, too big for efficiency, but after that it was usually about ten regular students. Others would come and go, but when they realised they wouldn't learn to play the guitar like Eric Clapton in one class – and more so, that the class involved genuine work – not all hung around. It was best that the classes were small. These were women who needed a lot of attention, and this way, I was able to attend to each of them individually. The songs and stories coming out were inspiring, healing, and beautiful. The love that flowed between us all was nurturing, to say the least. Underneath the hardened exteriors were people like you or me – people who loved their children, yearned for love and respect, wanted to feel useful and live self respecting lives.

Very few of the women were without guilt for what they had done. Most wanted to be better people. When I came to know each of their personal stories, though, all I could see were tragic histories, very low self-esteem, and a cycle they couldn't break out. They were in for various crimes, some for working illegally as prostitutes. In that regard, some women actually worked the system to their advantage. They knew the sentence length of many petty crimes so would commit one each year, enabling them to get off the cold streets for three months over winter, where they would at least have a warm bed in jail and regular meals. Others were in there for crimes ranging from drug use or possession, violence, fraud, shop-lifting (a habit she got into to feed her family then became addicted to), and driving under the influence of alcohol too many times.

Regardless of the actual crime, though, the prison system treated the crime, the effects, not their wounds, which were the underlying causes of their actions. While it was called a correctional facility, there was only limited help available for anyone seriously wanting to change their thinking and past patterns. This is the level where the healing was most needed, to break the cycles of low self-esteem, drug use, domestic violence, and the criminal life that had flowed from that. Perhaps some criminals would still commit crimes if given help. But those I came to know would certainly have changed their habits if given ongoing support in and beyond their jail-time.

There were some lovely people working in the system itself, but they were also up against it. There were also volunteers from church groups who managed to reach a few individuals, helping them to turn their lives around. The truth is that much more money was spent on security and red tape than on methods of healing and support. In a jail of about three hundred inmates, there were only two psychologists, and they were often unavailable because of lack of time and being overly committed. If you didn't already feel pretty low about yourself before you lived in a jail, you would certainly do so during and after.

Having watched an informative documentary about the success of meditation in jails and in turning people's lives around, I mentioned this to some of the staff and how I could put the right people in touch with them. The meditation path I followed had had success with teaching inmates meditation in other countries, but I was told 'Good luck', with a laugh and total discouragement. So instead, I worked within the capacity I could and that was with the students in my class, by helping them to start believing in their own beauty and goodness. I did this through teaching them songwriting and how to express themselves through original songs, songs they owned and could perform and share with others. Many of them had never had a compliment in their lives and were like a sponge with the positive feedback I gave them, all of which was genuine. Any suggestion for improvement of their songs was always delivered through gentle appraisal.

There were funny times, too, as they grew to trust me, educating me about life out in the yard. One day, one of the women was talking loudly to another about how she'd managed to score an extra pair of running shoes. When she realised I had heard her, she shut up immediately. With encouragement from me and other students, she explained the scheme to me. I commented that it was pretty clever thinking, only to hear, "Well, we are crims, Miss. Remember where you are," to which I cracked up laughing. By that time I had gained confidence and wasn't at all intimidated, so I found this statement rather funny.

Another student came to class one week looking quite wound up, yet exhausted at the same time. When I questioned if she was OK, she said, "Yeah, I'm fine now, Miss. I've just had a terrible morning. This chick has been giving me the shits for ages, so I put her head inside a clothes dryer. It's fine now." With slight astonishment I nodded, as if saying 'I see'. "Anyway, Miss, it's all good. I'm here and it's time for music. None of that matters when I'm here. If I didn't have this class to come to, I might have killed her. But they'd ban me from this class, and that would kill *me*." With that, she sat down and continued working on her song from the previous week. She was actually a brilliant songwriter with one of the nicest voices I've known. I wish we had met through other circumstances, as I would have loved to share songs around a campfire with her. That was never going to happen, though.

One week at a time, more and more positive transformations were unfolding. It was rewarding and beautiful to see. The staff members in the Education Department were also delighted with the success and positive changes in many of the students who came through the program. The class soon became the highlight of their week and mine.

By now I had ended the long-distance relationship I had been in, despite now living closer to each other. I was never going to be able to move in the direction my heart was calling by staying with that man. Our values were just too different. While there were tears shed and necessary growth through the sad process of letting go, I had come too far in myself to now start living a lifestyle untrue to my own values.

Home life was beautiful, and I delighted in playing host to friends who visited occasionally, instead of me doing all of the visiting as in the last decade or two. After so much roaming, it was not entirely surprising to find myself very much becoming a home person. It was rare that I would feel any inclination to go anywhere ,and I decided that in the long-term, I definitely wanted to work from home more.

So during my spare time, I developed an online songwriting course, based on what I was teaching to the women in the jail. My writing was also gaining momentum, with articles being published in various magazines, and I was writing a blog. This began gaining a lot of followers, which reinforced how much I loved connecting with like-minded people through my work. It also left me questioning if I wanted to keep doing the hard life of a performer. While teaching in the jail, my own music had slowed down a bit, though I was still doing some quality gigs now and then. When I was connecting with the right audiences and was totally lost in the music, I loved it, but writing and working from home began to bring more contentment.

Although the cottage and the jail job were wonderful, there wasn't much else to keep me in the area. Friends had moved on and life had changed since I'd previously lived nearby in Sydney. There was also a part of me that knew I would eventually end up living back in the country one day. In more than two decades of roaming, I had never lost the yearning for space that farm life gives. I didn't make many friends in the new area, as I was becoming more reclusive and loving being in my own place after years of roaming.

So without any true conscious awareness on my behalf, the students became my most local friends. Over time, the walls between teacher and student, or employee and inmates, fell down considerably. The class simply became a place where a group of women played music. I felt there wasn't that much separating the inmates from me, and at times, I could have just as easily been one of them. That's how it felt sometimes anyway. Certainly there were other moments when I didn't feel quite so much that way. I hadn't committed a crime to validate me being there, but there was always closeness between us, as women who were bonded by the honesty we experienced. My own fragility and painful past was also still shaping me in some ways, although nowhere near as much as previously. So this possibly strengthened the connection with the students, as their own pasts were full of pain, various kinds of abuse, and a lack of self worth also resulting from that.

When first arriving in the jail, I was guided how to deflect questions about my personal life. While I never told them where I lived, when they had asked I'd simply said I couldn't tell them, rather than point in some abstract direction or lie. The women were respectful of this, as trust now existed, but I answered the questions I could. Through all of the honest conversations with dying clients in the past, I'd also come to enjoy being more open. The emotional walls of privacy just block goodness out. Truth brings people together. They asked questions about my past, and I replied honestly, explaining what I had stupidly tolerated from others and believed for too long.

The kindness from these women as a group and individually woke something up in me that had been dormant for a very long time. Simply, I didn't know how to receive kindness. I knew how to give it, but not receive it. So when I felt their love for me, and their genuine understanding of my pain, it was overwhelming. These really were the kindest and most beautiful of women. They had all suffered, and many of them were missing their children and families with enormous longing. Yet their hearts were incredibly kind. Sure, they had messed up and made mistakes, ending up in jail, but few were without regret and none were without a good and loving heart.

The funding was running out, and after almost a year in the jail, I accepted that I wasn't only burning out from looking after dying people. I was actually burning out from life. There was just too much sadness around me. When tragedy happened to a couple of close friends and I tried to be there, life became even harder. Knowing how difficult it was to get the first round of funding, I wondered if I had the energy to do it all over again. Falling asleep that night, listening to my new neighbours having a screaming match with each other, my decision was made. It was time to return to country life. I had done all I was capable of doing at this point.

Most of my original students had been released by now or were about to be, so this freed me up a lot. Having the clarity and energy to teach new students was not going to be possible. It was time to learn how to look after me. So I gave my notice at the jail and to the landlord, and began making plans.

My parents were getting older. Mum and I were as beautifully close as always in our friendship, and I was enjoying a lovely relationship with my dad. So I wanted to be closer and more accessible to them, at least within a few hours' drive. This is not far in an Australian's perception of distance. I also wanted to live somewhere nearer the coast.

The suitable area was chosen and I began scanning the Internet pages of house rentals. I decided which two towns I wanted to live between and what my rent limit would be. When nothing suitable had presented itself within a couple of weeks, I put an advertisement in the local paper, stating clearly what I was looking for. A couple of situations were offered, though neither felt right, but I made new contacts and the availability of a great little cottage came to my attention very soon after. It was exactly where I had wanted, for exactly the amount of rent I could afford and before I knew it, I was living on a two thousand acre farm.

DARKNESS AND DAWN

❧⊙❧

A running creek passed in front of the cottage, which brought an ever-changing scene of wildlife and beauty. Magnificent, enormous trees dotted the landscape. Birds sang to me all day while frogs sang all night. Millions of stars, not streetlights, shone brightly overhead as each evening arrived. It was absolutely bliss, particularly when I played my guitar watching the sunset from a perfect verandah, or when the rain pelted down on the tin roof. I was in heaven and said many, many prayers of thanks.

Country life obviously has a lot of sacrifices when it comes to easily accessing live entertainment and the arts, but there was enough around to suit me. My lifestyle would always take me away travelling somewhere on occasions anyway. It didn't matter. I was moving in rhythm with nature again and finally living the life that made the most sense to me. Five houses, including the farmer's, were dotted over the hills and valleys on these vast acres. As a tenant I simply had to enjoy the space.

Things felt easier and lighter immediately. It was such a homecoming to be living in the country again. My energy was very low after caring for so many dying people and then working in the jail, so I was happy to have a break and live off my savings for a little while. In the meantime, I would do some research on my new area and decide which direction to take when I was ready, following each step as it would come to present itself. With each passing day I felt better, slowly rejuvenating. Positive energy and thoughts were flowing again. Wandering over hills and paddocks, delighting in the simplicity and complexity of nature, my healing and restoration was underway.

The previous years of growth, sitting at the bedsides of so many wonderful and wise people, had definitely created a lot of positive shifts. I smiled in the memories, often recalling tender moments and beautiful conversations. Although that life seemed a long way behind me now, particularly as I walked the hills and valleys, it had shaped me hugely and I continued to feel overwhelmingly grateful.

Other than needing to spend some time at home and to continue my creative journey, I was out on a leap of faith yet again, trusting that the next steps would surely reveal themselves at the right time. After all, this was what had usually happened previously. With so much natural beauty around me, the writing and music started to flow through marvellously. The abundance of natural life around the cottage and the creek helped me adapt to a very simple lifestyle in no time.

Well below levels of my own consciousness, though, destructive patterns of my low self-worth still lingered. On a conscious level, my thinking had been changed a great deal over the last decade, and life felt easier than it had in years. In that regard, I was in a place of peace and gratitude, restoring myself with each new day. Emotionally, it was all flowing well. Or so I thought.

Then out of the blue, things took a twist in an unforeseen direction. I had been cruising along fine, so it buckled me completely when all of a sudden I was then flung into the darkest depths of my healing. Up it all came from places far deeper than ever before. My remaining (and I had thought, restoring) energy disappeared *completely,* almost overnight, as if someone unplugged me from the power socket and I slumped into a pile on the floor. It seemed to happen so suddenly. Every ounce of energy was *absolutely gone.*

Ideas of finding any casual work to make some local contacts flew out the window. The thought of facing anyone at all seemed impossible. Ideas of working in any job for even a short while became out of the question. I simply wasn't capable. I was forced to enter the very core of my being to face these changes, and it was a heck of a rough ride. I didn't have any choice, though. It was coming up whether I liked it or not, and once the tears began, there was no stopping them. I needed to heal so that I could become the real person I had been born to become, to completely break free of my past. These months became the hardest of my life, as I unexpectedly slid headfirst into a deep pit of suicidal depression.

Those who knew me best could not believe that this was me. If I hadn't been there myself, I may have felt the same. I'd seen depression firsthand in others previously and could never have imagined myself in such a place. But that's the thing with depression, and that's what makes it so hard initially for many sufferers – the shock that it is happening to them.

Some friends refused outright to believe it. How could this be Bronnie, the one who always lifted everyone else up, and was now on the crash and burn? Some simply didn't know how to handle it, to see me in such a vulnerable place. The suggestions from other friends who phoned, people I thought who knew me very well, were so far from what I was capable of that it left me feeling even more misunderstood. If I could have been any sadder, it would have made me so. But I couldn't be, so it didn't. The least of my worries was other people. All I was capable of attending to was myself – and not even that at times.

The suggestions continued from all angles, though, as to how to change my situation. But what people with depression most need is acceptance. Depression is an illness that can be the most catalytic gift for positive transformation, if one is allowed to move through it at their own pace. Depression is the name given to it in modern society. But it is in fact an opportunity and enormous time for spiritual transformation and awakening. It may be a breakdown. But it can also be a break-through, if approached with determination, the willingness to surrender, and faith. Of course, this doesn't actually make it fun.

Waking up sobbing before I'd even had my first thought for the day, I needed compassion and patience from those who knew me. Sometimes my waking thoughts were not even conscious, the tears just poured forth the moment I awoke slightly. At other times, it was the sadness for myself and my situation - that life just felt *so* impossibly hard these days, and really, had for years. Acknowledging that I didn't have the energy to start all over again yet knowing I had to also overwhelmed me, as I couldn't even *imagine* having the energy to do this, let alone *find* the energy. Nobody was going to walk to my front door, though, and offer me the perfect job, particularly when I hardly knew a person in the area.

No one in my closest circle really knew how to deal with my depth of sadness and lack of strength, so they continued to phone with suggestions to get me out and about again, to see me functioning. It just added pressure, though, as I was definitely not ready for that yet. If I managed to vacuum my house, which took *so* much energy, it became a massive achievement, one I would acknowledge to myself – 'You did well today, Bronnie, you achieved something'. In previous times, I could have vacuumed five houses, gone out to lunch, walked a few miles, and swum for an hour. But this is what depression is like when it first hits. It calls the shots initially.

The best thing friends and loved ones can do is to accept that this is where the other person is. They may or may not come out of it. There is a good chance they will come through, especially if they want to. The acceptance from those they love supports this potential, but pressure just hinders it. The person suffering also needs to accept that this is where their life is at, in order to not put pressure on themselves, which in turn only exacerbates the symptoms. It took a while for me to reach this place of acceptance in myself, though, as I grappled with my inability to function in regular life.

Returning to live on the land tapped into somewhere so deep within me that it accessed pain buried from my youth and days as a young adult, when I had lived in a similar setting. It seemed that by slowing down and returning to my roots as such, as well as not putting all of my energy into looking after other people, the lid had burst open from a tin of pain that had been securely and somewhat forcefully shut decades ago. It had been seeping out gradually over the past decade as I had embarked on healing and releasing what I was conscious of. Now the utter sadness that surfaced, so raw and painful, was from places not only conscious, but unconscious as well. Pain from years of criticism in my youth, from not being accepted as who I was even then, from all of the yelling and ridicule

I had been exposed to – all of the pain that had been stored without me even realising it surfaced. I cried and cried.

To benefit from true healing, there is no other option but to face what is in front of you – the pain, the acknowledgment of your suffering, the opportunity for growth, the need for healing, and the need to find strength by eventually becoming stronger than the pain. No one can take our learning away, though. No one else can do it for us. Love from others helps, of course, and this flowing from my dear mother and a couple of old friends, was great support. Yet there was no escaping my own healing. It was time to face myself. It was also time to release things from the very deepest levels.

The release came in a variety of ways. Of course, there was crying. There was also writing things out. For the first time in my life, I screamed, too – not yelling, but truly screaming. (Actually I had squealed once, involuntarily, when I jumped out of a plane). But this was screaming, in a primal way. I was so grateful to be living so far from other houses and to have the privacy to go through this turmoil in whatever way each day dictated. I screamed all of the things I wished I had said when I was younger and growing up to people who had hurt me. I also screamed sounds of pain, with no words attached. I screamed for my utter frustration of being in the situation I was, for the level of pain I was experiencing. I sobbed uncontrollably. I lay exhausted . . . but little by little, I healed.

In more sentimental times, I had often likened learning to be like a rose. We unfold layer after layer of our beautiful, delicate selves, and eventually get to the centre, the bud of who we are. In such a state of utter sadness and hopelessness, though, I threw that theory well and truly out the window and decided that growth is more like peeling a very large onion. As we remove each new layer, it becomes even more painful, and each layer just makes us cry harder. That's what was happening to me. I was peeling a full-strength onion, and a mighty big one at that. Every tear shed, every sentence written, every thought shared, assisted a new layer to be peeled away.

It wasn't happiness I was aiming for every day, just the strength to accept where I was. There was little energy for anything initially except for crying, and then from the verandah, watching as the world of nature unfolded before me. Exhausted from the waves of release that continued on a daily basis, every day was one of living presently. It was simply too hard at times to think beyond the moment I was in. Just surviving the intensity of emotions was enough on a day-to-day basis. I was numb, emotionally worn out, and very, very tired with life.

While I was reminded that happiness is a choice, choosing to challenge myself and get out of bed, or to see a moment of something beautiful in between the tears, were conscious choices in that direction. Choices and successes that appeared as insignificant to others were now huge achievements for me. Things that were once simple – like choosing to get out of bed, returning phone calls, getting the knots out of my hair, wearing nice clothes, and preparing healthy food when all I wanted to do was eat baked beans out of the tin – were all now massive achievements.

I wasn't who I used to be anymore, and if I was to become who I was on this earth to be, I had to accept my feelings, not reject them. I needed to allow them to surface in order to be released forever. We all have to heal our own way. While swallowing happy pills was not the path for me, though I judge no one for choosing that option, I still had to move through it in my own way. Each day was different. Some days were full of darkness, tears, and heartbroken sorrow. Some saw me functioning mildly, in an exhausted haze, but with determination to prepare a healthy meal and freeze some, ensuring I would still be eating well on darker days. Other days, when I found the energy, I would walk over the back hills and paddocks, far from sight of humans, and just breathe in the sounds and sights of the natural habitat.

Meditation remained a part of daily life. I hate to imagine what I would have done without that skill. It had previously taught me that suffering is a result of the mind. The preceding years of practice had already helped to let go of an enormous amount of unhealthy thinking. So it had to remain as an integral part of my healing now. I wondered how anyone actually copes with this illness without meditation. It teaches the skills to observe your thoughts and realise that they are not you. They are just your mind, and while your mind is a part of you, it is not all of you, nor are all of the thoughts your own. Many have originated from the thoughts of others projected onto you.

This awareness helped me enormously as I sat to meditate at least twice a day, with the intention of taking true ownership of my own thoughts and mind. It took enormous determination to focus on my practice when so much pain would surface and try to distract me. But for the majority of those hours in meditation, I owned myself. By observing my thoughts while meditating but not attaching my focus to them, I returned to a place of stillness, a place of love and certainty, knowing that this turmoil would surely pass one day, realising that the peaceful part of me still existed within. I just had to work harder to access that at the moment, much harder. The discipline of meditation was also very good for me. It meant that despite my fluctuating moods, I had a commitment to honour daily, meaning I had to challenge myself to sit and continue my practice, regardless of how lousy I was feeling. For some people, it may be the challenge of going to work that gets them through, or continuing some other routine. For me, it was my meditation practice.

Of course I cried, too, from the very depths of my soul. Trying not to lose sight of a beautiful life potentially waiting for me, if I could get myself through this level of pain and healing, I held onto hope when I was able. When the present moment is so hindered by pain from the past, it is only hope of a different future that sometimes brings any prospective joy. So hope played a large role in my healing. In moments of semi-stillness, I dreamed of functioning again, of using what talents I had been blessed with (as we all are), earning good money doing work I loved, laughing with friends, owing my own acreage by a fresh-water river, daring to love again, and having a child. But most, I simply dreamed of knowing happiness again, of waking with joy and excitement purely for the gift of being alive. I dreamed of being happy, yearning to remember what that felt like for more than a rapid, fleeting moment. Yes, I hoped for happiness.

The only true thing that could really be done well, though, was to stay as present as possible, when I could, and just continue to deal with the moment of now. Living in such a magnificent setting helped greatly, as there were so many intricate things happening in the natural world around me, enabling me to become totally absorbed in such moments, watching insects and birds, listening to the breeze in the trees, watching the sky and its constant changes.

A wonderful social worker, whose help I came to seek, was also a blessing. Not only did she practice the same meditation technique as me, but in a way she also held a mirror for me to look at. Through her assistance, I came to see myself from different angles, in kinder ways, acknowledging my own beautiful heart. I also saw how much energy I had put into looking after others and not myself, not believing on the deepest levels that I deserved it. Much of this was due to past opinions of others still affecting me on subconscious levels, people who did not know me despite thinking they did. A part of the current transformation was the determination to break free *completely* from these hindrances. I had also taken on way too much pain from a friend who was going through a hard time herself, thinking I was simply being a good friend. But in swimming out to save her, I was drowning, too. I needed to separate my compassion and empathy for everyone a little, by applying more detached compassion to those I empathised with.

Being reminded again of the need for my own compassion was significant and liberating, too. This brilliant social worker also helped me to see the bad habits I had previously developed in excusing other people's behaviour, previously out of wanting to keep the superficial peace and more recently out of compassion. Her wonderfully direct counselling style was definitely needed, and her honesty worked, particularly when she asked me if I was going for a gold medal in the carer's Olympics?

I had too often forgotten to share some of my compassion with myself, both in thought and deed. All of the previous years of growth and letting go had not been wasted though, even if it sometimes felt this way. Instead, I had the reached the true core of my wounds, the crunch of where many of them had truly originated from, and was able to start releasing them permanently.

Acknowledging my pain, the effects of decades of criticism from those whose love I most needed, ceasing to make excuses for unkind behaviour, and talking it all out took courage, my own permission, and my willingness to step free of those patterns forever. The way to do this was by learning how to be kind to myself, also learning how to *receive* that kindness. I deserved goodness and happiness, completely. Even if others did not believe so, they did not know the paths I had walked, and it no longer mattered. I *now knew* I deserved amazing goodness to flow my way. It was in coming to this significant acknowledgement, that *I did deserve it,* which allowed me to start receiving my own kindness. I had believed this already on other levels, but not at the depths I was now beginning to operate from. That was where the refocusing was now underway, towards the levels that *truly* drove me. It was time to allow my own kindness in. After all, I deserved it, too.

The old thinking patterns of low self-worth were holding on fiercely, though, and some days it still took *everything* I had to be stronger than the emotional and mental pain. With each layer conquered, glimpses of beauty and euphoria also started creeping in occasionally, which was both refreshing and inspiring. Something as simple as the sun shining on leaves in nearby trees became so incredibly beautiful, it would move me to moments of unexpected bliss. New parts of myself that had been incubating for years were becoming a more natural part of me now. Some permanent changes had truly happened, with some of my old thinking patterns indeed being left behind properly.

I realised that I had dealt with particular angles of my previous mental shaping and *had* actually released them, so I acknowledged all of this with gratitude. The beauty of where I was living also continued to keep me very present. The remaining pain tended to do that, too, of course. But the natural life unfolding around the cottage nurtured me daily. As each layer of pain fell away, my senses became more heightened and even more in tune with the natural world. This encouraged me immensely, even though bad moments still lingered.

Sometimes I became angry towards myself because I wasn't past the depression as quickly as I wanted to be. But anger directed towards anyone is just frustrated expectations. So I would let the expectation go and bring myself back to the present, by acknowledging something beautiful out my window, putting some music on and singing along, or just bringing my awareness back to my breath or the sounds around me. Then I could accept my situation again, knowing I was working through it all at the right pace for my own growth.

One of my old friends sent me a constant supply of divine organic skin care products. So I would then take time to carefully rub in the lotions, caring and nurturing myself, both mentally *and* physically, to balance out previous unkindness towards myself. This always left me feeling better, not to mention smelling gorgeous. Attending to my body with such pampering reminded me of how I had nurtured my dying clients. I was now starting to give myself some of the same love I gave them.

But being stronger than the pain was very challenging, and while good days were definitely creeping back in after some months, the depression and the negative thoughts that accompanied it seemed to then fight back with even more determination afterwards. It certainly wasn't willing to let go easily. After all, it was fuelled by negative patterns of self-condemnation that had ruled now for more than forty years, created by my allowing too many opinions of others into my belief system. My mind seemed to operate like an independent master ,and this master did not want to lose control over me.

I was becoming my own master now, though, truly realising my worth and beauty, and consciously choosing to direct my mind into more positive belief systems. Rather than focus on old ways, I treated myself with respect and love. Ditties about my own goodness started to flow from me as I pottered about the home singing funny things to myself. Saying hello to my beautiful self in the mirror when I'd walk past became a fun and entertaining habit, too. Ensuring my body was nurtured regularly with baths and healthy food also brought me back to happier moments. Little by little, happiness was returning. My old mind did not like this at all, though, and depression dug its ugly claws in, refusing to let go completely. This restructuring of my thinking had already been happening for years. But now, a final dual was underway, where only one side could survive.

It was during this climax, this wrestle to say goodbye to my old self completely and forever, that I eventually gave up. It just became *too hard*. Despite the improvements to my day-to-day life and increasing moments of happiness, I was utterly exhausted emotionally. It had taken *so* much energy to get to this point that suddenly all of my remaining strength disappeared, delivering me to the final occasion of contemplating suicide. Not one ounce of strength remained for any more mental discipline or hope. I had tried my best but was just *too tired* of it all. I wanted to die. I wanted this life to be over once and for all.

A friend of more than twenty years was an angel, ringing me up regularly. Thankfully he had his own approach. "Pick up the phone. I mean it, you'd better not be *#@# killing yourself. Pick up the phone. Stop ignoring me, and pick up the *#@# phone," he would say, until I couldn't help but pick it up, laughing through my tears. While his approach was somewhat unorthodox, his heart is one of the biggest I know and humour had already helped us both through things in the past. His approach worked. I needed laughter, and I knew he loved me dearly, as I do him. Laughter is a very underrated tool for healing.

On a day that he didn't call, though, I did reach the absolute bottom of anywhere I had ever been in my whole life. Scrawling a farewell note, unable to even write clearly, I gave up on life. It was just too hard.

They say that the darkest hour always comes before the dawn. This was the darkest hour of my life. I just could not live this life anymore. It was not possible to ever feel any worse in myself than I did in this moment. I hated myself for the weakness to not conquer my mind despite all of my efforts. I hated that I had tolerated so much bullshit in my life from others. I hated that I had settled for such a hard existence so often. I hated that it took *so* much courage to create the life I wanted and deserved. I hated almost everything about myself. It was indeed the darkest hour.

At the very instant that I finished scrawling my farewell note of apology and utter sadness, the phone rang. I considered not answering it, but I did, with great reluctance. It wasn't the friend I thought it would be. It wasn't anyone I knew. Instead, what I heard was a chirpy voice from a woman saying a bright and happy hello to me. She then proceeded to offer me ambulance insurance!

'Great', I thought. 'I can't even do suicide properly. I'll probably need a damn ambulance'. I had chosen a crevice in the local region that I was going to drive my van into, ensuring I would not survive. I had given a decent amount of thought to the act, as I did not want to half-do it. Fine details had been considered in the planning.

The offer of ambulance insurance (which I declined through a haze) truly reminded me that I may or *may not* succeed in my attempt. I thought about all of the lovely ambulance workers I had known over the years and realised how insensitive I had been, how consumed by my own pain I was, that I hadn't considered the effect my act would have on whoever found me and on those who loved me. I also knew that I didn't want a life of paralysis if I was unsuccessful, particularly self-induced paralysis. But it wasn't just the symbolism of the ambulance – though of course you couldn't ask for a better wake-up call – it was that the phone call broke the spell, the haze I was in at the very bottom of my pain.

That pivotal moment was indeed the turning point, the biggest turning point of my whole life. I didn't want to damage the body that had provided me with so much freedom and mobility, the beautiful, healthy body that had carried me through everything. I didn't want to die either. As I started to love my legs for all of the miles they had already carried me, I then began to love all of me.

In the same minute of that phone call, I had a moment of pain in my heart area. It was then I realised that my poor, tender, beautiful heart had already endured enough. It couldn't take any more suffering or self-loathing. It needed love to heal, and that love, above all else, had to come from me first.

NO REGRETS

The speed in which things changed after this was phenomenal. Depression slipped away in the night, taking its heavy cloud of darkness with it. It had only ever been waiting for love to arrive, and when that happened, it knew its role was completed and left. I spent the next few days restoring my energy through meditation, gratitude, and reverence for my beautiful self. This nurtured my heart, while soaking in the bath nurtured my body. I took long, easy walks over the hills, not pushing myself, just walking gently as I marvelled at life through the eyes of someone reborn. It was like waking up in a world so beautiful that it was difficult to remember the world before.

To signify the beginning of my new life I decided to carry out a formal farewell and welcoming ceremony. I collected wood from the paddocks and lit a beautiful fire. There were things that needed a proper farewell from my life, aspects of my old self and the circumstances that had risen from that. So I wrote these things down as well as things being welcomed. Then as the sun went down and the first evening stars came out, I happily stood by the healing, warming fire. Old parts of myself were thanked and given farewell as I then dropped that piece of paper into the fire. Each welcome was also acknowledged. Sitting out under that country sky after, staring into the fire, I felt immense love for myself and for life. I also felt incredible gratitude.

The firelight continued to burn warmly. Grinning, I looked at the vast cover of stars above me and acknowledged that through all of this, someone new had indeed been born. The person I had been working towards being for years was now who I was. She had finally been allowed through. The person who had made too many excuses for others, had carried decades of pain, and who hadn't accepted that she too deserved every happiness was no longer needed. Her role was now complete. She was gently thanked for her part in my evolution, and was now gone.

Every day following continued to reveal delight on fresh levels. It was almost like discovering life for the first time. Never had I felt so free. Happiness, as I had never known happiness before – completely unhindered, joyous, and guilt-free – became my more natural state. New birds came to sit on the fence and sing to me. Old ones followed me when I walked the paddocks in a state of bliss. All of my senses became more heightened, feeling like I had just finished weeks of silent meditation, except that this more alert state remained. Natural sounds were clearer, and colours brighter and more alive. I noticed as least thirty different shades of green in the country surrounding the cottage.

There was space and clarity within that I had always believed was there, but had never quite known. My past was now of little relevance either. The wisdom gained along the way was a part of me. The past has served as an incredible learning tool and none of the learning had been wasted. But the suffering that had come to shape me had played its role and had now disintegrated. There was nothing to prove, nothing to explain, nothing to justify. My face ached from smiling. Almost overnight, life shifted onto a completely different plane. Living presently had also now become a way of life, after years of practice.

The doors of opportunity then swung open. All of the past efforts on my creative journey, of focus, resilience and sacrifices, started to be rewarded. My work gained huge momentum and new writing opportunities arrived from unimagined sources. Love for myself had opened the doors, allowing great things to flow my way. It had all been waiting patiently for years, simply for my own readiness.

As time has since unfolded, the natural flow of goodness continues to grow. New support systems have also built themselves around me, both professionally and personally. Of course, there will always be new things to learn about myself, but I never take even the tiniest blessing for granted now.

Over the previous years I had been consciously creating the life I imagined, by releasing my hindrances one layer at a time. Getting very clear about the life I wanted to be living and the person I wanted to be was also a necessary part of this process. If occasional blockages now surface, I am patient and loving with myself whilst working through them. Self-discovery is a joyful process, and I can smile at my humanness.

With all that happening, I found myself feeling closer than ever to every one of the beautiful people I had cared for in their passing. This new life unravelling for me was the kind of life they had each glimpsed as having once been possible, when they had looked back and spoken of their regrets. In their final weeks and days, when all else had fallen away, they could see what potential joy life had offered them, if only they had lived differently.

Not every person spoke of regrets, though. Some people said they would have done some things differently, but were not consumed with any actual regret. Some were beautifully content with the life they had led. Or in the least, beautifully accepting of the life they had led. Many others *did* have regrets, and had a strong desire to be heard, to have their thoughts known. The length of time I spent with each client was possibly a catalyst for the honesty that each relationship came to know. For those large amounts of time, I will always be very grateful.

The regrets they shared left me determined to not feel the same at the end of my own time, whenever that was. There was no way I was going to be given the gift of this wisdom and not learn by it. But having now endured the biggest tests, I understood just how difficult the challenges could be. I also now understood, though, how joyous the rewards were by making it through.

The potential of fulfillment and pleasure, which each of these dear people caught a glimpse of towards their passing, is what is on offer to every one of us now, before our own time to pass arrives. Each new day that unfolds leaves me even more enchanted with the natural flow of goodness. It wants to come through, and it does so when you learn how to allow it, through faith and self-love. It awaits everyone. You just need to get out of your own way first, and that is where the real work is – learning to own your own thoughts by clearing away the debris that stops you from letting it all flow.

Learning will always continue. It's not like you'll reach a stage of growth and say, "Great. Now I can sit back, know everything, and cruise through every day without ever having to learn another thing." Even Stella, who had done so much work on her inner journey, was reminded of the need to let go and surrender at times. In doing so, she was able to become more peaceful in her remaining days, before leaving with a radiant smile on her face when the time to pass over arrived.

So if the learning never stops, we may as well embrace it rather than resist it. Not one day goes by that I don't learn something new about myself. But I can do so now with loving kindness, by loving myself in an unconditional way, with no self-judgment. Laughing gently and lovingly also allows the growth process to be smoother.

When Grace spoke the words, "I wish I'd had the courage to live a life true to myself, not the life others expected of me," she carried such sadness about her life turning out the way it did.

It is a pity that being who you truly are requires so much courage. But it does. It takes *enormous* courage at times. Being who you are, whoever that is, sometimes cannot even be articulated at first, not even to yourself. All you know is there is a yearning within that is not being fulfilled by the life you are currently living. Having to explain this to others, who have not walked in your shoes, may just leave you questioning yourself even further.

But as the wise man Buddha said more than two millennia ago, "The mind knows no answers. The heart knows no questions." It is the heart that guides you to joy, not the mind. Overcoming the mind and letting go of others' expectations allows you to hear your own heart. Having the courage to then follow it is where true happiness lies. In the meantime, keep on cultivating the heart while mastering the mind. As the heart grows, life brings more joy and peace your way. A happy life wants you as much as you want it.

When Anthony lay in the nursing home and admitted to not

having the courage to try for a better life, he sadly showed the consequences of being ruled by such fear. It doesn't mean that you too will end up in a nursing home before your time. But the lack of both stimulus and happiness that became a part of his life are no different from the lives of millions amongst us. Each day was just a mind numbing routine, safe and secure, but never satisfying.

It takes fortitude to create big changes. The longer you stay in the wrong environment and remain its product, though, the longer you deny yourself the opportunity to know true happiness and satisfaction. Life is too short to watch it go by, just because of fear that can be conquered if faced.

Like the vines trapping beautiful flowers in the garden of Florence's mansion, we are all capable of creating our own trappings. Obviously, many of these are not quite so easy to remove as her vine was. Most trappings have the strength of decades of growth behind them and do not take kindly to being removed. They will hang on for dear life, strangling your beauty if you let them.

Yet just as they were created over time, they can be undone over time, too. It is a delicate process of determination, bravery and at times, of letting go. It is having the courage to stop unhealthy relationships in their tracks and say "Enough." It is treating yourself with respect and kindness, both of which you deserve. Mostly though, to break free of your own trappings, it is about becoming an observer of your own thoughts and habits. This awareness helps solutions become more apparent.

Life is your own, not someone else's. If you are not finding some element of happiness in what you have created and are doing nothing to improve on it, then the gift of every new day is wasted. A tiny step or a small decision are great starting points, those and taking responsibility for your own happiness. A happy life can also be found without moving house or doing anything drastic in your physical world. It is about changing your perception and being brave enough to honour some of your own desires too. No one else can make you happy or unhappy, unless you allow him or her to.

Yes, having the courage to be yourself and not who others expect you to be may take a lot of strength and honesty. But so does lying on your deathbed and admitting that you wished you had done it differently. There were many other clients in between those mentioned. This regret, *wishing they had been true to themselves,* was the most common one of all.

When John said he wished he hadn't worked so hard, he was also speaking some of the most common words I would hear throughout those years. During his final weeks, sitting out on the balcony watching life on the harbour unfold, John was burdened with regret. There is nothing at all wrong in loving the work you do. In fact, this is how it should be. But it's about finding balance so that work is not your whole life. I can still hear that dear man sighing deeply, as he came to terms with the choices he had made.

Listening then to Charlie's insistence on the benefits of a simple life, I had to agree with his wisdom and life experience. True value is not on what you own, but on who you are. Dying people know this. Their belongings are of no consequence whatsoever at the end. What other people think of them, or what they have achieved in belongings, does not even enter their thinking at such a time.

In the end, what matters to people is *how much happiness they have brought to those they love and how much time they spent doing things they themselves loved.* Trying to ensure that those they left behind don't end up with the same regrets also became critical for many people. None of the life reviews I witnessed from their deathbeds were spent on thoughts of wishing they had bought or owned more, not even one. Instead, what most occupies the thoughts of dying people are how they lived their lives, what they did, and if they had made a positive difference to those they left behind, whether that was family, community, or whomever.

The things you often think you need are sometimes the things that keep you trapped in an unfulfilled life. Simplicity is the key to changing this, that and letting go of the need for validation through ownership or through others' expectations of you. Taking risks also requires courage. But you cannot control everything. Staying in a seemingly secure environment does not guarantee that life's lessons will pass you by unnoticed. They can still come out of the blue, when you least expect them. So can life's rewards, though, for those with courage to honour their hearts. The clock ticks for every one of us. It is your own choice how you spend your remaining days.

As Pearl understood, things flow when you need them. She believed that the most important thing is to work towards finding your purpose, to do your work, whatever it is, with the right intention and not get trapped into unhappy work situations by a fear of lack. It is about learning and daring to think without limitations and not trying to control how things will flow to you. Life is over so quickly, she said. It is. Some of us will live a long life, many of us won't. But if you can know happiness and fulfillment in this brief time, there is no need for regret when the end comes, as it inevitably will.

Learning how to express feelings is unfortunately a challenge for too many adults. It was also a deep frustration and regret for dying people, including Jozsef. He wanted to express himself but didn't know how, as he'd had no practice. The heartache this brought to the lovely man was his greatest regret, as he died feeling like his family had never truly known him. Other clients developed illnesses associated with the bitterness they carried, as they had also never learned to express themselves.

Like anything, you get better with practice. So by starting with small acts of bravery in expressing yourself, you become more at ease with opening up and even begin to enjoy sharing such honesty. You'll never be able to control the reactions of others. However, although people may initially react when you change the way you are by speaking honestly, in the end it raises the relationship to a whole new and healthier level. Either that or it releases the unhealthy relationship from your life completely. Whichever way, you win.

We can never know how long we are here for or how long those we love will be. So rather than have to live with the regrets before your dying time, ensure those you value know how you feel now. As dear Jude said, guilt is a toxic emotion to accompany your remaining years. Expressing your feelings feels good, too, when you get used to it. It is just the fear of how it will be received that holds you back. So knock the fear on the head and dare to reveal your beautiful self to others, before it is too late either way.

If you are already carrying guilt from things left unsaid to someone already passed, it is now time to forgive yourself. You are not honouring your life by carrying guilt forward. It is time to be gentle with yourself. That was who you were then. It does not need to be who you are now. Compassion for who you used to be, given from who you are now is the first seed of kindness towards self-forgiveness.

If people in your life don't appear to respond to your honest expression, it doesn't mean they haven't heard you or that you should not have expressed yourself. Nanci with Alzheimer's disease was a great example of this. But other relationships in my life have also been transformed through consistency of kindness and honesty. For a long time, it appeared that my words were not heard. But when the other people were ready to express their feelings, it was obvious that every word had been heard along the way. It wouldn't have mattered in the end, though. I was peaceful knowing I'd had the courage to express myself honestly. If any of us had been taken unexpectedly, I would have been without guilt. There was no one taken for granted, no one who didn't know that I loved them, even if they were not able to express themselves in return so honestly. Tell people how you feel. Life is short.

Locating her friend for Doris brought me true enjoyment and fulfillment. When she spoke of regretting not staying in touch with her friends, I had no idea how often I would also hear this regret through other clients to follow. Now having been through what I have and knowing how valuable old and loyal friends were in carrying me through, it is even less difficult to understand this regret. Most people have friends, but when it comes to the crunch, there are not a lot of friends who can be there through the absolute hardest times. When someone is dying, this is one such time.

History and understanding are what friendships offer. As the clients were looking back over their lives, it was often friends they missed to reminisce with. Life gets busy, and friendships fade away. There will always be people who come and go in life, friends included. But those who truly matter, those whom you love most dearly, are worth every ounce of effort to stay in touch with. They are the ones who will be there for you when you most need them, just as you will be there for them. Sometimes it is not possible to physically be there, but even phone contact gives people a lot of strength and comfort during hard times.

Acceptance and forgiveness from friends, particularly when dying, assisted Elizabeth in finding her peace after years of alcoholism. In the end, it is just about love and relationships. But not everyone was so lucky to track down friends at the end, despite the desire to. That's why not losing touch in the first place is important. No one knows what lies ahead or when the time will come that you are longing for your friends and in between, you still have the gift of them in your life.

Watching the roster of Harry's support team only continued to emphasise the importance of this at the end. While it can be a gloomy time of sadness for others, the person actually dying wants to enjoy their remaining time as much as possible. Friends bring humour to sad times, and this humour brings happiness to the dying person. Whether you are dying or not, friends are the ones capable of making you laugh through the worst of times.

Sitting beside me on her bed after she had screamed at me to go, Rosemary's admission to having never allowed herself to be happy was an honest one. It also improved her remaining time immensely. Rosemary hadn't believed that she deserved happiness, due to not being what her family had expected her to be. When she realised it was a choice, she learned to allow happiness through and was able to find a part of herself that had been dormant for most of her adult life. It was a beautiful smile that sometimes then came to escape her in her last weeks.

Appreciating every single step along the way is one of the keys to such happiness. As Cath contemplated her final time, she spoke of missing a lot of potential happiness by focusing too much on the results, rather than on the time along the way as well. It is so easy to think that happiness depends on something falling into place, when it is the other way around. Things fall into place when happiness is already found.

While it may not be possible to be happy every day, learning to steer the mind towards that direction is still possible. Acknowledging something beautiful outside of the sadness is one example, something that helped me to move back towards a place of peace myself. The mind may cause great suffering. But it can also be used to create a beautiful life, once mastered and used properly. Every single of us has reasons to feel sorry for ourselves. Every one of us has suffered. But life doesn't owe us anything. We only owe ourselves, to make the most of the life we are living, of the time we have left, and to live in gratitude.

When we accept that there will always be learning and that some of this will bring suffering and some will bring happiness, we reach a place of better equanimity. From this perspective, happiness becomes a more conscious choice, and the waves are no longer so tumultuous. Some that may have once left you crushed and wounded may now be ridden with the skills that come from experience and wisdom.

It is also perfectly OK to be silly and playful sometimes. You just have to give yourself permission. It is also more than possible to have fun without drugs or alcohol. There is no rule in place that says adults have to be serious and cannot have silly fun. Taking life too critically or being concerned how you will appear to others are going to be regrets you face at the end of your life, only if you let such thoughts hinder your happiness now.

Of course, your perspective makes a huge difference to happiness, as beautiful Lenny showed. Despite the losses in his life, he focused on the gifts he had received and saw his life as a good one. The same view you look at every day, the same life, can become something brand new by focusing on its gifts rather than the negative aspects. Perspective is your own choice, and the best way to shift that perspective is through gratitude, by acknowledging and appreciating the positives.

Despite the many regrets dying people shared with me, in the very end, each of them found their peace. Some were not able to forgive themselves until their last couple of days but they did manage it before they passed. Many experienced a variety of emotions leading up to this, including denial, fear, anger, remorse, and the worst, self-condemnation. Many also experienced positive feelings of love and immense joy for memories that surfaced as they lived through their final weeks.

Before the very end, though, they found a peaceful acceptance that their time had come and they were able to forgive themselves for the regrets they expressed, regardless of how tormented they had been. It was imperative to many of these clients, however, that others learned through their regrets.

They were all people who had been given the time to contemplate their lives. Those who go suddenly do not have such a luxury, and many of us will be amongst those, too. It is so important to consider the life you are living now, as there may be little time given at your passing to find your peace or for any contemplation. Instead, you will die knowing that you have spent your whole life chasing happiness through the wrong channels; with it always eluding you, always just out of your grasp, always depending on the right things or situations to come your way. You will die knowing that the opportunity to change your direction well before it was too late just slipped on by.

The peace each of these dear people found before their passing is available now, without having to wait until your final hours. You have the choice to change your life, to be courageous and to live a life true to your heart, one that will see you pass without regret.

Kindness and forgiveness are a great starting point. Not just to others, but to yourself as well. Forgiving yourself is also such a necessary component for this process. Without it, you continue to add fertiliser to the existing bad seeds in your mind by being hard on yourself, as I once did. But self-forgiveness and kindness weakens the strength of these seeds. Healthier ones replace them and grow stronger, in time overshadowing the old seeds until there is nothing left to sustain their growth.

The bravery needed to change your life is easier to find when you are kind on yourself. Good things take time, too, so patience is also required. Every single one of us is an amazing person with a potential limited only by our own thinking. We are all amazing. When you think of the numerous environmental and genetic influences that have shaped you, including the genes that have come to you through your own unique biology, it makes you a pretty amazing and special person. All of your life experiences so far, both good and bad, also contribute to you being unlike *any* other person on this planet. You are already special. You are already unique.

It is time to realise your own worth and to realise the worth of others. Lay your judgments down. Be kind to yourself and be kind to others. As no one has ever truly walked in another's shoes, seen through another's eyes, or felt through another's heart for their whole life, no one knows just how much each other has suffered either. A little bit of empathy goes a long way.

By being kind to others and tossing your judgment out the window, you are also being kind to yourself by planting better seeds. Forgive yourself for blaming others for your unhappiness. Learn to be gentle on yourself, accepting your own humanness and frailty. Forgive others, too, who have blamed you for their unhappiness. We are all human. We have all said and done things that could have been otherwise done in a kinder way.

Life is over so quickly. It is possible to reach the end with no regrets. It takes some bravery to live it right, to honour the life you are here to live but the choice is yours. So will be the rewards. Appreciate the time you have left by valuing *all* of the gifts in your life, and that especially includes your own, amazing self.

SMILE AND KNOW

When I look at my life now, there are moments that still blow me away. The life I imagined becomes more of a reality every day. The person I had imagined is now me. It came about through courage, resilience, discipline, and through learning to love my own heart. Life *can* actually be easy and joyous. It can in fact flow well. Even better is that as I have continued to adjust and grow, continuing to accept that I deserve all that comes my way, the more easily things keep flowing.

One little phrase kept my faith strong through that final, dark period: *Smile and know.* On one particularly hard day, my old thinking was holding on for dear life and telling me I didn't deserve all I had dreamed of. My new thinking, meanwhile, was trying to move in permanently, reassuring me I did. So I prayed for some very simple and clear guidance, something that would not be hard to remember in my tearful state, in order to conquer the hard days. I needed something to keep me strong and with hope whenever I was able. The words *Smile and know* came to me.

I wrote these words down and put them in obvious places around the home. Whenever I walked past them, a commitment with myself was honoured, and I would *Smile and know* that this time would pass and good would follow. It is also much easier to be strong in faith when you are smiling. So it would automatically lift my mood and reassure me that I would indeed find more reasons to smile again. There was no point reading the words without actually smiling, though, as the smiling itself allowed the knowing to be easier. So smile I did.

Later, I added underneath *Thank and know,* ensuring prayers of gratitude were said in advance, with confidence and faith that it was all coming to me. *Smile and know, Thank and know,* became my mantra as I went about my days smiling and knowing when I could. As I did so, I was walking in complete faith, which left me naturally wanting to thank as well. My prayers, dreams, and intentions had already been heard. My only job was to *Smile and know* and to *Thank and know.* Naturally this enabled me to smile much more than I would have otherwise.

Of course, there were times when I was not strong enough to draw on these words, including that final day of utter sadness and resignation. But that time of surrender was the ultimate turning point. It was true I could not live with the pain of my past anymore, and I was right in a sense. It was the end of my life, as I knew it at least. But I didn't have to die physically. Only that old part of myself died, spiritually. Those old ideas of myself could not survive the bright light of my own love. The new life that had been quietly manifesting for years was finally able to be born.

While I was smiling and knowing, my dreams felt real and became even more a part of me. That's why the doors of opportunity swung open when I was finally able to realise my own worth. The dreams had already arrived and were simply waiting for me to let them come through. So it was with a joyous heart that I opened up, allowing things to flow. They did in many and various forms: personally and professionally.

Some time later, as I sat in delighted shock at the suggestion of my dear, beautiful parents to have a vegan Christmas, I smiled wholeheartedly, having just been given the best Christmas present in the world. For more than two decades I had dreamed of at least a vegetarian Christmas. When it finally came about, it did so with such natural ease that we all agreed it was one of the most beautiful Christmas days we'd ever experienced. With my mum chopping vegetables beside me, sharing cheek and laughter, my dad sorted out the music. Country tunes from the 1950s floated through the home as we all laughed, chatted, and prepared a great feast. It was joyous and easy.

My work continues to grow and thrive, bringing satisfaction

and enjoyment. While it is possible to find work you love in being employed by others, in the times we live in, the best way forward for me is to work for myself. That is what I needed and wanted most anyway, to live life my way, including my work-life. High levels of motivation and amazing clarity accompanied me onto my new plane of existence, along with the best from the old life, including self-discipline.

Making contacts in the local area, meetings were set up all over the place. Inspiration and ideas poured forth. Excitement built as I re-entered the world, creating new and positive opportunities for myself. Through a couple of community groups, I taught some songwriting workshops to disadvantaged sectors of society. Teaching again, and being my own boss, was lovely, and of course, watching the transformation of the people in the classes was hugely rewarding.

After the seriousness of my past, it was time for more joy in my work as well. So I created a children's show, performing to children under five years old. Watching these delightful, uninhibited, little humans dancing and jumping around to my new songs has been delightful. Writing opportunities also flowed, as did a new album's worth of adult songs. It amazes me of what we are truly capable of creatively and physically when we let go of all that has held us back.

My blog experienced further massive waves, bringing more people to my work. I also created a happy and positive range of T-shirts, bumper stickers, and tote bags, drawing on lines from my songs and articles. Not only did the ideas flow forth, but motivated action also accompanied.

As I now share my autumn nights snuggled up with a beautiful man, I smile at how much life can change. He is a dear person. There were things we both had to let go of before we could find each other, but timing is an amazing thing. Life is now lived from new perspectives.

In the very best of ways I have been reminded about the cycles of life. Death has certainly been shown to me directly through others. I have known my own kind of death now, too, by watching that old part of me finally cease to exist. It was a spiritual death, a death of a part of me that had controlled me for decades. It was also the birth of a new spirit, one that I had always suspected was there, one that I wished to be. It was a painful death, yet it was what truly freed me from the conditioning of my past, of unnecessary burdens, of all that held me back.

With the real me now allowed to live unhindered, I continue to evolve into who I really am. It is only through shedding what I have that I am able to actually know who that is and I love her. I love her courage. I love her heart. I love her creativity. I love her mind. I love her body. I love her kindness. I love all of her.

Life moves in new directions. It is a new beginning, a new birth of myself. In the best possible way I have also been reminded of other new beginnings. A precious baby now grows within me. I have been blessed with the opportunity to become a mother. As my womb expands and my body swells in the divinity of womanhood, I am in bliss and overwhelming gratitude to know such an experience. It is a world away from the life I once knew - the isolation, the sadness, the hopelessness. Yet again, I am reminded of just how much we can fit into one lifetime. Thank goodness I did not end my life when I thought to. Thank goodness.

The bond between mother and child grows daily. I have also been blessed with great health throughout, much to the curse of other poor pregnant women suffering morning sickness. I absolutely love being pregnant, and soon will be guiding another soul through their human journey until they are old enough to fly in directions of their own choice. Life may certainly have its share of death and endings, but it has its share of birth and beginnings, too. I am grateful to have been exposed to both, literally and symbolically, on so many occasions.

Whenever out on a leap of faith, things have never turned out as I had imagined, but in the long run, things have always turned out better. Faith is a powerful force and one that creates incredible blessings. Letting go of limitations and of trying to control how things will flow is an immense gift to one's self.

Strangely one of the hardest things for many, as it was for me, is to learn how to receive, to realise you deserve it, then allow the goodness to flow. Most of the miraculous solutions that have flowed to me throughout my life have also come via other people. We are all much more inter-connected than we acknowledge, and play bigger roles in each other's lives than we know.

So learning to receive is a necessity if you are truly open to seeing your dreams realised. As any person who is a natural giver knows, there is great pleasure in giving. But if you are a giver without allowing yourself to also receive, then not only are you blocking the natural flow of things to you and creating an imbalance, you are robbing someone else of the pleasure of giving. So allow others to give, too. It is only pride or lack of self-worth that stops anyone from being able to receive, and every single one of us deserves such goodness.

If you are one who does not know how to actually give, then keep practicing. Just try it without expectation. It feels good. Just give for the pleasure of giving. To do so with accountability is not true giving, though, nor is giving then reminding people of it later in anger. Waiting for the good to flow back to you after giving is not it in its truest sense either. But giving with the sole intention of giving, whether that is in love, kindness, or action is where true pleasure comes in. And yes, those who give with this intention are rewarded, but not always immediately and not necessarily in ways you imagine. But you also need to know how to receive as well, allowing the flow to go both ways. Of course, this includes giving and receiving with your own self, too.

It is possible to change the world and us. As we improve our own lives, and work toward having no regrets, we naturally improve the lives of all around us. It is possible to reverse the segregation and disharmony we have created in society. It is possible to be happy. It is possible to work towards dying without regrets while still alive and well.

We are all fragile in our own way, like globes of delicate glass. Imagine the old light bulb with the roundish glass surrounding the globe. (It doesn't quite create the same image if you imagine the new energy-saving tube-like light globes, though either will suffice.) A part of all of us is like a delicate light globe. A beautiful light shines from within, one that can remove darkness from any place.

When we are born, we are shining bright, bringing great light and happiness to all. People marvel at our beauty and light.

Then over time, muck starts being thrown at us. This muck is not about us. It is theirs, the people who are throwing it. But they hurl it at us anyway. After a while, it is not only those close to us who throw muck on us. It is school friends, workmates, society, and many of whom we come across. It affects us all differently, some become victims, some bullies, some take it in and it stays within for a long time, some appear to let it go naturally. Regardless of how it appears to affect each of us, it still hinders our original light and goodness from shining at its absolute best.

With so many people throwing muck on us, we figure that they must be right. So we join in, throwing muck on ourselves, too. Why not? All of the muck throwers can't be wrong after all. If I am going to throw muck on myself, then it must be normal and OK to throw muck on others as well. Yes, I'll throw some more and I'll continue to let others throw it on me. Eventually, you are carrying so much muck that not only are you weighed down by it, but also your light cannot be seen at all anymore. Every inch of you is covered in muck, a lot of it from what others have thrown and some from when you joined in and started throwing it on yourself, too.

Then one day you remember there was once a beautiful light shining in you. But things have been dark for so long, you hardly remember that part of yourself. It can still be felt sometimes, though, when you are quiet and alone. The warm glow has remained shining all this time, regardless of the darkness surrounding it. You realise that you want to shine again. You want to remember who you are when you're not carrying other people's muck on you, or your own.

So you start saying you've had enough. You stop allowing anyone else to throw muck on you. People don't like this. But you are determined and move out of reach of the muck throwers. Slowly you start rubbing very gently to remove some of it off you. But it has to be done very tenderly, as you are incredibly fragile underneath. If you try to do it too roughly or hurriedly, you will shatter and never know your light again.

So you slowly and patiently work away at cleaning it off. A tiny ray of light breaks through, and you are given a glimpse of your own beauty again. It feels good. Then someone throws some more muck at you and you have to start removing it again. So you wipe that bit off and clean some more away. Frightened by what you see, though, you then throw some at yourself. You don't deserve to shine this brightly. Here, have some more muck. But the light has caught a glimpse of the outside again and starts to shine brighter. It wants to be seen.

With each bit of light that starts shining out, you start feeling better. It gives you a taste of how great it would feel to be free of all that you are carrying. This makes you recognise just how much everyone else is also carrying and you feel compassion. You decide that from now on you are not going to throw any more muck on others. After all, how can we all be shining at our best if we keep throwing it all over place and on each other? So you get back to work on yourself and very gently rub a little more off. It takes a lot of patience and gentleness, working on a little bit at a time. But excitement builds each time another pocket of light breaks through and you catch another glimpse of your own beauty and radiance.

At times you are tempted to throw some more back on yourself or others, as you have been in the habit of it for almost all of your life. But now you see how the little bits of light shining out of you are helping others, who are also becoming more courageous. They start cleaning off some of their own muck. They have to be very gentle, too, as everyone is delicate and fragile underneath and can shatter very easily. You also want to help others clean theirs off. But they have to do it themselves, as no one but them knows just how fragile they are underneath.

You can show others how you did it and maybe that will help them. But they have to do the work themselves, at their own pace, and in their own way. And of course, not everyone has the courage or strength to do it all at once. So you are patient, respectful, and compassionate, as you now understand that it can sometimes be a very painful and frightening experience.

You feel good in yourself. It is a new feeling, but you like it a lot. So you give up throwing muck on yourself forever, because you are beginning to love the beauty you have discovered, as your light continues to shine brighter. There are rays of light coming out of you at all angles now. But some of the oldest muck is still very stuck on you, making it the hardest to remove. It had grown very comfy here over the decades, thank you very much. It doesn't want to go anywhere. The closer you are to the glass, the more delicately you have to rub. Yet the more stubborn and determined the muck is at this level.

It has been such a big job and you are very weary. You are already an improvement on who you were, definitely. Maybe this will be enough. Maybe I can live with this last layer of muck and just shine as much as I am now. But the light is strong and determined, too. It wants you to shine at your brightest. So it gives you even more strength, and you keep cleaning away the last of it.

Finally, you have done it, and your brightness astonishes everyone, especially yourself. You had no idea you could be so beautiful and shine with such radiance. Now when you hang out with other light globes, they too want to shine brightly, as they can see your beauty and it reminds them that they also have such potential inside of them. They had just forgotten it with all of the muck they were also carrying.

Some light globes think it is too hard to let their light show, so they stick together in the darkness, trying to convince themselves and each other that they are happy this way. Who needs all that hard work when we have become used to carrying our muck? Why, I like it this way, they say, and I am going to throw some more muck around. I am going out there right now to throw some on those bright lights that are happy and having a good time out there. How dare they have so much enjoyment?

So the dark globes head outside with all of the muck they can find and start throwing it. They work better in a team, too, safety in numbers and all that. They can't see as clearly anymore, though, as everything is so bright with all of this cleaning going on. But they spot a few light globes that are now shining brightly and happily, as they have almost finished removing their muck. So the dark globes throw heaps of it at those bright ones. It doesn't stick, though. What's going on? It used to always stick.

What they didn't know was that even though the light was hidden for all of these years, it had still been growing inside. Now it shines so warmly and brightly that the muck will never stick again. It just slides off, without even leaving a mark or an impression anymore.

Your own glow is like that. You have a light within you that is beautiful and potentially radiant. But you need patience and tenderness with yourself to remove all of the muck you have been carrying for decades. As each little bit is removed, a little more of your true self will shine through.

Each of the regrets shared from the bedsides of those now dearly departed people takes courage and love to conquer. But the choice is yours. Like a light that wants to shine brightly and cheerfully, you have a guidance within that will lead you through, one step at a time.

Be who you are, find balance, speak honestly, value those you love, and allow yourself to be happy. If you do this, then you will not only be honouring yourself, but all of those who despaired in their final weeks by not having had the courage to do so previously in their own lives. The choice is yours. Your life is your own.

When the challenges are thrown your way and you are wondering how on Earth it will all come together, how you will find peace about a particular relationship, when the contacts you need will arrive, or how you will find the money to make something happen, just remember that what your heart wants, wants you, too. You just have to get out of the way sometimes. Take what action you can and then let go. Get out of your own way.

Then when you find yourself in this position, stand tall, put your shoulders back, and take a deep and loving breath. Walk on being proud of who you already are, with full faith and confidence you deserve it, that your prayers have been heard, and that they are already on their way to you. And simply remember one little phrase. Smile and know. Just smile and know.

We hope you enjoyed this Hay House book. If you'd like to receive our online catalog featuring additional information on Hay House books and products, or if you'd like to find out more about the Hay Foundation, please contact:

Hay House, Inc., P.O. Box 5100, Carlsbad, CA 92018-5100
(760) 431-7695 or (800) 654-5126
(760) 431-6948 (fax) or (800) 650-5115 (fax)
www.hayhouse.com® • **www.hayfoundation.org**

✈☙◉☙

Published and distributed in Australia by: Hay House Australia Pty. Ltd., 18/36 Ralph St., Alexandria NSW 2015 • *Phone:* 612-9669-4299
Fax: 612-9669-4144 • www.hayhouse.com.au

Published and distributed in the United Kingdom by: Hay House UK, Ltd., 292B Kensal Rd., London W10 5BE • *Phone:* 44-20-8962-1230
Fax: 44-20-8962-1239 • www.hayhouse.co.uk

Published and distributed in the Republic of South Africa by: Hay House SA (Pty), Ltd., P.O. Box 990, Witkoppen 2068 • *Phone/Fax:* 27-11-467-8904 www.hayhouse.co.za

Published in India by: Hay House Publishers India, Muskaan Complex, Plot No. 3, B-2, Vasant Kunj, New Delhi 110 070 • *Phone:* 91-11-4176-1620
Fax: 91-11-4176-1630 • www.hayhouse.co.in

Distributed in Canada by: Raincoast, 9050 Shaughnessy St., Vancouver, B.C. V6P 6E5 • *Phone:* (604) 323-7100 • *Fax:* (604) 323-2600 www.raincoast.com

✈☙◉☙

Take Your Soul on a Vacation

Visit **www.HealYourLife.com®** to regroup, recharge, and reconnect with your own magnificence. Featuring blogs, mind-body-spirit news, and life-changing wisdom from Louise Hay and friends.

Visit **www.HealYourLife.com** today!